Push Comes to Shove

The Escalation of
Student Protest

The Escalation of

Push Comes

Boston

Student Protest

to Shove

by Steven Kelman

Houghton Mifflin Company

Sixth Printing   C

Library of Congress Catalog Card Number: 70–108686
Printed in the United States of America

To Mom and Dad,
who prevented the generation gap
from becoming a chasm

Acknowledgments

THE IDEA for this book originated one morning in April 1969. Three-quarters of the Harvard student body was out on strike at the place they said it couldn't happen. I had been awakened at 8:30, after having gone to sleep at 2:00 A.M. the night before, by Professor Lipset calling to ask what I thought would happen at the stadium meeting. That morning a letter arrived in the mail from Anne Barrett at Houghton Mifflin, asking whether I thought "there is a book in all this." As a close friend and wonderful editor, first thanks for this book must go to her.

Other thanks are due. To Mike Harrington, Bayard Rustin, and Max Shachtman, who taught me what politics is really all about; to Elliott Abrams, Dave Guberman, Jon Ratner, Henry Fetter, and John Stephens, who provided a lot of the day-to-day camaraderie that makes politics worthwhile despite the escalation of unreality; to Mark, a great source of ideas, a wonderful brother, and my worst critic. And finally to my friends on *The Harvard Crimson*, without whom the Harvard confrontation, and thus this book, might never have been possible.

Contents

Introduction: What's Happened to Harvard?   1

Part One : The Pot Is Set Boiling — Notes from
          My Freshman Diary, 1966–67
          1. Harvard   11
          2. The Radicals   42
          3. The Alienated   77

Part Two : Push Comes to Shove
          1. SDS Prepares for Confrontation   105
          2. The Alienated Prepare for "Liberation" 162
          3. The Moderates Prepare for Active Non-
             resistance   176
          4. The New Left Takes Control of
             Our Mass Media   202
          5. The University Is Chosen as a Target 220

Part Three: Confrontation 1969, and After
          1. The Escalation of Unreality   237
          2. Has Sanity a Future?   277

Push Comes to Shove

The Escalation of
Student Protest

Introduction: What's Happened to Harvard?

WHILE I WAS HOME for Christmas vacation during my freshman year, a friend told me that at the first freshman assembly at his college one dean asked each student to look at the person to his left and his right. "One of the people you're looking at will flunk out before graduation." He was incredulous.

Nobody flunks out at Harvard. But if some dean had told me at our freshman assembly that one of those on my left or right would participate in an attempt to destroy Harvard before graduation, I would have been incredulous.

For one, two, or however many years ago, each student arrived in his dorm in Harvard Yard along with 1200 classmates, proud and happy to have the chance to be at Harvard. Some entered with a disgusting arrogance, a presupposition that their selection for Harvard conferred upon them the right to lord over the world and the people in it. But most had a more simple and straightforward notion of gratitude that they were *lucky* enough to have the opportunity to be here. Many knew that their friends from home could equally well have taken advantage of the wonders of Cambridge if they had been allowed to. So snobbish boasting was wrong; but, since we were where all our friends wanted to be, anything less than a normal pride was unbecoming false modesty.

One sign of the fact that we all felt uneasy about any trace of boasting was always the paucity of Harvard T-shirts or sweat shirts that could be seen around the Square. The Coop had a large section of their store devoted to selling them — and the emblemed shirts always appeared to disappear at a steady pace. Yet you couldn't find a Harvard student wearing one. Until April 1969. Then the shirts, hidden away in drawers, came out, worn by all the people who hated Harvard most — with bright huge red fists silk-screened over the front, partly obliterating the Harvard seal. They had cared about Harvard once.

Writing this book is going to be somewhat painful, for I discovered during the April days that Harvard students were not immune to the same types of emotions which made the Nazi rise to power possible. I regretfully came to realize that SDS had hit upon a tactic which was unbeatable, even at Harvard. I witnessed that SDS had succeeded in winning at Harvard, in having themselves accepted by all too many of the student body as our moral vanguard. And I realized how different my reaction to events was from that of so many of the people around me. While Harvard Yard was "liberated" during those ominously sunny and warm days, I felt chained up. While students believed themselves released from anxiety and pain, I was tense and depressed.

After a week and a half, I escaped Harvard — the "new" Harvard, the Harvard where "real learning was going on for the first time," the Harvard where the strike had proved "that we can get along perfectly well without the professors." The newspeak Harvard where stealing files was "liberating" them, and the "new college" Harvard where courses ranged from The History of the Self to The Political Relevance of Encounter Groups. This was the greatest thing that ever happened to Harvard, they said. I was at the end of a long frayed rope. I had to get away from campus. I couldn't stand it anymore.

The pain in writing this book will come as I try to piece out in my own mind how the April days at Harvard were possible. The events were much more than an inconvenience for me and a tragedy for Harvard. The upper-middle-class participants in the building take-over and the "strike" — and indeed the more than a handful of the sons of the ruling class among them too — will scatter out in their respective directions in the next months and years, eventually finding the traditional elitism of the bourgeoisie more to their liking than the New Left elitism of their college days. Many will look back fondly twenty years from now at the moldy T-shirts with their fading fists.

But most Americans lead a hard life far away — both emotionally and physically — from the antics on the campus. They are savvy enough to see through the hocus-pocus SDS jargon by which the New Left tries to portray itself as a friend of theirs. You might persuade the white taxi driver that Martin Luther King was his friend, but no amount of circumlocution will convince him that the Black Panthers like him. The auto worker doesn't see Teddy Kennedy as an imperialist agent or his union leaders as "sellout misleaders." He's smart enough to know that China and Cuba are no models for the United States. With more wisdom than the editors of *The Harvard Crimson*, most Americans see the extremists as pampered slobs gone amuck.

There is one side to most people that wants change and inspires them to a vision of a more just and free society. It is the side which leads people to look to an easing not only of their own lives but also of those of others even less fortunate — that wants brotherhood and not war. I remember vividly one evening driving home from Logan Airport in a taxi with my roommate, listening to the taxi driver bemoan the rat race "which all the big boys with the money try to get the working-man in on,": the struggle for existence which sets men against each other, "neighbor against neighbor instead of neighbor with neighbor." But it used to be different. "We were poorer then, but with Roosevelt you had a feeling that we all had to work together and build something."

Now we've got Nixon, and it's no coincidence. For there is also another side to people which demands an ordering to life, that shuns the uncertainty of chaos and confusion. There is nothing inherently wrong with this side of people — for it is this which allows many to be "poor, but respectable." Bored upper-class Harvard students may have "liberated" themselves from the shackles of bourgeois respectability during the April days. But respectability isn't only "bourgeois," and if you take away the "respectable" from many people all you have left is "poor."

So when people see themselves attacked by confrontationist students, they counterattack. They're not articulate enough to outargue, or loudmouthed enough to outshout, the activists. But they have their one man, one vote. SDS can't take that away from them. Their revenge is on election day.

But people bite their nose to spite their face. For order is a *precondition* for a just society, not a means of reaching justice. Justice requires change as well as order. Americans counterattack, and they restore the threatened order. But the politicians who make "law and order" their whole program won't deliver the decent jobs, houses, parks, or unpolluted cities which are at the foundation of a better America. To regain the respectability threatened by those for whom confusion is liberation, people sacrifice the side of them which strives upward.

While Harvard is "freed," the kids who want to go to state colleges are left out in the cold because popular resentment has led to cuts in state education budgets. And while Harvard awaits the revolution, black people in the ghettos, the poor in Appalachia, the farm worker in California, experience the counterrevolution. Around Boston the Wallace supporters I spoke to in the fall of 1968 were far more upset with punk students than with Negroes.

So people will accuse me of carping about students and ignoring the so much else that is wrong in American society. My answer is that the confrontationists are making it more difficult to build a better America. Eldridge Cleaver says that in the United States today you are either part of the problem or part of the solution. My bitterness comes from the unhappy realization that many of the people I know at school have become part of the problem.

Some seek to bring about a cruel and harsh regime where freedom of speech and democracy are replaced by terror and dictatorship. A larger number want the right things but despair at ever persuading Americans of their views, somehow believing that a decent society is so repulsive to most people that it must be introduced like an unpleasant medicine or snuck in through the back door while people aren't looking. These students are the victims of a self-imposed and self-perpetuating isolation, scornfully viewing almost all but themselves as "conned" into contentment with all aspects of present-day American life. Their tactics deepen their isolation, and their haughtiness turns ordinary people away from them.

I have been a socialist as long as I can remember. But it wasn't until I read a little bit and learned the first lessons from history that I saw that socialism must inextricably be connected with human freedom, and that I realized that socialism must be introduced by an optimistic and confident people. For the

socialism of desperation and despair never succeeds in over-
coming the disorder and coercion from which it was born.

I know that the road to socialism does not pass by way of the
destruction of Harvard.

In April of 1969 a large number of the same students who
had entered Harvard so ashamed in their pride at being there
that they wouldn't wear a T-shirt advertising their Harvardness,
decided that hurting Harvard would be a good thing for themselves and the world. Most sincerely viewed it as one of the
most idealistic and noble acts of their lives. In this book I want
to try to find out why.

The first part of the book contains, unchanged, excerpts from
a diary I kept as a freshman spending his first year in Cambridge. The excerpts have been chosen to try to give something
of a raw and unrefined-by-hindsight image both of Harvard as
a place to live and of the development of the New Left and
alienated students who, nurtured at Harvard, were later to lead
the assault on it. Some of the observations in the diary take on
an added significance in the light of what has happened since
1966–67, but I assure the reader that this is unintended, and
that the diary material has not been altered in any way, except
that some names and personal descriptions have been changed
to respect the privacy of the individuals concerned.

The second and third parts of the book were written in the
summer and fall following the spring confrontation at Harvard. In the first three chapters of the second part I try to
sketch the development, from my freshman year through the
confrontation year, of the forces which were to make up the
"confrontation coalition" — the New Left, the alienated "cultural radicals," and finally the moderates. While the New Left
and the cultural radicals provided the cutting edge for the con-

frontation coalition, it was the inclusion of the moderates which in the end made the strike possible. Therefore I must try to explain not only why SDS came to seek out confrontations — something that was not true when I was a freshman — but also why the moderates, always a force against confrontation at Harvard, came to join in. The answers to all of these questions, in my view, correspond hardly at all to most of the glib explanations which have been presented up until now.

Part One

The Pot Is Set Boiling—
Notes from My
Freshman Diary, 1966-67

1. Harvard

I ARRIVED *at Harvard — or more precisely in Matthews Hall number 44, right inside Harvard Yard — three days before freshman registration. Everyone, especially freshmen, needs some time to settle down and find a little bit out before things actually start.*

September 17, 1966

The Second Day

The formalities of unpacking and introductory settling down, and the infantlike feeling around of the new object which is Harvard, couldn't keep on holding all my attention beyond yesterday. This morning when I got up I knew that today I would have to go out and meet some people, pause and look at those faces that have been there all along. How do you make friends? What does it take for someone to become a friend or, alternatively, an enemy?

On the second day, it doesn't take very much either way. I saw a tall, blond, not-quite-fat kid around the dorm today. One time he was gazing down at the rest of the world from his pedestal on the ledge of the staircase one floor up, and once again later in the afternoon downstairs. His eyes eyed in a superciliousness so classic that I felt like photographing it. The lips seemed delicately positioned so that he could voice his contempt without saying one audible word. Puritanical, righteous anger flowed up to my head with the blood.

Disgusting *prep school* kid! What is he doing here, calmly

observing everything, taking a place away from someone who
deserves it? His look of contempt bred my own contempt for
him. His contempt was generalized to include the whole non-
prep world; mine was directed precisely at him.

By Tuesday, three days later, all the people on the top three
floors of the dorm were called together for a meeting with our
freshman proctor. We didn't know what to expect, but we
knew what we found would be telling us something about
Harvard.

September 20, 1966

I went to dinner tonight at Hayes-Bickford's, a small cafeteria
on Mass. Ave. right near the room. I ate at the place last year
when I was up for an interview, and I remembered the food to
be anything but distinguished. But it's relatively cheap, and I
wasn't in the mood to wander up and down Mass. Ave. looking for someplace else. After getting a meal at the counter, I
sat down opposite two kids speaking with each other. After
listening for a few seconds and noticing that they were uttering
introductory banalities, I decided that I could join in.

I spoke softly, cautiously, not trying to barge in: "Are you
people freshmen here?" It sounded strange to use the word
"people," but sometimes friends reproach me for using "kid" so
often to refer to anyone younger than an adult. They answered
that they were, so each of us introduced ourselves: Bob and
Mark. As if to reinforce my initial prejudices about the legendary qualities of those twelve hundred who had somehow made
it "in," Bob is British. And, to compound that, he's no son of
a lord or Member of Parliament. He had gone to the English

equivalent of a regular high school, outside of London, not to Eton or Harrow, and he's here on a $2700 scholarship. "I arrived in the States for the first time this morning. I left London yesterday."

The most important thing I wanted to ask Bob was why he decided to apply to Harvard and go to school in the United States, especially considering the high reputation of British universities. "I wanted to get a humanistic education, instead of coming out of a machine." He gave his answer quickly enough to sound like the first time he had a chance to use a reply he had rehearsed, and then continued, "Anyway, almost nobody from a state school can get into Oxford or Cambridge. And Harvard is a pretty good place."

But throughout the time we were talking one unarticulated feeling continued to swim back and forth across the waters of my spoken words. My God, he was in England just yesterday, and he's seeing a new country and having to learn to live in it all at once. With all the problem "getting adjusted to college" is going to be, I would have never wished a new country on someone at the same time. It's lucky that at least he speaks English.

Pete, our proctor, started off by passing out beer to everyone. "It's provided to us by the university for these proctorial meetings. But I'm not allowed to buy any liquor for you guys to have in your rooms." Massachusetts has a twenty-one drinking age. "Get friendly with some upperclassmen and ask them to buy it for you. Listen around for the names of stores that let you buy stuff without proof. None of the places right around the Square will, but the ones farther out that don't do such a big business might. And listen, fellows, don't play around with phony 'proof.' If the owner of the store asks you for proof of age, just search around your pockets and say you forgot it and leave the place. It's not worth it if they catch you."

A boy with a delicate face and blond hair parted almost down the middle, cried out, sarcastically merrily, from the back of the room, "Pete, is this what they call the proctor's duty to give freshmen *advice* on getting adjusted to Harvard?"

Pete didn't react except with an inaudible smile. "Oh, by the way. If any of you want Coke instead of beer, I have some in the freezer." One boy, sitting two people away from me, raised his hand, and Pete passed him a can of Coke. The boy seemed to raise his hand without any hesitation, and nobody made any comments — which was about the only time during the evening that anyone passed up an opportunity to make a crack. But I could sense by the unusual quiet that everyone was thinking the same thing: it must take courage to ask for Coke.

The whole proctorial meeting went on exactly like the un-expectedly non-"official" style of the beginning. Pete warned us about "townies" from Cambridge whom kids liked to pick up as quickie dates on the Square. "There have been cases of these girls blackmailing Harvard students they've gotten involved with. This problem of townie pickups is mainly one you have as a freshman, with the Square so nearby. When you're upper-classmen, you'll be farther from the Square, and temptation de-creases inversely with the square of the distance."

"Pete, is it hard for freshmen to get dates?" That was a good question; I had heard stories that at many schools freshman social life was almost totally barren, with freshman girls dating only upperclassmen. Pete said that there was no problem.

"What about parietals?" It was the same delicate blond as before. He appeared to be trying to set himself up as master of ceremonies. Almost everybody laughed nervously. "Parietals." I've never looked that word up in a dictionary (I'll have to do it someday), but I know what it means to me as a freshman — the hours when we can have girls in our rooms. I once read about the controversy at Harvard several years ago over the extension of parietal hours, during which President Pusey accused some students of abusing parietal "privileges" to engage in orgies.

Rather abruptly, Pete's voice became more serious. "First of all, you have to realize that parietals are strictly enforced. Now I don't go around knocking on doors at night, but if I happen to see a girl in your room or sneaking out of it after parietal hours, I have no choice but to report you — and violation of parietal rules means you're thrown out of Harvard for a year."

I discerned a generalized stiffening in everyone's posture. I had never suspected that parietals were really enforced, and the voice of the question asking "What about parietals?" indicated that he was *really* wondering how soon we could start violating the rules.

"When your date comes into your room, you have to sign her in on the sheet I'll be taping up outside my door, and sign her out when she leaves. I remember when I was a freshman, I always would forget to sign my date out when we left, until they almost took away my parietal privileges." Pete's at Harvard Law now. "So guys, watch out." He wasn't trying to threaten. "By the way, in addition to the parietals listed in your *Regulations*," — that is to say, 4:00 P.M. to 7:00 P.M. on weekdays, 12:00 noon to 8:00 P.M. on Saturday, and 12:00 noon to 7:00 P.M. on Sunday — "you are allowed to have extended parietals until midnight three times a semester for dorm parties. I think we should plan our first party relatively soon — after you've all had time to find girl friends, but before hour exams. We'll talk about that at our next dorm meeting, though."

Then we went through the little pocket-sized *Regulations for Students in Harvard College.* Our version of Chairman Mao's little red book? At first, I thought this part would be a dull letdown from the rest, because Pete insisted on reading the whole thing out loud, despite the fact that most of us had either already read it or else were sufficiently literate to be able to peruse it on our own. But the spirit of clever repartee which had already been established, combined with facetious renditions of some of the more pompous passages (the *Regulations* are written in the style of nineteenth-century university euphemism), continued to charm.

"Attendance: 1. Regular attendance at college exercises is expected."

"Credit for Summer Work at other Universities: No credit will be given for any summer courses except those listed in the Harvard Summer School catalogue." After all, how could Harvard accept the fact that any other university could possibly give as good a course as Harvard? You gotta realize they have a *name* to protect!

"Use of Harvard Name: No student shall be connected with any advertising medium or unrecognized publication which makes use of the name of Harvard or implies, without permission of the University, through its title or otherwise, a connection with the University."

Pete started to let various kids give their own dramatic readings of different points.

"Good order: 2. No boisterous music or playing upon drums or other harsh instruments shall be allowed at any time.

3. *No student may keep an animal, bird, or reptile in a College building.*" A kid in the back barked like a dog.

9. *No student shall refuse to give his name to an officer of the University. A student shall deliver his Identification Card to an officer of the University upon request.*"

Pete interrupted the parade of readings. "In spite of the sound of this, always remember that the campus policemen are your friends, and the Cambridge policemen aren't. The regular cops aren't allowed inside university property, though, so if a cop tries to stop you when you're jaywalking across Mass. Ave., just run into the Yard. The only time you have to worry about a campus cop is if there's a spring riot. They're likely to take away your bursar's card . . ."

The kid who asked for Coke: "What's that?"

"That's the plastic card they gave you in your registration envelope yesterday. They'll take it away, and you can get into trouble even if you're *at the scene* of a riot, so watch out. And look out for another thing that's not mentioned in the rule book. A few years ago some freshmen were throwing water balloons out of their windows, and one of them happened to hit Dean Monro. Since then, as you can imagine, he's been particularly harsh on kids brought in for that offense."

The biggest laughs from the rule book came in the section on "discipline." In it, they list *four different* ways of being thrown out of the university: severance of connection, require to withdraw (in these two cases, you can almost always come back after a year), dismissal ("readmission will be granted rarely and only by a vote of the Faculty"), and expulsion ("a student who is expelled can never be readmitted, and his name is expunged from the records of the University"). I yelled out, "It sounds like 1984. You become an un-person."

I finally got around to reading the Freshman Registration special issue of The Harvard Crimson *on Thursday. I was particularly interested in one long feature.*

September 22, 1967

The most fascinating thing of all was an explanation (exposé?) of the final clubs, the institutions which produce the "clubbies." "Colleges Final Clubs Enjoy Secluded Life In a World that Pays Little Attention to Them" was the title.

While other undergraduate organizations produce plays or publish journals, the members of Harvard's 11 Final Clubs devote their energies to maintaining a refuge from such endeavors. For the more conscientious members of the more prestigious clubs, it can turn into a full-time occupation.

Founded in 1789, The Porcellian is by far the oldest, the most exclusive, and the most secretive of the Final Clubs. Women are never allowed inside its doors. Distinguished guests of Porcellian members may visit — but only once. (The club turned down President Eisenhower's request for a second look.)

When I read that, I said to myself, I'm surprised they let that "hick" in even once.

The restrictions placed on discussions within the club make conversation meaningless. If you start to talk about issues, somebody says, "Go home and do that; the Club is for friendship." For Porcellian members, comradeship and intellectual relationships must be two different things . . .

The steeped tradition of the Porcellian hurts its members academically too, (one disgruntled member) feels. "To care too much about something is square. Big as it is, there's not one room in the place set aside for studying. This is part of a confusion between complacency and maturity." . . .

The clubs' exclusionist philosophy would seem to be out of step with the University's democratic ideals. Dean Watson answers that "only about one half of one percent of the people not in clubs are terribly unhappy about it." It is no doubt true that non-members are far more content than the undergraduate who wants to get into the Porcellian Club but is forced to settle for a club farther down the ladder.

Racial prejudice and anti-Semitism are still vital factors in the selection of Club members. The Porcellian Club is reputed never to have admitted a Jewish student.

There was a line at the beginning of *The Great Gatsby* where the narrator introduces Gatsby by saying something like "Gatsby, who represented everything for which I have an un-affected scorn."

I got to talk with the kid I had seen the previous Saturday looking superciliously around the dorm. His name is Al Gross. I also had a personal meeting with my proctor to talk about courses.

September 23, 1966

After talking, I don't react the same way to Gross — it would be impossible to respond as negatively to a living and moving person as to a personification of everything you hate, which is what he was last Saturday. But I don't know if I like him. His main topic in our conversation was the "celebrities" in our dorm.

"Have you met any of them yet?" He has a sort of upper-

class voice, deep and mature, but not especially "cultured." "On
the first floor there's Mike Bundy and David Bruce. That's
McGeorge's son" — he said "McGeorge" with an of-course-I-
know-McGeorge flourish* — "and David Bruce is the son of
the American ambassador to England. There are some families
that go back to the Mayflower around here, you know." Gross
was apparently ultraimpressed, and for once I had the chance to
act cool and unimpressed by comparison. "I wish *my* family
went back that far."

"Doesn't every family?" I put him down. "What happened,
did yours spring up only a few generations ago by spontaneous
generation?"

Gross wasn't flustered. "You know what I mean." He articu-
lated each word individually and exaggeratedly. "I mean how
long ago their families came to America."

*Before I came to Harvard, my natural rejoinder to Pete's com-
ment, "Well, Steve, it looks like you're in pretty good shape as
far as courses go," would have been, "Isn't everybody?" Three
weeks before I came up to Harvard, I began to feel nervous and
guilty that I hadn't chosen my courses yet. I read all the course
offerings in the interesting departments from the course catalogue Harvard had sent us and made up a tentative three-year
program for myself. Some things have had to be switched
around for different reasons, but I have been amazed to see all
the kids around here who, even now, with courses starting Monday, aren't at all sure what they're going to take. They plan to
"shop around" and look in at a bunch of courses, waiting an-*

---

* I found out later that Mike Bundy was not McGeorge's son but his
nephew.

other week to decide. (Study cards aren't due until October
4.) With my academic-centered mind, two of the first ques-
tions I've always asked new people are "What are you going to
be taking?" and "What are you going to major in?" After a
while, the incredulous responses to such a query have made me
stop asking. A typical response, by a curly-haired blond kid on
our floor in the bathroom: "I told Harvard I was going to major
in fine arts, but that's only because they asked. I really don't
know what I'm going to do."

The Crimson *"Confidential Guide to Lower and Middle-*
Level Courses" said the following about Government 146, Ur-
ban Policy Problems:

This is probably the last time that Edward Banfield will give this
course on the problems of urban policy . . . Don't let Banfield
scare you off; he is an avowed skeptic and many of his ideas come
out sounding (and sometimes are) ultra-conservative. Two years
ago, when he first gave the course, most students walked away from
the first lecture grumbling; most of them were stunned by the
questions Banfield had raised and some of the answers he suggested.

The description was fascinating; I decided to take the course.
It was my first Harvard lecture.

September 26, 1966

First Day of Classes

At exactly 11:03 this morning, Professor Edward Banfield
strutted onto the small stage in Emerson 105 and immediately,
suddenly, started lecturing. I was sitting halfway back and,

without my glasses, I couldn't see what he looked like. Here goes; for me Harvard is starting. But the undiluted brew of ecstasy, anxiety, and intoxication which I expected to have churning around my body and mind was weakened in its effectiveness somewhat by the presence of *so many* other students around me. Logically, I wasn't expecting to be alone in the audience with the professor — although my formless fantasies might have been something like that. But there were, really, too many people for such a small lecture room. There was in fact a mob outside the doors which couldn't fit in and others standing in the aisle. A crowd dilutes pure pulsations of emotion. Some of my energy was used up *looking* at the people.

Here goes. Will I have to learn shorthand in order to take notes? That's what all the teachers in high school always told us. I'm nervous, not in a down, butterflies-in-stomach way like before you take a test, but in an up, feet-are-collapsing-under-you way like before you get to shake hands with a celebrity.

I'm ready for anything Banfield can say to shock me . . .

But it's only because I had read the "Confi Guide," though, that I didn't walk out "grumbling" and "stunned." Banfield started off by asking whether, after all, there really *is* an "urban crisis." Traffic congestion? "A city wouldn't be a city if there weren't places where a lot of people want to be at the same time. And where people want to be at the same time, there's bound to be congestion." Urban sprawl uprooting our green landscapes? "If people want to live in single-family, detached houses, landscape is bound to be ruined. All the land we preserve as parks reduces the possible housing stock available and thus hurts the poor." Poverty? "This isn't strictly an urban problem. Poverty is much worse in rural areas." Cities the last bastion of culture and learning? "If Saint Louis or Kansas City disappeared tomorrow, our stock of high culture would barely be diminished. Actually there are only one or two cities where high culture is being produced."

And so on for a whole hour. Although the ideas were strange, it was nevertheless my ideal view of what a Harvard lecture would be like. Filled with new points of view, the type of thing you could never read in a book. Special thoughts of the professor reserved for his students. Fantastic, beautiful.

At just a minute before the bells started ringing on the hour at Memorial Church, Banfield stopped speaking, the audience started applauding (which startled me), and he walked off the stage. Before leaving he announced that he would try to find a new lecture hall in which to meet. "Watch the notice column of the *Crimson*. By the way, I'll have more reading lists on Wednesday for those who couldn't get them today." I was one. "As for administrative details, the course will meet in three lectures a week — there are no sections — and every third meeting I will have a 'question-and-yell-at-me period.' There will be an hour exam on Wednesday, November ninth. Grad students taking the course will be permitted to write papers in lieu of taking the final exam. You can discuss that matter with me during my office hours, which are, by the way, Monday through Thursday, two to three P.M. in Littauer three twenty."

As I walked out, I heard one kid say, "Did you see the front row? There it was, the whole football team. This course is supposed to be one of the biggest guts in the school. Two years ago, when the median on the hour exam was B–plus, he *apologized* to the class and said he'd be easier next time!" I smiled to myself and headed off to Lowell Lecture Hall, where Ec 1 meets. Innocent freshman that I am, I had wandered into Gov 146 because it looked novel. And took two neat pages of notes, without shorthand.

September 27, 1966

Our second proctorial meeting

The elections for freshman council took place tonight at our proctorial meeting. If one accepts the theory that candidates emphasize those issues of most concern to electors, there would be no choice but to conclude that the primary preoccupations of Harvard freshmen are scatological.

The blond kid who had constantly interrupted the dorm meeting last week gave the first speech. The first part was devoted to what he would do to get the freshman council to improve bathroom conditions. The second part centered, in a manner of speaking, on the role of the freshman council in improving the freshman's social life. He told us he was from Boston and knew there was "a lot of ass" to be had around. If elected, he intended to see that we all got some.

Some of the applause was obviously embarrassed. The kid speaks in the peculiar sexual idiom of preppies. Already, I've learned other quaint preppie expressions like "He craves her bod."

The other candidate, Harry Brand, presented himself as "a budding writer," adding that "with my creativity, I should be able to think up many new ideas." Although he wasn't able to upstage his rival on bringing girls to Harvard — he merely promised to do as much — he did present a new "idea" for the bathroom. "I will suggest if elected that sanitary and clean towels be introduced into the bathrooms. Sometimes a girl is in your room" — he glanced at Pete and chortled, "during parietals, of course" — "and for one reason or another you suddenly need some towels." A few gritted to prevent laughter, but most kids just let out the roar of disbelief that comes from somebody saying something too gross to be spoken. "You wouldn't want to use your *own* towels for that?" Applause. The election speeches were over; that was their entire "content."

Harry Brand won. I voted for the blond one but, for lack of other criteria, the most daring obscenity won out.

September 29, 1966

For no particular reason, there was a "menacing" gathering of Matthews South freshmen around the stairwells tonight. My roommate Mike was standing outside next to me, in blue jeans and a green pajama top. Kids were talking; the noise intensified each second. A few kids weren't talking, just yelling incoherently to add to the racket. The different conversations had only lack of content in common.

I could only think of how riots start from restless crowds. "How come you're not working?" "When I get organized . . ." Everybody was staring at everyone else when they were babbling. Or staring over the stairwell looking suicidally down to the lobby. It was inevitable that something would happen tonight, but I never expected to see what did take place.

A *water fight.*

"It's just like Andover, only sooner," Mike chimed in. Perhaps this is another stupid custom introduced from prep schools; maybe it develops naturally from a group of kids confined together with pressures to get working beginning. But explanations can't dull my disappointment at seeing Harvard freshmen squirting water at each other with squeeze bottles, dropping balloons full of it, whipping wet towels — like six-year-olds. I'm well beyond that old part of my life when I frowned upon "having fun" in any but an intellectual way, but I can't see how an eighteen-year-old can "have fun" in a water fight. For the first time, tonight I allowed myself to state inwardly the question of whether the Harvard stereotype isn't really only a stereotype.

October 4, 1966

I had my first tutorial in my "field of concentration," government, tonight. My tutor is a grad student named John Berg, and there are only six of us in the class. I didn't get much idea of what tutorial — the famed individualized tutorial of Harvard — will be like. We're going to read a book and write a brief paper about it for each class, which meets every two weeks. Today I mainly discovered the unusual fact, which I should have expected, that not everybody goes into government as a major out of desire to change the world. Of the six kids in the tutorial, three said tonight they wanted to study chiefly American government, because they were planning to go into politics. I guess government can be a how-to-do-it major just like engineering.

October 9, 1966

Sunday dinner, probably to make it feel like home, has been unpalatable leftovers for the last two weeks. And we were all treated to the third straight night of kids clinking glasses when a girl entered the dining hall. Tonight's performance, despite the relatively small number of girls, was the most cacophonous yet. At one point, freshmen began to beat out the beginnings of familiar rhythms and wait for others to complete them.

It was amid all this that the kid sitting opposite me remarked, obviously piqued, "Grow up, Harvard men!" And, as if confessing failure after repeated attempts, he added, "Frankly,

I'm disappointed with a lot of the kids here." That blunt admission made me wonder if perhaps I wasn't also and just refused to admit it. I don't know: all the people I've met seem great, but "the class" in an impersonal way seems typified by glass-clinking and water fights.

There is so much going on at Harvard beyond classes — like all the public personalities who come to speak here.

October 13, 1966

The Grand Old Man came to speak at Harvard tonight. I had seen the signs on the bulletin boards as early as last Monday announcing that Norman Thomas would speak at a lecture sponsored by the Law School Young Dems. I've never seen him before in person.

Last night I got a phone call from a boy from Harvard Law School who told me that he was an officer of the Law School Young Dems. Someone from the Young People's Socialist League in New York — the "Yipsel" I had joined as a high school socialist — had given him my name. "Would you like to come to the airport with me to meet Mr. Thomas?"

I was just as thrilled as if he had asked me to come to the airport to meet the President. He was supposed to pick me up at seven-thirty in front of Holyoke Center. But his car never came. Finally, at almost eight, I left for the Austin Courtroom.

The car with Norman Thomas arrived shortly before eight-thirty, and I went outside as soon as I heard. In his eighties, Norman Thomas can barely walk up stairs — he has to rest after every third one. His hair is brilliant white, the bald area on top is freckled, and his eyes are surrounded by a pinkish

color which gives the illusion he's an albino. He is legally blind
— newspapers and books are read out loud to him, I learned
tonight, by his companion Tim Sullivan — and he moves around
guided by a cane and by Mr. Sullivan's arm.

I was very close to crying when the law school boy whispered,
"Mr. Thomas, this is Steve Kelman, who's a Yipsel here at
Harvard."

His mouth quivered. I shook his warm hand so tightly. Even
though I had never met him before, there was no other way I
could address him but "Norman." I think that he preferred it
that way.

As he came onto the stage, almost crawling it seemed, I discerned that the audience was feeling as if they were sitting down
to listen to a pathetic old man. The large room was almost
filled.

Unexpectedly, miraculously, came out tones which were full
and youthful, words which were quick and lucid. It was almost
a mystical experience: Norman Thomas's speech was coming
full-blown from a body that was only a ghost. Where was the
energy coming from as he stared blankly into the distance, his
words coming unhesitantly and rapidly out of his mind? He
had not a single written note.

He spoke on Vietnam, not on socialism as I had expected.
"If I die before this *terrible* war is ended, I will feel that my
whole life's work for decency has been a failure."

Every person in the auditorium was fixated on the body of
Norman Thomas.

"Tim," I whispered to his companion, feeling I had to express some of the emotion I felt, "he is *fantastic*. I can't believe it." I was enchanted.

"He's not at his best tonight. He's a little tired."

When it was over, Norman Thomas got a standing ovation. A large teardrop finally came up, after building itself up all this time, from my right eye. I was sweating. We sold fourteen copies of Norman Thomas's pamphlet, *Democratic Socialism: A New Appraisal*, at fifty cents each to people leaving the hall.

Norman had given YPSL a brief pitch during his speech. "I'm glad to see there's the beginning of a revival of socialism on this campus. I wish the YPSLs all the luck, and hope to see them doing their part to end this war." As he was leaving for the shuttle, he apologized that the Law School Young Dems had to pay for the air fare of Tim Sullivan as well as his own. "But I'm just a weak old man who has to be watched all the time." His teeth, mostly still there, although feeble-looking, shone as he smiled.

One night David Bruce knocked on my door. I remembered him from the day Al Gross mentioned him, and I had met him once, casually, at the Freshman Union. He had skipped the Ec 1 lecture on Friday, and someone downstairs had suggested I might have the notes. The next night I met him again, by chance.

October 17, 1966

As I went out at midnight to get a roast beef special at Elsie's, I saw Dave Bruce outside his room, and we went together. He said that what disappoints him most about Harvard is that there are "few people who you can have a serious discussion with — about philosophy, or politics, or anything. Most of the people I've met are virtual illiterates." Dave sounded like he was delivering a speech. "And the preppies really annoy me. They have no motivation at all." He was speaking disdainfully now — you can tell he is when he turns on his British accent. "They spend all their time trying to appear 'in.' To be 'in,' you have to have a certain amount of dilettantish knowledge. But," he paused, smiling cynically, "not much."

I had met John Kuerner of Brooklyn, N.Y., and Groton School, during freshman week. Attracted by a common interest in French and government, we became good friends. But John began acting strange rather soon. He had asked for, and gotten, a roommate from France. But René wasn't perhaps the best thing for him. He made a confession one night late in October while I was in his room.

October 24, 1966

John was in a morose, pessimistic mood at dinner tonight. Comparing his way of life with René's epicurianism, he wasn't sure whether René wasn't right. "Look at him. He doesn't care if he's faking the whole university out. He's going to try to graduate from here in *two* years." John laughed a laugh of admiration. "And then he'll go back to Bordeaux and get a fancy business job in his father's law office. He never works, and he goes to parties almost every night." He lit up a cigarette. "You know, he looks old, and with his cute French accent," he continued somewhat contemptuously, "he goes out with twenty-two-year-old girls."

René was in his room smoking a Gauloise and reading the *Crimson*. "The nineteen-year-old girls in America are simply not serious," René said. "*Pas sérieuses, tu sais?* I got a letter from my home today that an old girl friend of mine died," René added laconically.

"Oh, I'm sorry to hear that."

"Oh, don't mention it. I took away from her her virginity before she left." *Je lui ai emporté sa virginité.* "She didn't want to go all the way with me. But I persuaded her. I needed only fifteen minutes."

"See," John interrupted, "that's my point. René doesn't care about humanitarianism or anything like that. I've been thinking and all — you know, socialism is what I believe in, providing you want to help people. But I'm not sure I want to help people anymore." He paused. "I'm becoming very cynical about politics. You know, I like to find out what's happening in the world, but that's just for curiosity. I don't know whether I want to *do* anything. I just wish I could feel *committed* like you." John was staring hard on me, inhaling very deeply with his cigarette. "It's not that I don't want to be, it's just that I can't *feel* it."

He looked so much the oversensitive, oversuffering artist with his black hair neatly parted down the middle. I was still staring at his cigarette.

"Stop staring at the cigarette!" he ejected suddenly. "I know I'm smoking it like a marijuana joint. Don't stare! I only wish I could find some pot somewhere."

Everyone has his own "Harvard myth." For a New York area public school kid, the Harvard myth is of the good school, center of genius and inspiration. But other people's Harvard myth is different — the only agreement seems to be that there

is a Harvard myth. One night I spoke with Al Gross about his
ideas on the subject.

November 2, 1966

"I've been to the Harvard-Yale football game every year since
I was six. My grandfather and father both came here. My
grandfather was a Jewish immigrant to the United States who
lived in Boston, and Harvard was closer to his home than Brandeis, so he came here. And family tradition has put us here
ever since." Unfortunately for Al's story, Brandeis wasn't around
when his grandfather would have gone to college.

But at that moment only the fact that this preppie scum is
Jewish occupied my mind. It's so out of place it's almost immoral: it's as if John Harvard himself were posthumously discovered to have been a Marrano.

"For me Harvard has always been a land of sophisticated
superstuds, who can handle girls, liquor, literature, and politics
without flinching." He stood up; he's about six feet tall. "The
big flaming crimson *H* in the sky, you know. The place where
I would finally be able to dine in the Porcellian Club." He
hesitated for a split second. "You've heard of the P.C., haven't
you?" He remembered he was talking to a peasant.

"Yeah, I read the article in the *Crimson*. But don't you remember that they never admit Jews?"

"Alas, that's tragic. Anyway, at Harvard I imagined dining
at one of the clubs, discussing a cool poem with a professor over
a cup of expresso. Just coolness all around." He showed me an
article he had written for the first issue of the *Yardling* on his
first impressions of Harvard.

"Why'd you go out for the *Yardling*?"

"Well, I hoped to meet some literate people there, but unfortunately they're all from Brooklyn or something."

I met Tom Young of Cohasset, Mass., and Andover by chance one night while I was writing. Defensive about being a "preppie," Tom Young invited me to a party at his home the evening after the Yale game, so I could see "preppies were human." With me came two friends from high school, Joe Samuels (Yale '70) and Kate Little, a freshman at Brandeis.

November 19, 1966

The party was different from what I had expected. If you ignored the surface differences, it wasn't remarkably different from the type of party I had always gone to at home. No psychedelic lights, fancy buffet tables, minks, or suave orgies.

But the surface differences — differences which reflected a whole different way of life — were enough to put Kate into a trance of disbelief. She wasn't *impressed;* she was *stunned.* Neither negatively nor positively, just stunned. Struck silent almost — she stared all evening from her position on the couch right opposite the fireplace. Her mumbling sounded disjointed, bubbling, and high.

Surface differences: Tom Young admitted that until last spring, he didn't know that not every girl had a coming-out party. "I thought that even in the slums the girls had little deb balls."

Small differences: Many of the boys came with dates, and there weren't any "unattached" girls. All the girls were fantastically tall and universally blond — and, like the boys, good-looking. Kate couldn't get over their size. I said to her, "Look at it this way, Kate. Our grandparents were poverty-stricken Europeans, and we've only been eating well for one or two generations. Look at them: eating hearty for two hundred years? What do you expect?"

Surface differences: According to Kate, every girl was dressed in a very expensive suit. (She was wearing only a ten-dollar corduroy dress.) But she got her "message" out of it. Staring at a sullen thing up from New York for the weekend especially for the party, wrapped protectively in an asexual thick wool emerald suit and sitting by the fire away from her date, Kate became philosophical. "Look at her. She has a hundred-dollar suit, but she's still not happy."

Small differences: Tom Young likes Kate, it's obvious. Maybe he'll ask her out. We four tended to stay together most of the evening, and somewhere in the middle, Tom spilled some wine on her dress. "Oh, don't worry, I'll buy you a new one." Tom has a very unpreppie cuteness behind his dimples and glasses. I don't know what Kate thinks.

Surface differences: They speak a different language. It features verbs like "to summer" (As in, "Where do you summer?") and nouns like "caretaker" (someone who takes care of your house, like a gardener or servant).

Small differences: Parents live in Europe, permanently or partially. Actually, one girl's father is currently stationed in Vietnam — as agent in charge of security for American personnel. (Before going to Saigon, he was in charge of security in the Congo!) The girl is remarkably beautiful; I know some kids in her Gov 1 section, and that section is said to have almost perfect attendance.

December 1, 1966

When I saw a notice in the *Crimson* on Tuesday that Banfield would have dinner at Dunster House with interested Young

Dems, I immediately called for reservations. With all the people in Gov 146, I was sure that it would be necessary to hurry out so as not to be frozen out. But over the phone the person whom I called was very nonchalant when I offered to spell my name. "Don't worry about a reservation. We just want to get an idea of how many people are coming to see if we'll have to drum up any of the old faithfuls."

The dinner was arranged by a Negro Young Dem. His name, I found out tonight, is Harlon Dalton, and he's taking Gov 146.

"Frankly, Professor Banfield, I arranged this dinner tonight," he began with a very parliamentary voice, "because I personally am disturbed by a number of the theses which you seem in fact to me to be propounding in Gov One Forty-six."

Although Harlon ranged over the whole gamut of Higher Banfield Criticism, he concentrated on attacking what seemed to me to be a rather nonessential part of the course — Banfield's idea that there is no aspect of the "Negro subculture" which distinguishes it in important ways from white culture.

In a voice more humble, serious, and quiet than I've heard him use all year, Banfield asked Harlon to describe to him where he thought the Negro subculture is basically different. But all Harlon could produce was a disjointed and halting elegy to "soul parties" (which he said were completely different from white parties) and the fact that Negroes don't go steady.

He sounded apologetic at bringing up such examples. His phrases began like, "For example, it has been argued that the so-called soul parties . . ."

We were all seated around a big oblong table in a private dining room, and once we were through eating, the question-answer-reply flowed and ebbed incessantly. The one or two non–Gov 146 people there were interested in discussing Banfield's recent condemnation of the 2–S deferment, in a statement issued with some other professors, mostly liberals or radicals.

"Professor Banfield, as you are probably aware, several professors have taken this position on the draft as a tool of opposition to the war. Professor Walzer, in particular, sees the prospect of politically influential middle-class parents facing the possibility of their sons being drafted as a big stimulus for antiwar activity. Do you have any comment on that?"

"Well, Professor Walzer is entitled to his reasons, and I have my own." He sounded like an old New England farmer.

Once the school routine gets established, there are few new topics of conversation — except midyear exams — until the time comes to "apply" for living in one of the nine upperclass houses. The process resembles somewhat applying for college, but it beats fraternity rushing. (There are no frats at Harvard.) Each house has a different reputation. Winthrop is for jocks, Eliot for preppies, Adams for Bohemians. One cold March night I spoke about the whole procedure with Dave Bruce.

March 3, 1967

"I'm applying to Adams. What about you?" I was answering Dave's query.

"I am too." I was a little bit surprised. I expected Dave, despite his sometime break with tradition, to go for Eliot. I asked him why he wasn't.

"Oh, God, that would be my *last* choice. Those are just the kind of people I want to get away from — I had enough of them at Groton. Their intellectual horizon abruptly stops at any point beyond snowball fights and getting drunk at a party."

"Is this get-drunk-every-weekend here at Matthews a carry-over from prep school?"

"Well, at most of the prep schools, liquor is forbidden. It's mainly pent-up desire unleashed here. Speaking of Eliot House, by the way, did you see that story on Master Finley in the *Crimson?*" Professor Finley is the nobility-loving old man who is the most paternalistic of the house masters, most anxious to keep the distinct images of the houses intact, and most responsible for the character of Eliot House. He's proud of his "boys."

"I thought you didn't subscribe to the *Crimson*." That has always struck me, because it represented to me a clear symbol of self-exile from Harvard.

"I read this one in Bundy's room. Anyway, there was a feature about him which told about the winter afternoon he was walking over the bridge on the Charles outside of Eliot House, and he saw some Cambridge guys fishing through a hole in the ice. So he raised up his arm and called out" — here Dave snickered — " '*Salve piscatores.*' And the fisherman yelled back, 'Screw you, mack!' "

Because I had written a piece for the New York Times *on the Harvard freshman class, I was invited to speak to a huge group of prospective Harvard freshmen at the Harvard Club of New York. I spoke with Don Chiofaro, captain of the football team, who spoke on how easy Harvard was academically ("there are really a lot of gut courses around"). Two other students also spoke.*

March 17, 1967

I was the only one with long hair. I was representing the freakouts and rebels to everyone in the audience. A Harvard

Club official introduced me by saying that my *Times* article on Harvard "had created more stir about Harvard than anything since the activities of the late senator from Wisconsin." When he identified me with the *Times* piece, there were a few out-of-place, almost movie-star-like ohs and ahs.

"There'll be some surprises when you get up to Cambridge. You'll find that most of the student body consists of normal kids. You'll even find some conservatives, which may shock you." Laughs. "But don't worry; a lot of them will change — eventually." Laughs, again. "One guy I know in my dorm had never gotten drunk even once in his life before he came to Harvard. Now he smokes pot almost every night." Laughter.

I had been asked to talk about the question of big versus small schools.

"The most amazing thing about Harvard is the amount of activity going on there. Sunday, when I go back, former governor Pat Brown of California will be speaking to one group, and 'Sing Out!' — that's the 'Up With People' extravaganza which you might have seen on TV with Pat Boone — will be, I guess, singing out. There are speeches and meetings constantly. The movie theaters are half the price they are in New York. And there's always the Square if you're desperate for girls."

I paused and ha-hummed. "Some people speak of the supposedly intimate atmosphere which exists at certain schools in, uh, Connecticut and New Jersey, which they compare with the alleged impersonality of Harvard. Well, you might say that there's an enforced intimacy at those places because there's nothing else to do. But at any rate the atmosphere at Harvard isn't really impersonal. The freshman dorms have anywhere from thirty to a hundred kids in them, which isn't very big, and you can really get to know the kids in your dorm. Relations with professors are as close as you want to make them."

The old, distinguished, and rich alumnus who had paid for the whole dinner — and who was honored for that with a silent seat at the center of the dais — was very worried that I had given the fathers a false impression of what Harvard was like by talking about the alcohol virgin now on pot. "You wouldn't say that this is any more than an isolated case, would you?"

"Well, I'll have to be honest and say that there are many kids who smoke pot. But the case I described before *is* unique and rather strange. And I think that the pot problem at Harvard is certainly no worse than it is at other colleges."

"Could you assure the fathers here that there won't be any social pressures put on the boy to experiment with dangerous drugs?"

"Oh, don't worry about that. Nobody's going to turn on who doesn't want to. You just don't have to go around with the kids who are taking drugs. You can ignore them if you want."

"I would also like to point out to the fathers here that the Harvard administration takes a very serious view of those who indulge with these drugs, and actively discourages their use."

He wasn't concerned about Chiofaro's advice on how to do Harvard without learning anything.

Someone in the audience asked Chiofaro how expensive the social life up in Cambridge is. "Oh, it's really cheap. You can get along on almost nothing. I'm a scholarship student," he proudly stated and repeated, "It's no problem. You can bring a girl into your house dining room for only a dollar thirty-five, if you're willing to let her submit to the horrible food. And —"

"Could you give a specific figure on how much your social life runs a week?" the questioner interrupted.

"Oh, it's really not much. It's no problem at all. Look, I only have three sport jackets up at school. It's no sweat."

That startled the questioner (as it did me) into more insistency. "Well, I might be an exception, but three sport jackets strikes me as a lot. Could you give a dollars and cents figure on how much it costs?"

"Well," Chiofaro's voice slowed down, "I'm sure if you skimp you'll have no problem getting along on — say, ten bucks a week."

Most of us gasped.

June 1, 1967

What's the balance sheet for the year? What have I learned?

I've learned a lot. First of all, everything I've learned from my courses. Ec 1 introduces you to a whole huge category of knowledge unobtainable from newspapers, radio, or general books. Banfield was fascinating. I read mounds of great Shakespeare for Daniel Seltzer's course and learned what Shakespeare was trying to tell us about philosophy and life. My tutorial was the only bad course I took.

I learned that Harvard isn't just Great Neck South Senior High School intellectuals writ large. Harvard is full of non-intellectuals, jocks, future businessmen, *and* absolutely brilliant kids who between them have been everywhere around the world and done virtually everything there is to do. I learned that Harvard is a gut. The hardest thing is to get in here; once you're in exams are easy and grading is light. The diversity can be both exciting and disappointing, because diversity of necessity includes not only kids whom you have a lot to learn from and admire, but also kids whom you wonder how they ever got into Harvard.

I did a lot. I saw huge numbers of movies, endless speakers. I thought up the idea of issuing a critique of the conservative biases on the reading list in Ec 1 — and helped write it only on the basis of what I had learned in Ec 1 itself. We distributed the eight-page critique in March. Chances look good that the new head of the course, Otto Eckstein, likes the critique and will make the changes we asked for. I staged, publicized, and ran an appearance of Michael Harrington, author of *The Other America*, co-sponsored by Young Dems and YPSL. Six hundred kids paid a dollar each to come hear him. Just last week — in the middle of final exam period — I organized a support picket line for striking workers at the Harvard University Press. Ten big-name and small-name professors and thirty students showed up. There was a front-page article in the *Crimson* about it. I did it despite all the studying I had to do.

The freshman year is the hardest, the most uncertain, the most anxious for everyone. There is so much to get used to, new things to try to figure out. Every upperclassman I know says that his freshman year was his worst at Harvard. Water fights, constant drunkenness, and so forth are reported to decline drastically as soon as freshmen become sophomores. Next year we can give girls a Harvard house address rather than a desultory address in the Yard's freshman dorms. It's been a pretty good year, and from here on it's all uphill.

2. The Radicals

I CAME TO HARVARD *with, among other ideas, the intention to set up a democratic socialist club at Harvard, independent of the already flourishing SDS chapter, with which I had too many disagreements. Ever since I had come in contact with it through a friend in high school, the YPSL's mix of political morality with tactical realism had impressed me. The organization had recently been revived by disillusioned veterans of SDS. Oblivious of the many difficulties of starting a chapter of the Young People's Socialist League — when hardly anyone but a few old-time SDS cadres had even heard of the organization — I talked up the YPSL (pronounced Yipsel) with everyone I met and trudged to the first SDS meeting of the year. One of the people who first hit my eye was Mark Dyen, a freshman living right upstairs whom I had been trying to interest in the YPSL.*

September 30, 1966

My arms were full with YPSL literature when I arrived in Emerson 105, a classroom in the Yard. It looked different with students in control. Hastily, I displayed the various literature on the seats near the door, opposite the table which had been brought in by SDS to sell memberships and their own literature. SDS didn't react kindly to my display. "This is our meeting, you know."

"Certainly you don't object to the free dissemination of minority views?" Mark Dyen walked in. He stopped at the SDS table and looked intently at the literature.

"You know, you need approval to sell literature at a meeting."

"Don't tell me you would turn a radical in to the *Administration* — the Establishment?" I called Mark over. "How's it going?"

"All right. How are you?" Mark seemed a little colder than usual.

"Did you get a chance to read the stuff I lent you?" He nodded. "What did you think?"

"I'm going to join SDS." The way he said that, so calmly, felt like the way a hired gunman might come up and say, "I'm going to kill you." Before the meeting, seven kids signed the interest sheet and a few bought literature. I suppressed my feelings about Mark.

The meeting appeared confused partly due to the parade of unfamiliar people taking and leaving the microphone to give reports on different branches of SDS activity, and partly because it *was* confused. Most of the reports were disorganized. At the end of one of them a tall, blond kid who had himself given one report, stood up from several rows in back of me and broke in, "I'd like to say that I don't think that was a very good report." That startled even the leaders on the stage. Actually, I shouldn't speak of "leaders," since every speaker was extremely self-conscious about using that word. One apologized that he was talking from a platform that was on a higher level than the audience.

Most of this was amusing.

The meeting, naturally, started a half hour late, and I kept staring at the clock, waiting for 8:45, which is when I had to leave for a date. I counted the number of kids there, around 150. The only time I was shocked rather than amused was when the chairman of the SDS foreign policy committee began his remarks by saying, "We think that the NLF in Vietnam is fighting for the same things we are fighting for here in America." The simple-minded would conclude from this that the SDS is fighting for a communist dictatorship. The pathetic thing is that for SDS it means something else — that the Vietcong is fighting for democracy. I glanced at Mark Dyen, but he didn't flinch at all.

David Bruce had gotten himself elected to the Young Democrats Yard Council, which is the special freshman Young Dems body, and, according to the flyer the Young Dems distributed, "the traditional first step for those interested in Young Democrat politics." But when I met him for the first time at dinner and we introduced ourselves, he had other things on his mind. He's tall, aristocratic-looking, and speaks with a slight British accent.

October 1, 1966

David had heard I was interested in politics and wanted to talk some. If Al Gross only knew! He asked me what I thought of SDS, explaining that he had attended their first meeting and enjoyed the high intellectual level of their ideas. I wondered to myself whether he had been at the same intellectually sterile and clichéed SDS meeting I had attended, but out loud I merely commented that he should give equal time to YPSL when we got started.

"What are the differences between SDS and YPSL?" A strand of his long hair kept on falling over his face, and his fingers kept on pushing it back.

"Well, for example, we would never say, like SDS did at their meeting, that the Vietcong is fighting for the same goals as we are. Did you think that statement was of stellar intellectual quality?"

"No." But he went on to cite some other things said at the

meeting. While a few made sense, the majority were hackneyed New Left arguments and phrases. But I presume David hasn't traveled extensively in New Left circles, and a cliché sounds original the first time you hear it.

"Let me take an example from California politics, which I guess you've become pretty familiar with." He had told me he had been working over the summer on a construction gang in San Francisco. "SDS takes the position that it doesn't matter whether Brown or Reagan wins for governor, and some even take the disastrous position of 'the worse, the better,' and hope that Reagan wins!"

I assumed that this would really shock him, but he responded, "Well, you know, I can see their point. Brown really isn't such a flaming liberal." He said "flaming liberal" with a mixture of continental urbanity and SDSish sarcasm. I felt at ease with David, but I certainly don't really understand him yet.

The *Crimson* is obviously controlled by SDS. That was my first, irrational response to their story on the SDS meeting last night. No mention was made of any of the idiocy. And the article implied that SDS had eleven hundred members at Harvard and Radcliffe — that figure being only the number who had signed the "no obligation" SDS interest card at registration. I bet that most of those people were showing little more than intellectual curiosity. The bigger SDS seems, the harder it's going to be to set up a YPSL chapter, which will obviously be small at the beginning.

I saw that best today when Mark Dyen came in after dinner to return the articles I lent him. "Why don't you join SDS instead of trying to set up a new organization? If you disagree with some of their policies, just fight within." Mark was already

speaking as an SDS militant, trying to sell his organization
to me.

I explained to him how YPSL people helped found SDS but
were soon far outnumbered by kooks. "One of the people who's
remained almost got beat up at the last SDS convention by PL
kids — you know, that's Progressive Labor, the pro-Chinese
Communist party. Anyway, so a lot of these people got together
and refounded YPSL, you know, which was around from the
thirties. Anyway, I couldn't join SDS because it's against my
principles to work in the same organization with communists,
whom you'll no doubt find in this chapter. Do *you* think the
Vietcong is fighting for participatory democracy?"

"No, I don't agree with that either, but you have to work
within SDS if you're a radical."

*I met Doug one night during freshman week at a meeting
which we were all required to attend, in order to meet assorted
deans. He introduced me sometime later to his roommate
Ernie, a suave black who had been a Capitol page in Washington, D.C., a mixture of on-the-make politician and with-it nationalist. We all met one night at dinner.*

October 11, 1966

"Steve, what is YPSL's position on Black Power?" Ernie
queried without preparation or preface.

"Hey, did Doug tell you about YPSL?" I didn't wait to have
my question answered, realizing that perhaps I had mentioned
it to him. "Well, obviously we're for Black Power in its literal
meaning that black people should have power. The YPSL official position reads something like, 'While supporting full

democratic participation of American Negroes in politics, we reject the slogan of Black Power as divisive and harmful.' " But more than wanting to recite our position, I wanted to hear Ernie's. Do Negroes at Harvard, having "made it" of sorts already, rush into apathy toward politics, careers in science or business, and conformity? There was also one other Negro kid at the table, whose name I can't remember now, but who comes from a southern city, was wearing a beret, and had grown a goatee onto his already pointed chin. I continued, "That perhaps cryptic statement means, essentially, that we don't think that the program — to the extent that there *is* a program, and one of the problems with the slogan is that it's a substitute for a program — of Black Power will aid in bringing about a situation where black people have real power." Many Negroes don't like to be described as "Negroes" anymore. I always try to use the preferred expression, "blacks" or "black people."

"What do you mean?" Ernie asked.

"Let me reverse the question. What do *you* mean when you say Black Power?"

This time the other black kid spoke. Throughout, he was so angry, and maybe contemptuous, that I was almost expecting him to start calling me whitey. "What you white folks don't dig, man, is that blacks want to control their *own* organizations now. You know, man, we like don't *like* a situation where the president of the NAACP has been, ever since it was founded, a white Jew."

"Come on, don't give me the speech. OK, I'm for Negroes controlling their own organizations too. But that's not all there is to Black Power, is it?"

Louder, more convinced. "Man, remember that Negroes are a majority this very day in Newark, and in ten years they're gonna be a majority in most big cities, 'cause you white folks is all moving out to the suburbs. Now, when I say Black Power, I mean Negroes should take power wherever they're in a majority."

I was carefully heightening my responses. "But that's not a *program!* Obviously, Negroes should have full representation based on their numbers. That's *democracy* — I realize it hasn't been implemented yet — not Black Power."

"Man, you have a system now where black people don't even control their own stinking ghetto. The stores aren't black-owned. The landlord is white. The black man is dependent on the white man for everything he needs."

Doug joined in. "Steve, let me give you an example of what Black Power is. You should get the Negro middle class to get together and buy up stores and apartments in the ghetto from whites. For example, Bill Russell — you know, the basketball player for the Boston Celtics — is working on a cooperative thing to buy up sections of Roxbury in Boston, renovate them, and put them under Negro control."

The goateed kid added, vehemently, "Black Power means that blacks should control their lives where they live!"

"OK." I swept my hair back from my damp forehead. "Unfortunately, if *everything* you all say happened, the condition of black people would be hardly better than it is today. Because local power only can't really do much. So what if Negroes control the decrepit housing or the corner grocery stores that are a rapidly declining segment of the economy? What the black needs to fight for is jobs, low income housing, good education — *real things!* It's unbelievable how 'Black Power' drives whites to their shotguns with its radical sounds, but when you dissect it, it turns out to be Bill Russell rebuilding Roxbury or a new traffic light being installed on a ghetto street! How can Bill

Russell rebuild the ghettos when you need billions of dollars to do it, Doug? You need federal money and national power. And Negroes can't get national power alone, no matter how united and militant they are. Negroes have to be in *coalitions* with groups that also want big federal programs to end poverty and achieve full employment — like the labor unions and white liberals or radicals. Now I realize that's not so simple to achieve, but it's to build such a coalition that YPSL is working." There was a hiatus, during which I could feel that the body of the boy with the beret next to me was getting hotter, and his breath faster.

"But how does Black Power prevent national things?" Ernie asked.

"Well, first of all, by implying that the solutions to black problems are local. Second, by alienating possible allies through slogans that appear to be antiwhite. Third, most Black Power leaders are against coalitions."

Ernie spoke again. "But what about the *psychology* of the ghetto? For me, that's the most important problem. You know, there are all these cats around the ghetto who actually believe they're inferior. And they don't want to work to improve their lives. When they cry for Black Power in the ghetto, they're freeing themselves from their lack of self-respect. They're saying they have their own culture — and you know how important a sense of a cultural identity is to people. You know, it's like the cats who wear their hair natural, African-style now instead of straightening it constantly. They're not ashamed of being black."

"Yeah, or lightening their skin — I've seen ads for that stuff in *Ebony*," I cut in, to lighten the air heavy from adversary debating.

"Yeah, right. Well, of course that's the publication of the

black bourgeoisie. The thing is that black people must realize they have their own cultural heritage." The boy from the South nodded. "Yeah, tell it like it is."

"Again, I agree with you about that. But the basic problem of the ghetto is *not* bad psychology. That's shit." For some reason, that flowed out inexorably, without trepidation. "It sounds like the old white moderate saying that what the Negro needs is self-improvement, not real solutions. Shit, man, most Negroes in the ghetto work *harder* than the average white bum — they're doing the dirty jobs and getting ridiculous pay." (The southern kid laughed, "You're not kidding, man.") "You're going to tell me that their basic problem is bad psychology? Man, the way to solve any problems like that is through attacking the objective causes of them. Giving a man a job in helping to rebuild his own community is one of the best cures I can imagine." My voice had lowered just perceptively from a shout. "To tell you the truth, I think you're projecting your own problems on ghetto Negroes. I can understand that the basic problem of the middle-class black is to find his own identity — you know, *negritude* and all that. But don't project your hang-ups on the guy who's sweating to find a job that isn't there. If black people adopt a go-it-alone attitude and if you ever get the local control in Harlem or Lowndes County, you'll see a psychological problem then, because after a while the people will see that they've hit up against a wall" — I pounded my left fist against my right palm — "of inability to solve basic problems without money. The people will be more demoralized than ever, because they've cried 'Black Power' and the walls haven't come tumbling down."

We seemed to have reached a climax. There was an even longer pause. I hadn't finished my chicken yet, but everyone else was preparing to leave. There was no advance indication of what the other Negro kid said as he left. "How do I go about joining YPSL?"

I'm positive that what he was really telling me, unconsciously, was something like, "You are the first white to have ever *argued* with me, rather than treating me like an object you could never disagree with or speak anything but platitudes to."

The newly established Kennedy Institute of Politics — function unclear, operating out of a two-room office at 1737 Cambridge Street — announced at the beginning of the year that they were setting up an "Honorary Associates Program," wherein various government official types would come to Harvard for a few days to take some time off thinking and getting ideas and views (translation — shooting the bull) with professors and students. It was announced that the first honorary associate would be Secretary of Defense McNamara. SDS wants more than a private meeting with a handful of randomly selected students and carefully selected professors.

October 28, 1966

The SDS had a general membership meeting last night. It was reported in the *Crimson* this morning in a lead story titled, SDS ASKS MCNAMARA. They're going to ask him to debate with Robert Scheer of *Ramparts*.

Students for a Democratic Society, acting on a vote by its membership last night, will send a telegraph of invitation to McNamara this week. Scheer has assured SDS that he is "willing to debate the Secretary of Defense at any time, any place."

Many members of SDS feel that McNamara will not accept their

invitation, but they have made no plans for any protest demonstrations during the Secretary's visit. They felt that contingency plans
would make their invitation appear "disingenuous."

Early last week, SDS was informally contacted by an official of the
Kennedy Institute who wanted to know what plans SDS was making
for McNamara's visit.

One reason for the official's interest in SDS plans was that there
had been a good deal of talk among SDS members about "blocking
House entrances and running McNamara off campus." However,
last night it was officially decided not to anticipate unpleasantness.

To support its invitation, SDS was already circulating on a
table outside Sever Hall today a petition asking McNamara to
debate Scheer. Their sign read:

DO YOU WANT TO LISTEN TO
McNAMARA?
Join the Request for OPEN DEBATE
LET US HEAR BOTH SIDES!!!!!!

Next to the McNamara petition, which I signed, there was
a table with that Vietnam petition which had been circulated
back in September but which I hadn't seen since. The freshman
who was manning it was Michael Kazin, son of the literary
critic Alfred Kazin. He was strikingly handsome, though he
needed a shave. He was dressed neatly in a jacket and tie. You
can always tell a radical around this place, because he's almost
the only one who's neat. You have to impress people.

He began with the standard complaint about how slow
signature-gathering was going. I continued by praising his father's books, and he grimaced. He has to establish his own
identity, I guess. He recognized a pretty Cliffie who walked
by and left the table, asking the SDS guy who was on the other
table to take over for him.

I told him about the YPSL meeting on Tuesday. He has a Young Dems Yard Council meeting that night but will come if it's over in time. It's good to see that someone against the war is on the Yard Council.

November 3, 1966

MCNAMARA IS NOT DEBATING WITH ANYONE; SDS WILL DEMON-STRATE IN QUINCY COURTYARD, was the headline in the *Crimson* today, and I think something interesting will be happening soon, though nobody is sure what. All we know is that there will be some vague, inexplicit "disruptive demonstration." At their hastily called meeting last night SDS decided for that. Beyond that, there is only confusion.

Barney Frank, special assistant at the Kennedy Institute in charge of liaison for McNamara's visit, didn't even let Mc-Namara reply. Frank declined for McNamara, saying that such a debate would violate the "spirit" of the Kennedy Institute invitations. This seemed slightly flimsy to me, since this is the first "honorary associate" visit, and any "spirit" must mainly be a sprite in Richard Neustadt's eye. The word from Mark Dyen is that Frank and the SDS leadership are meeting constantly to see if they can avoid "trouble." Apparently SDS co-chairman Mike Ansara has good "contacts" and rather friendly relations with administrators. (His recent bride is the granddaughter of a senior partner of Merrill, Lynch, Pierce, Fenner, and Smith, Inc.)

In Barney Frank, SDS has found a Satan much more to their disliking than any stuffy old administrator or dean. The deans are too high up to dally in the gutter by entering into contra-putal polemics with SDS public school boys. But Barney Frank, '62, an enormous cigar-smoking hulk who looks as if he's just stepped out of a smoke-filled room and speaks with a heavy New York City accent, relishes, I hear, the exchange of verbal atomic bombs. Worse than that, Barney Frank is a Left-liberal who can speak a radical's vocabulary. And SDS knows people like that are the biggest enemy.

November 6, 1966

I'm going to go to the McNamara demonstration tomorrow to see what happens. Mainly today I tried to find out from Mark Dyen what will happen tomorrow. The outline is that there will be a rally outside Quincy House while McNamara is inside talking with the fifty students. SDS has mimeoed a series of questions about Vietnam for McNamara, which they're distributing around the school and especially to sympathetic ones among the fifty who'll be inside.

Meanwhile, SDS will have commandos staged around all the exits to the building, and they will signal when and if McNamara comes out of one of them with the walkie-talkies that they will all be provided with. Then SDS kids will block McNamara as he tries to leave, and a representative of SDS will ask McNamara to answer some questions about Vietnam before they let him go.

But obviously he'll refuse, and I can't get any answers on what will happen then. It's either a secret, or else they don't know.

At any rate, SDS is trying to call up today every one of the 1100 who signed his registration interest card and ask him to come tomorrow. They are so desperate for manpower that Mark Dyen even asked — I should say bludgeoned — my roommate Mike into making ten phone calls for him. Mike, unfortunately, is too good-natured to refuse anyone, even though he opposes any potential disruption. But Mike finally stopped calling after the fourth straight person on the list hadn't even remembered signing an SDS interest sheet or else angrily told him that he had heard rumors that there was going to be violence against the secretary of defense and that he was strongly opposed to that.

November 7, 1966

Quincy is the most recently built of the Harvard houses. It is colloquially known as "the Harvard Hilton," I found out, because of its modern, garden-apartment appearance. As if to fit the appearance of the house, Quincy House "men" have a midwestern, suburban, conservative image. Perhaps that explained the messages carefully painted on bed sheets and draped out of the big picture windows to greet the demonstrators.

NAPALM SDS.

KILL THE CONG!

To be fair, there was also one that read, VIETNAM — ANOTHER EDSEL FOR MCNAMARA. Before the action started, someone near me playfully commented, "Gordon Linen is sure in for a big cleaning job next week." Harvard's collective sense of humor never leaves it.

When I arrived, McNamara was still inside, but the events had already started. Scheer was speaking, to the steady jeering of some tough-looking jock types. Their impoliteness went unnoticed by the press. They were counterjeered by antiwar people and at times it was impossible to hear Scheer and the other speakers over the loud monotone of the jocks and the shouting of the others.

"Shut up, you shitheads!" one person yelled out so loud that his voice boomed over the cacophony. The antiwar people cheered.

Around me was the unconcerned air of "after me, the deluge."

There were several hundred people there, most of them anti-McNamara, and most everybody, on both sides, was eager for action. But nobody knew exactly what was going to happen.

"Get your copy of *New America*, America's democratic socialist newspaper! Only ten cents!" I yelled.

I saw one of the Trotskyists, burly and smiling, near me. "Beat that kid over there up, Jim," he indicated to the person next to him. I didn't think he was serious.

"Hey, don't you believe in freedom of speech?"

"Freedom of speech for counterrevolutionaries?" He chuckled and walked away through the thick crowd.

"We call Khrushchev the 'Butcher of Budapest' here in the United States," Scheer shouted into the microphone of the hastily prepared stand. "The United States Air Force has bombed the North Vietnamese city of Vinh out of existence. I think it's time to start calling LBJ the 'Butcher of Vinh!' "

Acting like Walter Cronkite, or some other anchor man at a political convention, David Loud of SDS took up the microphone every few minutes to say, "We have spies inside to tell us from what exit McNamara is leaving. As soon as we receive the word from inside, we'll tell you." Now back to the speeches.

The main entrance to Quincy House was locked up. We were demonstrating on Plympton Street, not inside the courtyard. The grass inside the courtyard was green. The pro-McNamara jocks were sitting in a row on the fence. I saw a helicopter fly overhead — I don't know if it had anything to do with us.

The Kennedy Institute had hoped that by keeping McNamara's exit point secret they could allow him to escape undetected. But actually they were merely increasing the chance of "trouble." Then there was the squad of student bodyguards selected by the Kennedy Institute to protect McNamara. Although the institute denies it, the guards claim they had gotten instructions to beat up any students who tried to block McNamara's path.

The SDS people got tired of talking. Mike Ansara took the microphone. "Will everyone please move from Plympton Street onto Mount Auburn," he ordered slowly. Mt. Auburn is just perpendicular to Plympton. "We've gotten word that McNamara will be coming out of there." The PA went dead for a minute, and nobody could hear him. By the time it came on again, the crowd was already moving, and Ansara was already off the platform, pushing his way over to Mt. Auburn Street so he could be at the center of the action.

I was right next to him. The PA came on again, but I heard him without it. "When McNamara comes out, everyone lock arms so he can't leave!" His voice projected through the microphone was an ominous echo of his unmagnified voice as I heard it. He was calmly angry, playing around with the mike.

He told the crowd to keep quiet so they could hear him. "When he comes, I'll say to him, 'Mr. McNamara, there are several questions we'd like to ask you.' Now I don't want any yelling or screaming when he comes. Everyone keep silent."

Since I was right up front, I was marked for the group to be locking arms. I inched myself away from the front.

But before the chain could get established, one of the SDS commandos at the back garage exit from Quincy House started yelling. The chain unchained, and everybody started running. Feeling like an Indian surrounding a wagon train, I ran along, arriving in time to see a car rushing out of the garage and a mob scene around the car.

"Holy shit, they're going to run over that kid!" I screamed

out as someone seemed to be caught under the black limousine.

So here was McNamara.

Dyen had been the commando who had yelled. He's advancing fast in SDS. His hair was plastered down with sweat.

The kid escaped from the path of the car.

But suddenly people started running again, on around to Mill Street, almost completing the rectangle. What was going on? Shit! (Later I found out that the car from the garage was another decoy.) I kept running, outside the perimeter of the crowd. My copies of *New America* were still in my hands, getting sweated up. Hold on tightly.

When I got onto Mill Street, most of the crowd hadn't arrived yet. There was a limousine at the center of the street, and a group of twenty kids were sitting down in front of it. One kid from SDS was yelling, "Everybody sit down! Stop the car!"

But most people were simply surrounding the car, being pushed inexorably into the vacuum which had existed when I first arrived. The crowd was rushing to see the "real thing"; now it was forced into the middle of it. A few were screaming.

"Hey, let me get out!"

"Let me out of here. I don't want to block the fucking car!"

I almost felt like a newspaper reporter.

None of the circumstances leading up to the confrontation on Mill Street favored, to say the least, a peaceful demonstration. I didn't know at the time whether the sit-down had been originally planned by SDS; at any rate, it wasn't publicized. (Tonight Mark Dyen admitted to me that it had been a secret part of the plans.) But there was a lot of fighting going on, and screaming from both pro and anti kids. An older guy in front of me was yelling, "Down with American imperialism!" It seemed stridently out of place, even here.

I was about five feet from the car, but I couldn't see Mc-Namara inside. There was no question about it: the car wouldn't be able to move. The noise crescendoed.

Then McNamara climbed, slowly, out of the car.

In all the plots I had imagined, the idea of McNamara giving in and coming out of the car was never considered. I still don't know exactly how he got out — the guy in front of me was too tall — but I could catch him finally as he jumped on top of the car, aided by Mike Ansara.

McNamara was smiling. I'm not sure whether he was more excited than I was. As people saw him, there was a cheer of victory on Mill Street. As if it were a cheer for him, McNamara held up his hands like an actor requesting the audience to stop the lengthy applause because he wants to get onto the next number.

He was still smiling.

The noise never died down enough so that I could hear what Ansara and David Loud were saying to McNamara. But soon Ansara grabbed the mike and yelled out, "Secretary McNamara has agreed to answer a few questions." Cheers. Victory. Again, I never expected that. I was sure he was getting out to politely ask everyone to disperse. And then, maybe, the fire hoses would come.

McNamara took the mike. He completed Ansara's sentence for him. ". . . for five minutes, and then I'll have to ask you to let me get on to my next appointment." His hair was perfectly in place, as always. Ansara told everyone to keep quiet, and for the first time there was silence. It came only slowly, but it came. The guy in front of me shouted, "Don't listen to him! He's killing the people of Vietnam! He doesn't even have the right to speak!" But for the time being he was a small minority.

Everyone was raising his hand to ask questions. The first question was about civilian casualties, the second about whether the war had really started as an invasion from the north. Afterward people claimed the questions were stupid. But the fact was that nobody expected ever to be able to ask any questions, so nobody was ready to pour on the rhetoric.

The audience didn't like the answers McNamara started to give.

"I'm afraid I don't know how many civilian casualties there have been in the Vietnam conflict."

"Don't you *care?*" someone shouted from the back, and that was the signal for the end of the silence. I could still hear McNamara talking, but people a little farther away said that McNamara's voice had become completely drowned out.

"The war in Vietnam didn't begin in nineteen fifty-seven, as you said in your question. It began earlier than that, in nineteen fifty-four, when the North Vietnamese sent down cadres to infiltrate with the refugees who were leaving North Vietnam." That was the first time anybody had ever heard *that* argument from the government. Some people laughed above the noise. I heard one cry of "bullshit!"

Suddenly SuperMac broke.

He yelled out, pointing at one person who had said I don't know what, "Look, I went to school at Berkeley and spent four years there doing a lot of the same things you here are doing." I couldn't help thinking something unserious to myself: I wondered whether the Defense Department knew he had been a subversive at Berkeley when they hired him.

The shouting grew louder. Almost all of the kids with rooms overlooking Mill Street had opened their windows, looking over the proceedings with box seats. Strange, I thought, there didn't seem to be any policemen around.

McNamara continued, "I was doing the same things as you are, but there were two big differences." Pause. "I was *tougher*, and I was more *courteous*." The computer had shattered. The man was fighting back.

The television cameras were taking it all down. Total confusion. McNamara pointed to another face. "And I'm *still* tougher!"

The play was over; after that it was downhill. McNamara asked, after a pause, without any noticeable sarcasm, ". . . you ladies and gentlemen to please let me get on to my next appointment." The press conference was over. Ansara conferred with David Loud a moment and then asked the crowd to leave. They did, rather quickly. I stayed around until almost everyone had gone.

Within the next two days, 2700 Harvard undergraduates — an amazing number, really — signed a petition apologizing to McNamara.

November 15, 1966

The great SDS apologia, "Courtesy and the War," came out today, in the form of a flyer announcing their public meeting tonight. It was subdued in tone, almost penitent.

The recent SDS demonstration against Secretary McNamara has stimulated an encouraging amount of discussion on campus concerning the war and the tactics of dissent . . .

When the debate was refused, SDS had to decide what form a demonstration should take. Everything was offered us. Barney Frank would block off the street for us, give us police protection. All we had to do in exchange was to march quietly and in orderly fashion. As the *Crimson's* Bob Samuelson put it, we could have done this any time, McNamara or no McNamara. It was hardly an offer on Mr. Frank's part.

In discussion of our plans, it became clear to us that we could not accept Mr. Frank's definition of the situation. He would have had us become just another college extra-curricular activity, a practice group for later participation as "good citizens." SDS would be allowed, at its will, to hold mock demonstrations, perhaps full of sound and fury, but signifying absolutely nothing. SDS sought to make the point that an architect of a controversial American foreign policy has a duty to confront criticism of that policy in public, especially when the Johnson Administration has continuously evaded this criticism . . .

We are, as Barney Frank of all people should have understood, involved in real politics, in efforts really to confront establishment people with the injustices of the system they run. We are organizing labor, we are organizing in poor communities, we are organizing in middle class communities. On campus we are running seminars, inviting speakers, stimulating debate. We are organizing students against rank in class and against the draft by which the government continues its war in Vietnam. Through these efforts we hope to contribute to a better society.

After last Monday's confrontation, I had heard talk that an extreme group in SDS was going to try to throw Mike Ansara out from the co-chairmanship — for "letting McNamara off too easily"! (He had asked the crowd to disperse at the end, and this without even taking a vote of the people there.) I expressed outrage to Dyen, and he said that if I was really concerned, I ought to go to the meeting and participate in the vote, since anyone who shows up at these meetings can do so.

So I went tonight. I sold *New America* outside. But when Ansara passed, his wife holding on to him and his teeth smiling, he blurted out, "How can you sell that rag?" I left early. No challenge developed to Ansara.

Mark Dyen's voice has changed when he talks to me. It's become monstrous, malicious, cackling. It's become petty· last week he saw me taking in a bundle of New America's *from the mailbox and oozed, "Still at it with your little YPSL? Some people never give up." He grins like the villain in silent movies who's come to foreclose the mortgage.*

November 18, 1966

After dinner Mike told me that Mark Dyen had come in earlier to ask if I wanted to come up to his room and have a talk with Mike Traugot, an SDS co-chairman, who'd be in Dyen's room at ten. As I was leaving for Lamont Library, I said OK, I'd come back at ten.

I hadn't been invited up for private conversation. It was the "first of a series" of SDS dorm meetings to get the immovable freshmen interested in SDS. Mike Traugot had been invited by Mark because the two personally like each other. I commented that he seemed to have been chosen for his relatively moderate views — as a "show radical." Be enticed and then enter the kook show.

Around twenty kids from the dorm sat in a circle on Mark's floor. We passed around bowls of popcorn and bottles of Coke. Kids, mainly skeptical, argued against the McNamara demonstration. But Mike Traugot, mercifully, tried to turn the discussion away from McNamara and toward the "larger question" — Vietnam and the draft.

Mike acted like a dedicated schoolteacher, trying to encourage even the shy to say what they were thinking. On the draft the general non-SDS consensus was that students deserved defer-

ments, because they are more important to society than the
uneducated.

There were different shades of opinion on Vietnam. Most of
the kids were moderate doves — they wondered why we were
there, but were hung up on simply "abandoning the country."
On Vietnam, Mike Traugot talked more than others but didn't
attempt to impose his views. Maybe because he was alerted
by Mark (he knew my name already), he tried to include me
on his side as much as possible.

A boy named Ed started off by apologizing that "I shouldn't
be here, because I'm sort of a conservative myself." ("Don't
worry," Mike assured with a smile. "This isn't an in-gather-
ing.") He continued by saying that he didn't think the Vietcong wanted to end the war, so what could the United States do?

Mike gave his answer. He didn't support the NLF or rant
against American imperialism. "The important thing is that
the government change its attitude so that it *wants* to end this
war in Vietnam. We believe, Ed," Mike squeaked, "that there
is considerable specific evidence which shows that the American
government is insincere in its professed desire to negotiate." He
pecked at his goatee. "I personally don't think it's up to the
peace movement to present a detailed program for ending the
war. That's the government's responsibility. Do you see our
point?" He was almost talking through his nose. Would he do
a tap dance as part of the soft sell?

The discussion went on until after one, but I left early. Mark
says that Mike always cuts his little goatee and his not-too-long
hair before going back to his small-town home in Pennsylvania.

Kazin to me: "I liked what you said in some YPSL thing
about changing the Democratic party to 'a real people's party.'
You know, I want to go into politics, run for office, maybe like

Bobby Kennedy. Try to change the Democratic party, you know." At least he's not self-conscious about his ambitions.

"You're from Great Neck, aren't you?" he continued.

"Yeah, why. You know anyone from there?"

"Do you know a girl named Joan Steiner?"

"Yeah, she's probably the most beautiful girl at South."

"I went out with her one summer." Kazin ran his hands through his hair.

"Really?"

"We were on the same teen-age tour to Mexico. She was the first girl I ever loved. I wrote her some poetry." He mused. "She sure did have beautiful tits."

"Is that all you know about her?"

"That was all she would let me know. We were only juniors in high school."

I changed the subject. "Did you see how SDS is going to rechallenge McNamara to a debate? Some people don't know when to stop a bad thing."

"Didn't you think the McNamara confrontation was a good idea?"

I had been on the "Mike Douglas Show" to talk about something I had written for the Saturday Evening Post *called "You Force Kids to Rebel." I invited Mike Kazin to watch the pre-taped broadcast with me in the television room on the second floor of the Freshman Union. He seemed more interested in what I wore than in what I said.*

December 5, 1966

Kazin wasn't impressed that I had expounded SDS-like ideas of participatory democracy on the air, though one friend of

Kazin's who was with us was. Kazin was most turned on by the way I looked on TV: "You really looked good, except — how can you wear *white socks?*"

"OK, Kazin, I apologize. From now on, you can be my dress adviser."

"I can see it, Kelman. You're going to get letters from all over the world. 'My love — you were beautiful on the Mike Douglas Show, and I want to sleep with you. But white socks? Signed, Jean Shrimpton.' And 'Please let me come and meet you. I crave your bod. But don't wear white socks, please. Marion Gram, Radcliffe '70.' Or 'Come to Italy and make love to me. No bianco socks, OK? Gina Lollobrigida.'"

Kazin was making that speech to me as we were walking past Lamont after watching the Mike Douglas thing on the TV set at the union together. I had eaten lunch with him, and he came upstairs afterward to watch the show.

Kazin is a very strange mixed bag — a playboy radical. He's conscious of his good looks and often finishes up our arguments over immediate withdrawal from Vietnam or Black Power by saying, "I don't care, Kelman, I'm better looking than you!" His ravishingly beautiful (by his description) date to his senior prom wore a "Bring the Troops Home Now" button on her long gown. He couldn't come up to my room to talk after the "Mike Douglas Show" because a girl was coming up to his room to cut his hair. (He doesn't care if it's outside parietal hours.)

It was reading period — the two classless weeks we have to prepare for exams — and everyone was desperately studying, especially freshmen.

January 11, 1967

I had assumed that student politics, like everything else un-connected with studying for exams, ceases during reading period. But SDS is completely unmindful of traditions of formal study-ing. So they had a speaker come tonight.

As is fitting when you break convention, the speaker himself was unconventional. He was an English guy named Crook, an expatriate teaching at Peking University. His topic was "The Cultural Revolution in China."

As soon as I found out that SDS was sponsoring the meeting (the publicity put the SDS sponsorship in tiny, virtually un-noticeable letters, very atypically for SDS), I blew up at Dyen. I found him at lunch, eating with my roommate.

"How can SDS sponsor a speaker supporting the purge in China?"

"How do you know he's going to support it?" Dyen inquired with mock naiveté. "Why are you judging in advance?"

"*Please*, Dyen. You know what he'll say." His smile is slime. "I think it's a disgrace that SDS invited this character, as if the barbarities of the so-called Cultural Revolution were related in even the most remote way with democratic radicalism. Whad'ya invite him for — advice on how to rough up public officials, for the next time McNamara comes?"

"Look, YPSL always makes such a big deal about being a *democratic* organization, and you always criticize SDS for hav-ing communists in it — supposedly because communists aren't democratic. Now you're saying we don't have any *right* to invite a pro-Chinese speaker. What about civil liberties? Shouldn't we hear both sides?"

"It's not a question of your *right* to invite him. I favor

George Lincoln Rockwell's right to speak, but that doesn't mean I would personally favor an organization's choosing to extend him a platform on campus. If he wants to speak, OK, but we don't have to provide a forum for him."

Mike joined in, always the uncommitted third party. "But, Steve, I think you're backing Mark's point. Remember, the Law School Young Dems invited Rockwell to speak earlier this year."

I paused for a moment to think. "OK, OK, Mike. Good point. But there's a difference between the Young Dems and SDS. The Young Dems are mainly a forum organization, providing all sorts of speakers without endorsing any of them. In my high school I was head of a thing we had called the Forum Club. The year I was president I invited Herbert Aptheker for the Communist party and a guy from the New York State Conservative party without agreeing with either of them. But SDS is a political organization, not a forum. And when it presents a speaker it's implying political agreement with what the speaker is saying. It's not the same as a forum."

"That's not true," Dyen rebutted, raising and sharpening his voice. "There's no agreement implied."

"No agreement? When is SDS going to present a speaker for the war? You never will, and I don't expect you to, because that's not your position. No matter how you attempt to justify this disaster, you can't — unless you want to set SDS up as the Cambridge Red Guards."

"Look, we refuse to share YPSL's obsession with anticommunism," he gloated devilishly. "We're a forum for every shade of opinion in the Left, and that's why we invited Crook but wouldn't invite a prowar speaker."

"In other words, you consider a Maoist a legitimate part of the Left?"

"Yes."

"That's unbelievable," was my simple, shocked reply. Then I paused for a moment. "And this 'forum of the Left' is a lie too. I'd like to see you invite a speaker with democratic socialist politics!"

We both returned our lunch trays and were both present in Burr B that night to hear Crook. There were about two hundred kids there, and Crook's speech was largely predictable. "Selflessness" was the great ideal of the Cultural Revolution, and the purpose of the whole affair was simply to get rid of selfish elements and spread the community-spirited thought of Chairman Mao. "So-called authorities" who were pushing professionalism rather than proletarianism naturally became a big target. The whole affair was extremely democratic, because anyone could put up a big-character poster denouncing the selfish.

I was so angry that I wrote "A Story" upon returning to my room and pushed a carbon copy under Dyen's door.

"Once upon a time in the land of Us there grew up a man named Lin P. Mak Kar Thee. Now Mak Kar Thee said that there were individuals in the land who were not living up to the thought of Gee Sus Kryst — the spiritual leader of the country who, although over 1900 years old, was still 'alive and in good health' and even occasionally seen walking on the waters of the Yangtze. The thought of Gee Sus Kryst said that men must abandon their selfish concerns and serve the people instead.

"But some people (only about 5 percent of the population, to be sure) were ignoring the thought of Gee Sus. Inspired by brilliant essays like 'In Memory of Jun Byrch,' Mak Kar Thee instituted The Great Cultural Revolution. Big-character posters arose across the land, with different people contributing different things about the misdeeds of various men, until a total picture grew up. Some citizens pointed out that certain anti–Gee Sus elements were even homosexuals. All in all, there was extensive Krystian democracy: not only were top officials exposed, but even local 'authorities' (librarians, professors, etc.) were denounced by big-character posters. Those exposed were naturally disposed of and even exiled.

"Soon the Cultural Revolution made its way to the very highest leaders of the country. Criticisms were not made before long thought and investigation. People were not just condemned overnight. After all, there had been twenty years of treason. But the people decided it was time to make the decision to condemn them too.

"In a neighboring country, which was looking on these events with horror (having undergone a very much milder form of the same phenomenon several years earlier), a student group which called itself 'conservative' invited Will Yum Buck Lee, a teacher at Us State University, to speak on the Cultural Revolution. Just a question of free speech, of course! (So what if 'God and Man at Us State,' 'In Memory of Jun Byrch,' and 'The Us Review' were the only publications for sale outside?) Some, who perhaps recalled the country's own form of the Cultural Revolution — not to speak of the record of the Us government in the past — were skeptical of the invitation. But they were laughed out of town."

In February I had been elected to the Young Dems executive committee, asked to run because I had become friendly with Larry Seidman, the Young Dems president who was soon to join the YPSL. Mike Kazin, who had been on the Freshman

Yard Council since the beginning of the year, was also elected. Our first meeting was in mid-March.

March 13, 1967

Mike Kazin brought up a resolution putting the Young Dems on record as favoring immediate withdrawal from Vietnam. Arlene Popkin, doyen of the executive committee, reminded the new members that the club had no official policy at all on Vietnam, and that last year the club had spent hundreds of hours in debate and committee report but had still failed to come up with any policy. "You will notice that many of those prominently involved in that debate have not participated in our activities this academic year." She recommended that we vote down the resolution until the club could consider more fully all the policy alternatives during the spring.

Only Kazin and one other kid voted for. Kazin immediately began scribbling something on a sheet of notebook paper and, after the next order of business, raised his hand to read his statement of resignation from the executive committee. "An organization which does not take a clear position in favor of immediate and unconditional withdrawal of the American occupying army which is in Vietnam fighting the Vietnamese people cannot possibly be a vehicle for significant or radical political change in the United States. The Young Democrats speak about working within the System, but, contrary to the usual argument, this method will yield fewer practical results than independent action outside. I will be quitting the Young Democrats to be able to devote my full time to SDS, which is the only organization on campus which I believe is seriously committed to changing American society."

Then he just got up and left.

For the week after the first great Central Park be-in, in the dawn of the age of flower children, a huge Spring Mobilization to End the War in Vietnam was planned for New York. I finally ended up going, but I was hesitant because of the many Trotskyists and communists in the mobilization. I had an angry argument with Kazin and Dyen about the whole thing. A newcomer was Barry Margolin, a recent freshman convert to SDS (their third freshman activist) from the lib-radicalism of community organizing for the Phillips Brooks House, Harvard's social service umbrella organization.

April 11, 1967

"Steve, look. There are going to be all sorts of innocent housewives and ministers there. And *you*, who call yourself a radical, are hesitating about whether to go! I can't understand it." Margolin speaks the softest of the three. "Don't you think you're being a little stupid?" He sounded now as if he were imploring. We were on the step outside my room, and the various freshmen were walking past, talking about anything but politics. They won't be going to the mobilization.

"I'm sure there'll be a lot of very nice people there — and that's why it's such a shame that the unclear political stand of the mobilization is gonna mean that the march might not help end the war. Or at least not as much as if it had a clear political program. Look," I went on after pausing, looking at Dyen, "anyone who's legitimately for immediate withdrawal — that's fine. I think there can be legitimate differences of opinion on that. But what I'm opposed to is the influence of communists and people who believe in a Vietcong victory at a *peace* demonstration."

"Kelman, what you social dems don't realize," Kazin broke in harshly and contemptuously, "is that the antiwar movement has already rejected your old red herring about excluding people and loyalty oaths. Marty Peretz told me how your friend Bayard Rustin tried to redbait SDS's first antiwar march out of existence. Look, you think you can control things, but the New Left doesn't believe in excluding *anyone* from demonstrations."

"Look, the John Birch Society is against the war!"

"What . . ."

"Yeah. They say that since the U.S. is ruled by communists, what we're doing in Vietnam must be helping the communists. Would you be in favor of including *them* in your antiwar demonstration?"

"If they wanted to come," Margolin purred.

"Look, I'm not talking about *coming*. I'm not in favor of a loyalty oath on the picket line. What I'm saying is that in the *leadership* totalitarian groups should be excluded."

"There should be no exclusion of any groups on the Left," Kazin retorted with the uncharacteristic dogmatism of an old devotee. I didn't think he'd have the catechism down so pat already. "I worked for the ADA two summers ago, and what I discovered is that you liberals are so hung up with this exclusion thing that you'd rather see no radical movement develop at all rather than one with some communists in it."

"*Some* communists? The Trots and the CP are just about running the show! And what about here at Harvard, with all the PL people running around SDS, with their Mr. Crook speaking on China? That's a disgrace to radicalism! Don't you think there's something incongruous about people whose idea of a good regime is China being in a group called Students for a *Democratic* Society?"

"Don't you think they should have any freedom of speech?

I suppose you agree with Sidney Hook, who . . ." Kazin was preparing himself for a polemical punch in the stomach.

I struck. "Of course they have freedom of speech! They have a right to speak and organize themselves in *their own organization*. But they don't belong in any *democratic* organization. Kazin, do you think China is any sort of model of a 'democratic society?' "

"Kelman, you can't judge an Asian nation by Western terms. Fairbank may not teach us very much in Soc Sci Eleven, but at least I've learned *that* from him. China doesn't have any *tradition* of Western-style parliamentary democracy."

"You know, that can be used to explain away *anything*! No tradition! Did China have any 'tradition' of industrial development? Does South Africa have any tradition of racial equality? That's a typical apologia."

Kazin was silent, with an occasional "Well . . ." punctuating the silence of the next seconds, and finally an, "I don't accept that analogy at all."

Margolin cut off the embarrassment of Kazin's inability to reply. "Steve, you're making a mistake, because you think the PL and CP people are plotting to try to take over SDS. But in fact nobody pays attention to anything they say. They're completely harmless — everyone listens patiently to them and then ignores them. How many are there? Five? They make a lot of noise, but they're not trying to take over SDS. I think they learned their lesson from the thirties."

"They spend all their time arguing with each other!" Kazin interjected, stopping for a moment from playing with his hair. "Jared Israel of PL spends all his time at the SDS executive committee meetings denouncing the mobilization as a revisionist trick, because that's the PL line. So Pete Orriss of the CP has to spend all his time arguing with Jared and making sure that nobody else on the executive committee accepts his arguments. You know, I guess the mobilization is a big project for the CP, and he's probably under some sort of discipline to try to make sure that Harvard SDS supports it."

"Oh, I'm surprised you think communists are under discipline."

"Look, Steve, I'm an independent radical. I'm not a Marxist-Leninist."

"I never . . ."

"I remember Sunday night at the executive committee, Orriss and Jared were arguing with each other, and Orriss finally said to Jared, 'Look, Jared, do we have to always argue with each other more than with anybody else? You know, we're both communists.' That was pretty funny." The walrus smile came out on Kazin's face.

"What about the Crook China meeting?"

"Look, it's SDS policy to give the SDS sponsorship to any speaker who can't find any other group to sponsor him. Jared came to the executive committee and told us that he had this speaker on China, but he'd only be able to speak if SDS sponsored him. If you were at that meeting, you know that all the members of the executive committee asked Crook hostile questions after the speech."

"Look, I think there's a matter of principle involved here. I don't think totalitarians belong in SDS, and I don't think people who support the Vietcong belong in a *peace* demonstration. They're not for peace — they're for victory."

"What do you want — only pacifists?"

I hesitated. I was forgetting the arguments. I couldn't remember what to respond to that.

"No." I hesitated. Finally it came. I breathed more slowly again. "You can have, uh, political objections to the war. But people who would *rather* have a Vietcong military victory than peace don't belong. They should organize their own demonstration in support of the NLF."

"They're for peace. They don't want the war to continue. They want America to get out."

"Johnson wants peace too!"

3. The Alienated

The alienated are not always immediately obvious.

September 26, 1966

I walked down the stairs one-by-one with Doug, because I was slightly queasy from hunger. Down in the lobby a medium height, somewhat bizzare-looking chubby kid with glasses and a nonpolitician air was tacking up on the bulletin board a "humorous" campaign poster he had made. LYNDON JOHNSON, AND OTHER FAMOUS AMERICANS, SAY: "VOTE FOR HARRY BRAND FOR FRESHMAN COUNCIL."

"Is that recommendation supposed to help you get elected? Are you Harry Brand?"

"Yes, I am." I expected him to extend out his hand and ask whether Doug was a registered voter in this district. "And this is Herb Smith, my campaign manager."

"Is this for Pete Lehman's proctorial?"

"Yes. Can I count on your vote?" This kid must have been G. O. president in his high school, even if he was reciting the clichés jocularly.

Harry Brand was elected our representative to the Freshman Council. In addition to his other responsibilities, this made him in charge of organizing our first "extended parietals" dorm party.

October 13, 1966

The party wasn't an organized Harvard orgy; in fact, it wasn't an *organized* anything. The action was going on in too many separate rooms to ever really gel. Successively a certain room might be used mainly for dancing, drinking, talking, and making out — and then it would gradually empty. I didn't see any drugs.

For most of the evening my date and I sat on a dilapidated sofa. Brand was around us most of the night. A very good-looking boy whom I had noticed around the dorm but never met was making out with a very beautiful girl outside of the window right near our sofa, on the fire escape.

"Will you stop breathing so hard, Adam?" Brand giggled, high. "It's disturbing us."

"Brand, if you were going to fuck a girl in five minutes, you'd be breathing hard too," the boy answered, poking his head up out of the girl's breast. She blushed.

"Adam, if you're going to fuck her, at least go back to your room." They stayed there.

"Brand, shut up. You're stinking drunk."

"Yes, isn't it wonderful? My mother would never believe it. This is the first time I've ever gotten drunk."

"Brand, you're making a fool of yourself," I interrupted.

Brand's behavior at the party — his self-mocking and self-conscious drunkenness, which contrasted with his previous suavity, made me want to get to know him better. I went to "interview" him a week later for the story on the freshman class I was writing for the New York Times Magazine. *Then, as he requested, we went together to interview other freshmen on my "list."*

October 22, 1966

Brand gave out his sardonic, negative impressions of Harvard freshmen willingly. "It's impossible to tell what criteria they are chosen by. Certainly," he giggled, "Harvard freshmen are not chosen on any criterion of intelligence. In fact, it would be hard to say that they are 'best' by any criteria."

I asked him to turn down the record player a bit. He was playing *December's Children* by the Rolling Stones.

"It's quite a shock," he continued, as if I hadn't interrupted him, "to see all these jocks around. But even *they* couldn't be the best jocks in the country." Brand was wearing a thick gray sweater, thick glasses, and long hair. He was munching Ritz crackers still left over from the party last week and at one point asked me whether I wanted any leftover Coke.

He surprised me by claiming that he himself had been a "freak" admission.

"I thought that there were no freak admissions from the East." Brand is from Delaware.

"I was the class underachiever," he knowingly replied. "I was only twenty-fourth in my graduating class, but I had two eight hundreds on my SATs" — that's incredible, two perfect scores — "and Harvard must have taken me as a gamble. George deserved to get in." He pointed to his roommate, George Harrington, who's from the same school as Brand, and who was sitting — placid and Buddha-like — in a corner of the room, listening to a record on his stereo through earphones. There are two stereos in the room and a tape recorder.

"George and I are completely different. He's ultrastudious and political, and I'm a flipped-out aspiring novelist." He took out a comb from his pocket and began combing his hair. "Have you read any John Barth?"

"No, I haven't. He's the one who wrote *The Sot Weed Factor*, right?"

"Yeah, well he really turns me on. He and George Plimpton. You've gotta read them. Really. Once I corresponded with

John Barth. It was probably the coolest thing I ever did. I'll
show you the letter later."

"OK."

Our last interview of the night was with Andy Schlesinger. His
room is in Matthews North, and we just knocked and hoped
he wouldn't mind. He didn't; he thought it was a "cool idea."
From his face in the *Register*, I had imagined him to be short.
But I could tell he was taller than I even though he never left
his position lounging across a couch in his room.

"Are you interested in politics?" I asked.

"Oh, I'm a liberal, but I'm not really an activist." He sat
up for a second to tighten the wide belt on his brown corduroy
hip-huggers. He's a mod. There's a wide paisley tie on the
floor.

"Steve, I hope you don't mind if I say something," Harry
Brand interjected. "You know, you're not asking kids the
right questions. All night you've been asking them about their
views of the Establishment, about politics and stuff."

"What are the right questions?" We were sitting on the floor,
beneath Schlesinger.

"Well, the questions I would be interested in reading about
are like, 'Do your friends smoke pot?' or 'Where do you get
pot around Harvard?'"

"OK. Andy, where do you get pot around Harvard?"

"Yeah, sure there are places to get it. It's a question of
knowing people. Once you know the kids who are into the
drug scene, it's very simple."

"Can you get it at the Square?" I was interested in checking the rumors.

"Well, sometimes you might meet the person you're buying
it from at the Square and then go somewhere else. But a kid

would have to be stupid to just sell some stuff to a stranger at the Square. It's too dangerous. The guy could be a cop."

Brand looked fascinated. "Have you ever smoked pot yourself?"

"I tried it once," Schlesinger mused philosophically, with detachment. "But it didn't affect me at all. I could try it again if I wanted to, but I don't know if I do."

"I've yet to meet an avant-garde writer here at Harvard," Brand told Schlesinger. "And you're the first person I've met who's smoked pot or taken LSD. This school is too fucking straight."

November 12, 1966

Shortly before ten Harry Brand came into the room "to talk." I had heard vague stories from Herb that recently Harry had begun sleeping late and skipping classes, but I didn't expect to get from him a complete, ultra-honest self-criticism verging on self-degradation.

"Steve, I'm not really happy like you. I'm one of the uncommitted. You know, I'd like to take a year off from school and work at a book publisher's or something. But unfortunately I'm scared shitless of the draft."

"I presume everyone from where you live goes to college."

"Naturally. My older brother got drafted after he graduated from college. You know, at that time there weren't very big call-ups, and he was working as a book editor for a year before they got him."

"What happened to him?"

"They sent him to Vietnam for a year."

"Shit. Really?"

Brand asked if he could have some pretzels. "Yeah, but he

was just a typist. He was never in a battle. That's the thing, if you're anything but a retard, you'll get some good job."

"Is that right?"

"You know," he continued, "some kids say they don't want to be drafted because they're opposed to the war in Vietnam."

"Yeah, what about it?"

"Well, you know, I'm sort of antipolitical. I'm against the war, I guess, but I wouldn't want to fight in any war." He took his glasses off to clean them. That's the first time I've seen him without them. He grinned. "I'm a coward. If I only could be sure that I was four–F or something, I'd definitely take a year off. You know, like I once had a hernia, and I have bad vision and flat feet. If they only had a point system!"

"You mean, add everything up?"

"My brother had a friend who tried to get a four–F by eating a lot of sugar two days before he went for his physical and not pissing — so they'd think he had diabetes. They gave him the four–F, but that afternoon he fell into a sugar coma and died."

"Oh."

"I could try freaking out — you know, coming in high on pot or doing the homo routine. But they put that kind of rejection on your record, and that can screw you up for life. On the other hand," Brand continued logically, "if you're killed in Vietnam, you don't have any more life to screw up."

"Look — type, like your brother."

"I just can't see the government, or *anybody* for that matter, being able to tell *me* what to do with two years of my life."

"What about this thing about having to be in the upper half of your class or else they'll draft you? You know, half the kids at Harvard are on the dean's list."

"Yeah, well dean's list is a gut," he grinned. "Well, like I'm failing Hum Nine — the section man gave us this spot quiz once, and, like shit man, I hadn't done any of the reading, so all I wrote on my paper was, 'Since I know little about the *Epic of Gilgemesh* and even less about the other question, I merely beg your indulgence and will endeavor to do better next time. Your humble servant, Henry L. Brand.' "

"What did he say?"

"Well, he thought I was being sarcastic with the 'humble servant' part. He didn't get angry, though. But then I screwed up the hour exam and got a D–plus on it, so he's pissed off at me."

"Shit man, how could you have pulled a D–plus?"

"I didn't do the reading." I didn't ask him how he could possibly go into an exam he knew would be on a certain quantity of reading without having done that reading. "But it doesn't matter too much, because I'm doing OK in my other subjects, and I can drop my Hum Nine grade because of expo writing." You can drop your lowest grade if you have five courses.

"How do you like your courses?"

"They're shit, if you must know. I'm taking a stupid Latin literature course that is unspeakably dull. My course in American poetry eats it. I hate to admit it, but my best course is Nat Sci Nine."

"What's that?"

"It's astronomy, of all things. " Of all things.

I asked Brand about the stories that he had been skipping classes. "Kelman, you wouldn't believe how hung up I am. I am completely disillusioned with Harvard. I haven't done any writing since I've gotten up here. And I think too much. When you think too much, you're never satisfied with what you've got. You know, 'I've got my books and my poetry to protect me. I am shielded in my armor.' " He was quoting Paul Simon's "I Am a Rock." Everyone quotes songs. He asked me whether

I had that Simon and Garfunkel album. I said I didn't.

"With all the money you get from your articles, you really ought to get a decent stereo and some records. It's a crime what you do to your records."

"Yeah, you certainly have some good stuff."

"I spend around ten dollars a week on records."

"Shit, Brand, where do you get the money?"

"My father died last year, and I get a check for sixty dollars a month insurance money. I don't have anything else to spend it on."

"What do you get?"

"Well, recently I've gone on a kick of buying Nonesuch albums."

"What's that? Some new group?"

"*You've never heard of Nonesuch?* Steven, I'm shocked. They just put out the coolest baroque music in the world on really cheap albums — you know, about a buck fifty or so."

"*Baroque?*"

"Yeah, baroque is really great. I can't study to anything else. The harpsicord is the world's greatest instrument, tied with the electric guitar."

"*Baroque?*"

"Yeah, ask John Lennon." He stared briefly at my record player and then added with melancholy, "I wish I were one of the Beatles. Then I could be happy, maybe."

It was reading period.

January 13, 1967

I remember hearing disjointed and fragmentary stories from Herb Smith as early as November about how Harry wasn't going to classes. And about how Harry was staying up until 3 A.M. every night, talking with Herb or with anybody he could find, never doing any work. And about how he had a paper due in his English course the day before Christmas vacation, but he just couldn't do it, so he got an extension until after vacation. And about how he didn't write a word of the paper over Christmas vacation.

But I had talked with Harry so many times, really identified with him although we are superficially different. I never thought he was that different from me. He wanted to be a writer. So what if he didn't go to class and be happy like most everyone else. So what? I didn't understand any of that; I couldn't comprehend why he was doing it, but I didn't think it was anything deep. I conjectured it was just an extreme case of normal rebelliousness. Or maybe it was just because he was overtired; after going to sleep so late, he said, he could simply never get up in time in the morning. A simple adjusting to a new freedom? But . . .

Tonight, I didn't find out by opening a door and smelling it or gaping at kids in a circle passing it around. He just told me.

"Steven — I thought you *knew*. Remember when I came around with you last October when you were interviewing kids? Remember how I was asking kids — especially Andy Schlesinger, 'cause he looked cool and I was sure he'd know — about where you could buy pot? Yeah, I was looking for it then. Now — well like now I turn on all the time. It's the only thing that keeps me going."

January 17, 1967

Harry Brand is working again, but not happily. Over the past week I must have talked with him, both of us sitting on the steps of the staircase in the dorm, tens of times. It was about pot, about why he wasn't working, about alienation.

"Brand — shit man, you've got to snap out of it. You know, you're going to fail all your fucking courses."

"Steven, what you don't seem to realize is that I'm not sure anymore whether that matters to me. Whatever success-orientation I ever had," he spoke analytically, "has, well, vanished." Ghoulishly, he laughed. "You know, *nothing* is important to me anymore. I have no set of values, that's all. You have a set of values. I'm not sure we can understand each other."

"Brand, look — you might change your mind someday. Can't you just do your papers for a few days and stay in this place. Let me be selfish: I want to see you around. OK?"

"Steven, I simply don't have any motivation to do anything. I sit in front of my typewriter and tell myself to write a paper that's overdue, but no ideas come. You know, I haven't done any creative writing since the summer. I'm alienated."

"That's a beautiful word. What does it mean?"

"It means that the only things which can move me to action are immediate pleasures — eating when I'm hungry, sleeping when I'm sleepy, listening to beautiful music, or reading a light novel. The old routine things just can't motivate me. I need something that will give me immediate pleasure. That's all I'm interested in."

Brand is taking pep pills to give himself motivation artificially and allow him to stay up. He will be writing his two overdue term papers and cramming for his exams on pills.

Despite everything, I had decided to room with Harry and Herb Smith for next year. My mother didn't like it: "That boy has severe psychological problems. I wouldn't even be surprised if he takes pot." But my mother was assuaged when Dave Bruce asked if he could come in on our room arrangement. Everything looked fine. We were all applying to Adams House together.

February 13, 1967

This afternoon Herb came into the room, for the first time in a long time — when we see each other, it's usually in Brand's room. "Do you know Edward Watson and Simon Miller?" Herb began as soon as he had said hi.

"Just a second, Herb. Don't seem so out of breath." I told him to sit down and said that I didn't know those two names.

"Well, they're two friends of Brand's. You've probably seen them around — they're always together. Let me describe them. They both have very long hair. Simon's is very wavy and kinky, and it goes down to his shoulders. And he has sort of a cherubic face with bright red cheeks. And Edward — "

"Just a second. I think I know them. Does the other look sort of like Captain Davy Jones or something?"

"Yeah. And he has long hair and always wears a leather jacket."

I was afraid. "Herb, what's the point of this?"

"Brand wants them to be in our room also."

I had just cinched in my mind the certainty of who those two are. And I reacted quickly by saying exactly what came to my mind. "Shit, Herb, I've seen those two kids around the union all year. They're the two biggest" — I searched for a word — "*hippies* I've ever seen. I'm sure they don't do anything except smoke pot all the fucking time."

"Well, they do indulge pretty often," Herb giggled. He can

giggle in an adult way. "Look," he added slowly, "I've smoked pot too."

I hadn't known that before and was disappointed. I know that after Brand had started, Herb was still holding out. Herb waited to let the shock that he knew I'd feel penetrate. Then he went on. "Look, Harry is afraid that with you and Dave, the room is going to become too political and wonkish. He thinks you guys will influence me to turn straight or something."

"And he'll have nobody to share his alienation with."

Herb jerked his head around nervously and went over to the record player. He looked at the record that was on the turntable. It was *Revolver*.

I went on after he was through looking. "OK. Well I don't like it at all, but I'll talk to Dave about it." I was confident that Dave would be opposed. I don't want to be in a room where nobody is doing any work. I don't want to be caught in a drug raid because Edward Watson and Simon Miller are the biggest potheads on campus. And if Brand is worried about the balance of the room, so am I. Under their influence Herb is sure to freak out. And how sure could I be of staying sane with everyone else wildly psychedelic and turned on? Alienation is a contagious disease, spread by late nights and meaningless discussions.

"Oh, no. I don't want to room with two hippies," Dave was pleasantly emphatic. "We'll have to go up to Brand and put our foot down on this wild plan before it threatens to spread any further." Just this morning I made our appointment for an interview at Adams House. That's the only house we care enough about to bother with an interview.

Late that night Dave and I went up to Harry's room.

"Brand," I began, "Dave and I veto the idea of having Edward and Simon room with us."

"Steven, it'll be two triples. You won't have to be in the same room with them."

"Look, Brand, you know that even if there are two rooms, it'll be like one. Look at you and Herb this year, and you're not even rooming together."

"What do you have against Edward and Simon?"

"Look, it's not only me. It's Dave also. And how do you know Herb likes the idea?" Herb wasn't there at that moment. "Look, I admit that I have a somewhat conservative temperament. But I'm not dogmatically opposed to anyone who's not straight. Look, *we* seem to get along pretty well."

"They're just as wonderful as I am," Brand purred.

"Look, I admit I've never talked to Edward and Simon in my life. But I just know that the whole character of the room would change if they came in. It would be a zoo. Shit — twenty-four hours of records and alienation a day. Nonstop."

"Steven, Edward and Simon aren't alienated. They're two of the happiest people I know."

"You think so?"

"Remember when we had a discussion in January and you said that you'd smoke pot, except you looked at all the kids who smoke it and see that they're all doing it because they're unhappy? And I said that there were normal, happy kids who turned on too? Well, Edward and Simon are sweet, normal, un-hung-up happy" — Brand twisted his neck with a strange grin — "potheads."

Herb had walked back in from the bathroom. He had on only a towel around his waist. "Harry, I think Steve has a point. You'll have to admit that the room will be pretty freaked out if they room with us. And I don't think I've gotten to the degree of alienation yet where I want to give up doing any work." While he was talking, his towel fell off.

Dave and I got disgusted by the whole thing, and we pulled out and decided to room together in a double.

February 14, 1967

Dave and I spoke with Herb in the bathroom last night after we left Brand's room. We suggested that he room with us and let Brand room with Edward and Simon if he wanted to. Herb said he'd like to do that, but that he was afraid that we two would make the room "too political and too straight."

This morning Herb and Dave skipped classes, and when I came back to Matthews after lunch, Dave had a new suggestion. "Herb is willing to room with us if we can get Abe Marshall to be in the room too. He's planning to be a floater now."

"Abe Marshall?" I answered, saying exactly what was on my mind. "OK. Let me say in advance that I'm skeptical about him, but that it's OK with me if that's what we need to keep the room together."

"How could you be skeptical?" Dave asked.

"I'm skeptical because I can't figure out what he's all about."

Brand and Herb — as well as Dave, who knows him also somehow — have each told me at one time or another that they consider Abe to be the most brilliant person, intellectually, in the entire freshman class. He's taking, Dave once told me, graduate level math and phil courses. (That, he adds, merely symbolizes his brilliance.)

Marshall has a habit of living on two hours of sleep a night and spending the dark hours instead on elaborate philosophical and linguistic speculations in Brand's room. Brand tells me that Marshall can and does defend any one of the abstract positions in these abstract arguments and ends up reducing everything to a heap of dry bones. They argue about esthetics — and esthetics becomes something which connotes a painful noose of words, stifling beauty rather than letting it breathe and blossom. These "discussions" are subtle tortures really, concocted when a pure brain cell grows diseased from lack of concrete nourishment. I'm convinced they have contributed to Brand's motionlessness, to his inability to commit himself to anything. Why believe in anything, when Abe Marshall can prove you both wrong and right at the same time, depending on what he's in the mood to defend?

The bones of Marshall's words — the bones without fat and red blood — are *nothing*. At the end of a night's endless discussion of questions like Is communication possible? or What is the right method of literary criticism? words are dust, and dust can't move people to write the great novel or do schoolwork or be happy. *You choke on dust.*

Abe Marshall is so brilliant, says Brand, because he always "wins" the arguments. Wins! He can empty a room of air and make it into a life-killing vacuum better and faster than anybody else!

March 23, 1967

An article about people getting high from smoking the insides of banana peels was in the *Village Voice* this week. Bananas are legal, the author of the article gleefully reminded the *Voice* readers. But not that many people read the *Voice*. Even Brand hadn't heard of bananas when I mentioned it to him in the hall on Tuesday. Today, however, the *Crimson* ran an article, and everybody reads that, so bananas were the big rage in conversation at the union today.

Everybody was going to buy bananas. The price was already up to eight cents each when I checked them at the market this afternoon. On first reading the article I speculated about trying smoking bananas, but then I realized I had no way to bake the insides, which you have to do before smoking them. I don't have a pipe either.

Brand had just gotten out of the shower when I opened his door. His mat of hair was all combed back and plastered over his scalp. "You'll have to excuse my appearance. It's the only way I can get it to dry straight." He was in his underpants and looked like a walrus with his big hooked nose not covered as it always is with his glasses.

"I might have to try freaking out on bananas," Brand smiled. "Because everything's getting up tight with the drug scene. The university is really pissed off that so many kids are turning on so openly. Lehman and the other proctors are sending the word around the dorms to get rid of everything, because there might be a bust coming up."

"A bust?"

"That's a raid, Steven." I blushed at my ignorance.

"How come the word hasn't gotten around to me?"

"It only gets around to, let us say, those most directly concerned."

"So what are you doing about it?" It's very funny; some kids lock the door when they take pot, but most don't even take that elementary precaution. It's as if pot weren't illegal. Whenever I've thought about pot, the fact that it's illegal never enters my mind. Suddenly there's talk of a raid — Brand could go to *jail.* What if I were in the room when the police came? Sitting there, just observing. And there might suddenly be a knock, and in the darkness and loud music we would all be taken away.

"You can be sure, Steven," answered Brand, "that we are all cooling it, as it were. I haven't smoked any pot for the last week, which, as you may see, has had undesirable effects on my physical and mental condition."

"What do you mean? I thought that there were no withdrawal symptoms from pot."

"Well, I've been very nervous and tense, and my muscles have been twitching. I have a headache right now, for example."

"Brand, I didn't know you'd become so dependent on it. I thought you were better this semester."

"Oh, no, Steven. I'm afraid I'm — uh — worse — than — ever." Herb, next to him, chuckled. He had been reading from *Portrait of the Artist as a Young Man* on the big chair when I came in. "Didn't you know I've been smoking pot every night?"

"*Every* night?"

"Oh, yes."

"Hey, Herb, why can't you do anything about Brand?"

"Maybe because I have no convincing arguments to offer him. Maybe because I would admit that he's right if I weren't afraid to."

"Herb, why don't you tell Steven that *you've* indulged too?"

Herb stared at me and I stared at him. "Steve knows I have," he spoke, still looking at me. "But I haven't done it nearly as often as Harry has," he continued. "I don't see how you can be at this place this long and not be alienated, Steve. I really admire you; you can just keep on plugging along with your politics. You really feel you have something you can keep on being motivated for."

I remained impassive, not saying anything. Herb continued. "I wish I could feel as sure as you of believing in something. You know, something to keep you moving, keep you doing things. The New Left has it too. I'm alienated from American society as much as they are." He realized he made a faux pas. " — And I guess as alienated as you are too. But — " He stopped speaking then for a long time. Even Brand was listening carefully to his silence.

"No! Hell, Steven, I can't understand why you're a radical, because you're not alienated from America. You're right in the middle of American society — with the *New York Times* and the *Saturday Evening Post*." He paused again. "I'm sorry."

"What do you mean? You think you have to apologize for what you say?"

"Look, Steven, I didn't mean that. I don't like the kids in SDS. The only one I like is Ken Jackson, and that's because I play pinball with him."

"Ken Jackson's in SDS?" Brand cut in. "How can a good freakout like him be *political?*"

"Brand, you'll have to admit you're an extreme case of alienation," Herb turned to him. "We all talk about how we don't see any reason to go on living. None of us has any opinions we believe in. We can all see how death makes so arbitrary any commitment you make — "

Brand was angry. "But you keep on working. You keep on doing the reading for your courses!" Brand was raising his voice. "You all talk, and if you felt the meaning of the words you were saying you couldn't continue to go on living as if nothing has happened."

March 24, 1967

Brand was speaking to me with Herb next to him. "You holdouts are quickly becoming a minority. The situation is certainly different from last year. I have a 'head' friend who's an alienated sophomore — "

"At least he has an excuse. They have a name for it — sophomore slump," I chuckled.

"Yeah. Well he told me that a friend of his got reported to his proctor last year by the guy's roommate for turning on. The roommate thought that he was doing the guy a favor and saving his life!"

"Brand, what does it feel like when you're high on pot?"

"Steven, if you're so interested, why don't you try some? If you take it once, it won't ruin your life." I drew back and asked him please to tell me.

"Steven, it's just so difficult to describe it. The main effect is that you can concentrate unbelievably on what you're doing."

"What are you doing?"

"Whatever you want. If you're listening to music, the music is the only thing going on in the world. If you're talking, each word that you say or that somebody else says sticks onto you. If you touch your face, you can feel how alive and warm it is. Once I jerked off while I was high. I can't describe to you how concentrated the orgasm was."

It sounded so wonderful. My only defense would have been to yell out at him, "But Brand, you take pot all the time and look how wretched you are!" I kept silent.

March 25, 1967

This afternoon I was up in Brand's room while a friend of his from high school was sleeping on the floor. It was three in the afternoon. He's having his spring vacation now, a week earlier than ours, and he was sleeping there looking angelic and bearing no trace of alienation. Brand wasn't there, but Harrington was. I wanted to borrow Brand's copy of the Marquis de Sade, but when I saw Harrington the only awake person in the room I couldn't ask him for it. I asked instead if I could borrow Brand's copy of *Portrait of the Artist*. While locating it on the bookshelf, I snatched the de Sade. Harrington wasn't watching.

Herb said Thursday night that "Philosophy of the Bedroom" was the most obscene thing he ever read. Brand has been telling us that it's only immediate sense pleasures which motivate him to action.

I was reading de Sade tonight — I had already finished "Philosophy of the Bedroom" by then — when someone knocked on the door. I was alone in the room and had to come out of my small bedroom. I unlocked the door.

"We'd like to buy two ounces," one of the teen-agers whispered with a heavy Boston accent.

"Of *pot?*"

"Yeah, of course. How much can you give it to us for?"

"Who told you that you could get pot *here?*"

"We got your address from a guy at the Bick," the other said. He had long blond hair and was much better looking, except for his pimples. "This is forty-four Matthews, right?"

I paused. "Well, I don't have anything to sell you, I'm sorry. And I'm sure my roommates aren't dealers either. I wish I could help you. "

"D'ya have *anything?* Any pills or acid or anything?"

"No, I don't have anything to sell."

"Look, man, we're really desperate for the stuff. And y'know things are getting tight 'cause everybody's scared off his fucking ass there's gonna be a bust. How 'bout if we give you twenty-five bucks for an ounce of some stuff you smoke yourself."

"No, I'm sorry." I was so bewildered that I couldn't tell them I didn't even take drugs. They must assume that everyone at Harvard does.

"Look, could you do this for us? Could you tell us somebody else who might sell us some stuff?"

"OK. Go up to room fifty-seven and talk to Harry Brand. He should be able to help you."

"Thanks a shitfist. We're real grateful."

They let the door start to close, but I stopped it. "Are you high school kids?"

"Yeah," the untalkative one answered.

"Cambridge High and Latin?"

"No, we go to a private school." Exclusive, progressive.

They came and then left so suddenly that I didn't have a chance to reflect on what I was doing. It was so incongruous that it was only after they left that I pieced together the jagged bits of puzzle — the Boston accent, the insistence on buying something — and realized that they must be narcotics agents. I've read that they dress up as hippies sometimes and hang around where drug contacts are made.

Shit, Brand would be arrested. And I would be responsible. If I went up to his room now, he'd know that I sent the two guys upstairs. Fortunately, I hadn't given them my name. Immobilized, I stayed in my room and just hoped I was wrong, prayed that I wouldn't hear the sure-footed steps of policemen marching up the stairwell to get Brand. In a world where nothing else has meaning, pot, which allows you to live with meaninglessness, takes on a mystical significance. But getting arrested ends everything abruptly, because society has an "absolute value system" ready to impose, even if Harry Brand can't find one.

I waited until almost midnight. I hadn't heard anything. It was "to return the book" that I tiptoed up to Brand's room. They were all there, safe.

"Steven, did someone come to your room asking to buy pot earlier tonight?"

"No, why?"

"Well, two *high school* kids came up earlier and said they got my name from someone in forty-four. So I thought it must be you."

"No, I was out at Lamont up till now. They must have talked to Mike." I looked at Brand closely. "What did you tell them?" I asked with hesitation.

"Well, since they were from Ted Mitchell's high school, I sent them down to him. I thought it might be a joke or something. I told them we didn't smoke any pot here." Brand's friend, who was sitting awake now in the same spot he had been sleeping in before, laughed. "Anyway, Ted Mitchell told me he didn't know them, but that they knew some of the same people from high school. All the worst freakouts, he said. Anyway, he sent them to Ralph Lawes, and Lawes sold them some stuff. He'll sell to anybody. It's a big business for him."

"Ralph Lawes, Incorporated," Herb chimed. "Junk dealer."

Nobody at Harvard has friends from high school up so often as Brand. Riley, who's up now, from Trinity, and Thurston from Columbia — they always visit. He never has to go to them. But, he says, he couldn't keep on going without at least seeing them sometimes. I asked him about it while Riley was out taking a shower.

"In high school we three kept each other functioning. We were always together, and I didn't have to have my own value system, because the group provided it for me. We lived for each other, and we *could* live because of each other. Now that we're separated, we're all more or less alienated. Thurston hates Columbia and Riley hates Trinity. Sometimes I think it's this place that's brought on my acute state of alienation, but where else is there to go? Harvard is the pinnacle! That's what they always told me. And it's true. Where could I go that would be any better?"

Riley walked back in, completely naked.

"As you can see, Steven, my psychological difficulties date back a long time. I was just hiding them with my arbitrary commitments to my friends — and to my idea of being a writer."

"Arbitrary?"

"Oh, I don't mean that in a pejorative sense. Any commitment is arbitrary. And any commitment is equal in my mind."

"You mean some plugger's commitment to plodding ahead without questioning anything for a second is the same as Mark Dyen's commitment to SDS?"

"Yes. One is committed to making money and the other is committed to overthrowing the government. Their commitments are of equal merit to me. In a way, the first type strikes me as an appealing figure. He's so unconcerned that he's never even *questioned* his values."

"And you think that's good?"

"Well, of course my intellect tells me that such a person is a stupid fool and the average Harvard student is a stupid fool and I should look down on them. But I've gotten to distrust my intellect now, because I see where it's led me. And the rest of me envies the plugger."

"But doesn't their selfishness turn you off?"

"No, I'm a very selfish person myself, and I think Dyen's idealism is a very, very arbitrary commitment. In a way, I'm a conservative. I think the government is interfering too much in my life already — by telling me I can't smoke pot and by threatening to draft me. I'm not so sure that I wouldn't be more unhappy in Dyen's society."

"So you're not really alienated from American society like someone who hates a society which could end us up in Vietnam?"

"I don't give a shit about Vietnam, except now when it's threatening to draft me. I think if you transferred me now to any other society — say, the Navajo Indians — I'd still be as depressed as I am now. But I am resentful about this society because it brought me up without any values to believe in. If I had been brought up in, say, Nazi Germany — that is, presupposing I wasn't Jewish — they'd have given me an absolute set of values to believe in, and maybe I wouldn't be sitting here like this now." He paused. "Herb, could you turn on the Byrds album Steve brought up?"

"Brand, let's wait and play it tomorrow. It's one-thirty, and there must be some people sleeping already."

"Don't worry. It's Saturday night." Brand got up toward the record player himself. "Steven, we will have to do something about your sedentary life. Why don't you turn on?"

"Brand, you talk about smoking pot and how great it is. But I look at you and your friends. Are *any* of you happy?"

"No, I'm not happy. I'm miserable, to tell you the truth. I have to get out of this! I know I will. But that's not the point. I feel happy for you, Steven, that you have an arbitrary value system. I can't tell you what a hell life becomes without one.

But won't you realize at least that it *is* arbitrary, that it doesn't really mean anything? Just let Abe Marshall sit down up here with you and argue with you all night. You won't think your values mean anything after that. You run around like a little toy soldier and keep busy living with your commitment."

"Remember when you said, Harry, that Kelman must have a natural supply of amphetamines in his blood or something?" Herb laughed. His curls shook.

"Brand, have you ever taken LSD?"

"No. It can cause genetic damage, you know. It's dangerous."

Part Two

Push Comes to Shove

1. SDS Prepares
for Confrontation

The ranks of the Nazis were filled with young people. Those serious people who joined did so because they were for social justice, or opposed to unemployment. There was a feeling of restless energy about the Nazis. You constantly saw the swastika painted on the sidewalks or found them littered by pamphlets put out by the Nazis. I was drawn by the feeling of strength about the party, even though there was much in it which was highly questionable.

> — a German housewife, interviewed in
> William S. Allen's *The Nazi Seizure of Power*

> Build, not burn.
> — SDS slogan, circa 1966

> Build not, burn.
> — SDS slogan, circa 1969

> The joy in destruction is a creative joy.
> — Nazi slogan, circa 1933
> — German SDS (Sozialistischer Deutscher Studentenbund) slogan, circa 1969

SDS HAS CHANGED a lot since I was a Harvard freshman. But many people haven't recognized that.

Sure the kids you know in SDS sometimes may say some pretty hairy things. But one is a guy you grew up with. And there's another one you get drunk with, or smoke grass with, or play pinball at Tommy's Lunch with on weekends and when you just can't face those Hum 5 books. And what about that kid over there who's a big Maoist now? You knew him when he was a freshman apolitical preppy.

What is psychologically very difficult to cope with is that our friends are potential executioners and commissars, or PR men for the executioners and commissars.

History has never really been alive for us. The Stalins and the Hitlers are paper tyrants, the deaths and murders paper killings. Surprisingly, movies and television have not made things closer for us. Instead they have mummified live human beings, made them into celluloid celebrities about whom all we know is the public face. Celebrities are unreal because they are eternal, and we are not. We can imagine easily Adolf Hitler haranguing a crowd or giving the Nazi salute. But we cannot imagine the relaxed, human Adolf, boasting with a friend about his sex life and the cute girl he's going to screw this weekend.

The leaders of SDS will never, thank God, have the chance to act out the future they have in store for us. We can only glimpse it through the way they act now, and even then only on occasion.

John Berlow was a Harvard sophomore, one of the students who was to be most severely punished for his part in expelling deans from University Hall in April. In December, I attended a lecture by a Progressive Labor party "trade union organizer" in Lowell Lecture Hall. After the sustained applause (but no question period) which followed his interminable remarks, I got up and slowly followed the crowd out. John Berlow was standing at one of the exits selling *Progressive Labor* magazine.

"Is this the issue which says that the Russian invasion of Czechoslovakia was caused by a tactical division between the Soviet and Czech revisionists on how best to restore capitalism?"

Berlow's square-jowled business executive face, the hair neatly combed and the skin still tanned from his most recent trip to his Florida home, became contorted as his muscles tightened his cheekbones and lips. "Kelman, you're going to die," he began, seriously. "When we take over, you're going to be killed."

"Who's going to kill me? You?"

The answer, after a pause, was a curt, cut-off syllable. "Yes." He meant it.

On the Tuesday night in April when SDS met to decide on "militant action," John Berlow arrived with knapsack and sleeping bag, ready to take over University Hall that night, as PL was to propose. Miles Rapoport, a leader of the New Left caucus opposed to PL within SDS, presented their caucus's proposal that a building be taken over the following Monday. Lowell Lecture Hall was crowded, and PL people were gathered up front standing close at all times to the microphone.

The second Rapoport finished, Berlow ran up and lunged at Miles, knapsack on his back but unable to hold back any longer. He looked like he was about to spit at Miles. Instead, he took him by his blue shirt cuffs. "You yellow-bellied coward! You'll never take over the building. You stink, fascist pig. We're gonna *kill* you!"

I first met John Stephens at the beginning of my sophomore year when we were placed as semi-roommates with rooms separated only by an open fire door in Adams House. An incongruous product of a liberal humanist upbringing in Dallas, of all-Texas football and bell-bottomed trousers, John could never help but realize — as a liberal living in Dallas — exactly how important free speech protection for minorities is. And he was always too committed to reason (he's one of the few soc rel majors I know who's not majoring in soc rel because it's a gut), too psychologically contented with his girl friend (now wife) Jill, to be tempted by SDS. But because he was always lucky enough to avoid the bitterness which is part of me, he roomed with Mike Kazin, co-chairman of SDS, during the year of the confrontation. Indeed, he continued to be friendly with Mike throughout, although John was on the YPSL executive committee. (The confrontation broke up some friendships: one friend of mine slept in our room for two weeks during the strike because he was no longer on speaking terms with his roommate, who was supporting it.)

One Sunday in February I was eating lunch with John. "Hey, Kelman, you know what Kazin told me? He has this friend in SDS, and you spoiled the kid's mescaline trip last night." John laughed.

"How come?"

"Shucks, he said he kept on hallucinating about how he was an executioner holding an axe over your head and killing you."

My worst nightmares about the future of SDS, dreamable only in vague and horrifying outlines during my freshman year, have become reality now. Had I predicted them then, I would have even thought myself insane. It's not so much that Harvard SDS has been taken over by Progressive Labor as I feared then — although it has been, the entire Harvard sixty-man delegation to the 1969 SDS convention pandemonium and side show having consisted of PL people. But even worse, the ideology of the non-PL people, who came to be known as the chapter split into opposing factions as the "New Left caucus," has itself been transformed into something just as bad.

When I was a freshman I argued with Kazin, Margolin, and Dyen about whether it was right to allow people into the leadership of anti-Vietnam demonstrations who favored the Vietcong. Now militant support of the NLF is at the very core of SDS philosophy. Even ending the war, on any terms other than a Vietcong victory, is seen as unimportant or even pernicious. A leaflet of the "SDS Anti-War Committee," chaired by Mike Kazin, issued in November 1968, attacked the very idea of peace negotiations. (Slogan of the 1967 spring Mobilization, organized at Harvard by Kazin, STOP FIGHTING! START NEGOTIATING!) Peace negotiations, said the leaflet, weren't even a second-best alternative to immediate withdrawal, as some fuzzy liberals thought. "Some people ask," runs the leaflet, " 'But aren't negotiations better than continuing the fighting and the killing?' *We don't think so.*"

When I was a freshman, I argued that it was an ominous sign that SDS sponsored a pro-Peking talk on the Cultural Revolution and films from China. Dyen explained to me that I was oversensitive. Showing these things didn't mean SDS endorsed them. Jared Israel, whom I was assured everyone else in SDS despised, had just come to the SDS executive committee and asked to get an SDS okay so that the speaker and films could have some sponsoring organization and thus be permitted to take place on campus. "Surely I believed in free speech?" Dyen asked rhetorically.

Well, today Dyen and SDS have long since abandoned belief in free speech. And the ideological wars between the two factions within SDS are conducted via quotations from the *Little Red Book*, each side claiming to be the truer Maoists.

Since they have no chances to effect their schemes inside America, the goals of the new SDS can best be seen by their attitudes toward various foreign nations. They have come a very long way from 1965 when Clark Kissinger, then and now an SDS leader, told me that "We in SDS don't take positions on various foreign regimes or rank them on a 'goodness' scale. That's typical Old Left."

Now SDS knows instinctively whom the good and bad guys are. "What do you think of Sweden, Mike?" I asked Kazin once recently.

"I don't know much about it, but I'd like to find out more facts, because I know that with the social dems in power, it can't be very good."

As Carl Davidson, former internal "education" secretary in SDS, wrote in *New Left Notes* in June 1968, in an article on learning from the experiences of New Leftists in other countries, "From the Swedish and British New Leftists, we can learn from the apparent successes but actual failures of parliamentary Social Democracy." (No mention of what these failures were.) Davidson also said one could learn another lesson from the New Left in France — ". . . the need for revolutionary organization and leadership within mass insurgencies, given the treachery of a revisionist and trade union leadership." (The "revisionists" referred to were the French communists.)

One might have expected that Davidson's article, which was written while the eyes of the entire world were on the brave and in the end tragically halted attempt of the Czech people to build "socialism with a human face," and which discussed the experience of the New Left in every area of the world from France to Japan to Quebec, might have had a word to say about what the American New Left could learn from the Czech New Left. But not a word was mentioned.

It is utterly and shockingly revealing that SDS looked with scorn on the struggles of the Czech people. The files of *New Left Notes* from January to September 1968 reveal one bare and brief mention of developments in Czechoslovakia. A report on the communist Sofia "World Youth Festival" contains the brief sentence, "The Czech situation was a subject of lively discussion." Period. (A disgraceful way to refer to a situation where the Bulgarian border police confiscated all the printed literature Czech delegates brought with them for the festival, and Bulgarian authorities in Sofia made every attempt to isolate the Czechs.) SDS never condemned the Russian invasion, and when asked what he thought of it SDS national secretary Mike Klonsky (who, attacked as a Stalinist at an SDS convention, responded, "I consider that a compliment."), said that he didn't approve of the *way* the Russians "handled it"!

Socialism with a human face? No, the "New" Left prefers "socialism" in the glorious hours of massacres and mass murder. I remember our discussing in our junior social studies tutorial (the tutor was a New Leftist) what "reasons" Stalin had for liquidating the kulaks.

I protested. "When we talk about Stalin's reasons for murdering millions of people, isn't it somewhat like talking in a pseudo-scientific way about Hitler's 'reasons' for murdering the Jews?"

"No, it's different. The kulaks were trying to reestablish class patterns in the countryside."

"And a lot of Jews were big businessmen!"

The New Leftists don't admire Russia anymore. It's become too "soft" for them.

How can one capture the flavor of the New Left that has emerged in the last years? Perhaps best by quotations, since then it is impossible to be accused of falsifying what they "really meant."

New Left Notes, March 11, 1968:

Defining liberal racism: Basically, anytime someone opposes the liberation struggle of black people, he's taking a position in defense of racism, regardless of the subjective rationalization. The most prominent reason put forth for being against the black struggle on campus involved the question of violence . . . Pacifism plays into the hands of the ruling strata of the United States, because pacifism means not fighting for real change.

Pacifism equals racism.

Resolution adopted at SDS national council meeting in April 1969 by the "right wing" of SDS, after the Maoist Progressive Labor party bolted the meeting, entitled "Fight U.S.-Soviet Collusion Against China":

The recent Soviet imperialist attacks on the Chinese border are part of the overall U.S.-Soviet plan to encircle China. They are attempting to defeat the Communist Party of China and the Chinese masses, who have fought against Soviet revisionism and counter-revolution . . .

All chapters are urged to carry on educational work and agitate around this issue. Slogans such as

RUSSIA, GET OUT OF CHINA NOW!
FIGHT US-SOVIET COLLUSION!
US GET OUT OF TAIWAN NOW!

should be popularized and demonstrations should be built to make visible our vigorous opposition to this new imperialist trick.

At its June 1969 convention the right wing of SDS, in expelling the Progressive Labor party from SDS, set up, *inter alia,* the following "principle" as a *condition for SDS membership.* According to their official statement, those who do not "support the Democratic Republic of [North] Vietnam, as well as the Democratic Republic of China [*sic*], the Peoples' Republic of Korea and Albania, and the Republic of Cuba" are *"no longer members of SDS."*

In the fall of 1968 Lenny Lehrman, a sophomore pacifist who would have been at home in 1964's SDS but today finds himself in the extreme right wing, came up with the idea that the cure for SDS's problems would be for me to be SDS chairman. At first, I thought the idea was completely ridiculous, but on reconsideration decided that, although it *was* completely ridiculous, I should run anyway. So at the SDS meeting in early November set aside for chapter elections I came, with Lenny Lehrman ready to nominate me. Frankly, I didn't expect to win — or even to be a spoiler in the really serious business of the evening, the ongoing faction fight between the PL and the New Left caucuses on how best to install the dictatorship of the proletariat.

But somehow the rumor had spread that I was running. As soon as I entered Burr Hall, a surrealistically shaped lecture hall with the rows of chairs slanting up almost vertically from the podium, about ten kids surrounded me. Their representative, Barry Margolin, asked simply, "Is this some sort of joke?"

"No, of course not. I'm running as a reform candidate. We have to get rid of the treacherous ruling clique, the SDS misleaders." I kept a straight face while parodying SDS jargon, but I was lying. Of course it was a joke, I guess.

But my speech was going to be serious. I wanted to say something to the SDS people there, the ones who would or could still listen. I wanted to speak from one human being to another. I had worked hard on my speech. It wasn't a joke, but a plea.

There turned out to be more pressing business, though, for the evening. There was a confrontation to be planned, the Paine Hall sit-in at the faculty meeting, the first of an ill-fated year. So the elections were postponed.

My speech was thus never given. But I would hope SDSers could read it, for it expresses so much of the tragedy of SDS, both in human terms and in societal terms.

The founders of SDS were moved to action in the early days of the student movement by an insight that was both revolutionary and liberating — that the "normal" operation of the American social order was leading not to universal freedom and abundance, but to a practice that was often profoundly different from and even the opposite of its rhetoric. We saw, although often in a confused way, the outlines of a vision of another, of a new, America. We looked forward to greater equality between people, to an America on the side of those in the Third World seeking a better life, and — above all — to a society where the ordinary person, without benefit of elite claiming superior knowledge or "consciousness," would democratically help arrive at the basic decisions affecting the direction of our society. "Let the people decide" and "participatory democracy" were the slogans when I first heard of SDS as a junior in high school. Those slogans were insufficient, they were oversimplified, they often were a substitute for analysis — but let no one think that SDS is not worse off today than it was then because nobody ever uses those slogans anymore.

No, SDS was not perfect in those days. I remember Clark Kissinger, a leader of SDS, telling me in 1965 that SDS would not organizationally take a position on socialism, because it was up to the people to decide whether they wanted it. Obviously there is a distinction between saying that the people must make the decisions in the final analysis and saying that even trying to educate for a specific point of view is manipulative.

But whatever SDS's faults then were, it always stood up consistently in defense of the most basic, most precious, most necessary and beautiful concepts of democracy and democratic freedoms which must lie at the very *center* of any radical reconstruction of a humane society. SDS never flinched from a consistent and principled defense of democratic values and in opposition to those who would destroy radicalism by sullying its name with those of mass murderers, power-mad dictators, and the apologists always ready to hide the crimes with phony "on-the-spot" reports and photos of the tyrants kissing babies.

The Port Huron Statement, founding document of SDS, stated,

"As democrats, we are in basic opposition to Communism as a system." Listen to Tom Hayden, writing in the early days of the student movement: "Anti-anti-communism tends to seal off critical, freewheeling discussion in the worthless name of group unity. The danger of this course of action has been the subversion of the possibility of lending a persuasive, insightful intellectual concept to protest."

SDS is deeply sick today and is in drastic need of shock treatment. The current leadership of SDS has subverted the noble ideas of a just and humane society by making SDS into an organization for the propagandization of barbarism.

January 1st to 10th, I read, is scheduled as "Week of Solidarity With The Cuban Revolution." Will one day of this festive celebration be set aside in solidarity with the Cuban workers, whose free trade union movement was destroyed by Fidel Castro as early as 1959 when it refused to vote itself Stalinist leadership? Will there be a day of solidarity with the Cuban students who were sent in 1968, according to Radio Havana, to forced labor camps on Camaguey Island for listening to Beatles records and burning pictures of Che? Will a day be found for the Cuban peasants, who supported Castro because he promised land reform, only to have their land taken away by collective farms without their consent?

Or will SDS spend its time in slavish praise of a dictator who, only six months after coming to power on a slogan of free elections, denounced the very *idea* of elections as in principle "counterrevolutionary," the dictator who is responsible, according to a high member of the Cuban Communist party purged by Castro, for "economic chaos" in Cuba? How can we help but be sickened by what we are being asked to do? And why? Because of the reports of some no doubt very sincere people about the so-called socialist society being constructed by the Cuban tyrant?

We can be sure that Beatrice and Sidney Webb, two very fine and humane people, were not purposely lying when they returned from the Soviet Union in the early 1930s — at the height of collectivization, starvation, and mass murder — and reported that Soviet society was peaceful and progressing smoothly. Nor need we assume that Owen Lattimore was purposefully misleading us when he returned from one of Stalin's most horrible death camps and reported, not only that no killing or forced labor was taking place, but that the camp was a cross between an old-age home and a tourist resort!

This is just one example. I am deeply hurt by the perversion of the innocent ideals of democratic radicalism, crushed under the weight of totalitarian cynicism. But I am even more concerned with two other things. One is that the new positions of SDS deprive it of any opportunity to gain mass support for radicalism, and indeed discredit radical ideas to such an extent that today, when the *Crimson* wants to find a word to describe any proposal that is anti-democratic, ill-thought-out, kooky, or even psychotic — the word they use in description is "radical." SDS's newfound ideology has already effectively cut it off from the working class, the masses of black people, and most students. Imagine an organization once at the vanguard of the peace movement now supporting any war that dresses itself up in "revolutionary" verbiage and even calling a continuation of the fighting and killing in Vietnam itself a better alternative to peace negotiations!

But, from the personal point of view of each of us, there is something even worse. It is only so long that we can be guided down the path of support for vile and repulsive totalitarian regimes abroad and proposals at home — only so long before many of us realize we are being "taken." In the romantic flush of our search for something better, we have been conned into becoming henchmen for cynical dictators. Without thinking, we have come full circle. And at *that* moment of self-hatred, of fleeing the dirt and filth with which radical ideas have been associated, many will turn away from the Left entirely. They will become the Whittaker Chambers and the other witch-hunt witnesses left over from the thirties, the guilty and self-torturing — and most effective — tools of the status quo.

How did SDS come actively to seek a confrontation at Harvard during the two years that passed since I encountered SDS as a freshman?

A very strange thing happened over the summer between my

freshman and sophomore years. When we came back in the fall, suddenly *everyone* was against the war. As freshmen, those of us against the war had the feeling of being part of a large but somewhat suspect minority. I remember one freshman in Matthews South who used to take off his peace button every time he went to the Freshman Union to eat, because he was afraid that it might make the other people at his table afraid or hostile. The war was a constant subject of discussion among the most politicized, and especially on the Left. But it was something that most opponents of the war were hesitant to talk about with kids whom they didn't know in a political way.

I remember being rather surprised when the Young Democrats approved a mild stop-the-bombing resolution toward the end of my freshman year. A resolution supporting unilateral withdrawal presented at an earlier meeting by Mike Kazin got only his own vote, and one other.

Of the eight people who voted for the mild stop-the-bombing motion and against immediate withdrawal, four are today in SDS shouting "Ho, Ho, Ho Chi Minh!" one is married to a descendant of the author of the Bill of Rights, one is in Africa on a Harvard traveling fellowship, one is working full time in the "new politics" movement and arguing that "SDS and we are just using some different methods to get the same goals, so we shouldn't fight each other," and one of them is me. Of the eight who voted for the resolution, six helped purposefully to destroy the Young Dems at Harvard when McCarthy wasn't nominated.

The war was not escalated over the summer between my freshman and sophomore years. Nor did chances for ending the war seem any less bright. Indeed, it was one of the bright spots of the summer of 1967 that a steadily increasing number of people in Gallup polls were opposing the war. (This trend

was suddenly reversed in the poll taken the week after the
violent Confront the Warmakers "peace" demonstration in
Washington in October.)

One important factor did change, though, over the summer:
the draft laws. Starting with the class of 1968, the class that
was to graduate at the end of my sophomore year, students
would no longer be exempted from the draft past the first four
years of college.

In September the new climate was obvious. A peaceful campus, only marginally concerned with Vietnam, suddenly became
desperate. We felt boxed in. We were like the man about to
go into the gas chamber, with no way out and the walls slowly
but inexorably closing around him.

To be always talking about "the war" (no longer called "the
war in Vietnam") was no longer the sign of an eccentric. To
the exclusion of every other political question, the war became
the dining hall topic, and everyone groped together in the new
and oh so very difficult personal agony of deciding what to do
now that the war had come home to Harvard.

Now everyone, up to and including the Young Republicans,
was against the war. (Since September 1967, I have met, literally, a total of *one* Harvard student who supports American
policy in Vietnam.) Some were honest about the reasons for
their conversion. "Fuck, man, I just don't want to get my ass
blown off, not for nobody. That's all," explained one unlikely
blond-haired and bronzed surfer type as he signed a "Negotiation
Now!" petition I was circulating at upperclass registration in
the fall of my sophomore year. (This has always been the one
charmingly disarming aspect of the on-the-make apolitical types
one meets around the Yard. They don't even *try* to paint the
reasons for their political prejudices in idealistic terms.)

For many, though, it was simply that they had "thought

things over" during the summer. There's nothing wrong with that, even if it was only the change in the draft laws which impelled so many students to give Vietnam a thought. And it was nice, in a way, to see oneself suddenly part of a general consensus against what is, to be sure, a lousy war.

But in a way it wasn't so nice. It was the pressing and direct call for soul-searching which the change in the draft laws necessitated that caused large numbers of students first to "think things over" about the war. One would assume from this that students might have a certain amount of humility vis-à-vis those not put in a similar existential situation. As a young American deserter I met in Stockholm, arguing with a middle-aged tourist, put it honestly, "I can understand why adults can have opinions for and against Vietnam. But those are just opinions. You aren't faced with being ordered to go there and kill." I hope that adults can sympathize with such a direct and honest statement. I know *I* can — I was raised to abhor violence and have never in my twenty-one-year-old life been in a physical fight.

But students should have realized that in many cases it was not our oft-praised idealism and sensitivity — those traits which we frequently and stupidly believe we are the first generation in world history to possess — which led us into mass action against the war. It was something close to self-interest. An enlightened self-interest, nothing to be ashamed of — but nothing to become a self-righteous self-proclaimed guardian of morality over either.

But such a self-righteousness, of the type that engulfs either the newly converted or the guilty conscienced, a new Cotton Matherhood of burning frenzy, suddenly enveloped Harvard in the months between September and November of my sophomore year. On other issues the good old Harvard "cool" remained. But to say one supported the war in Vietnam quickly became a rough equivalent of saying one supported Bull Connor's police dogs in Birmingham — and certainly much worse than saying one supported, say, Mao's invasion of India. People who a year or even six months earlier had supported government policy in Vietnam were now shrieking like banshees gone berserk — or like the old ladies you see at peace rallies, yelling and strutting around psychotically — at even the slightest hint that some people might have good, even liberal, reasons for supporting the war.

Harvard tolerance stopped at the Mekong's edge.

Where did all this leave the old SDS, which had gained grudging respect as having been the group right about the war all along? (Even my roommate, who's about as anti-SDS as you can get, once told me, "You have to admit, Steve, at the beginning they were the only people who were speaking up about Vietnam. We all thought they were crazy then.") SDS had been built on the basis of antiwar activity and was still known on campus as an antiwar group, not a radical group. SDS could have — if it had stayed right where it had been during my freshman year — settled down as a large and respected organization.

But as the campus swung against the war, a new SDS was born. The new birth took place during the same months between September and November which saw the rest of the campus work itself into the state of desperation which was to cause the release of large amounts of energy into the McCarthy campaign. The new SDS was born with two events that followed one right after another — the Confront the Warmakers Pentagon mobilization in October and the sit-in against Dow Chemical Company the following week. Freshman year's antiwar mobilization in New York had been a peaceful and carnival-like flower child spring day affair. Freshman year's action against

Dow Chemical was a picket line. Tactics and ideology now escalated.

Why did SDS refuse to become a mass movement? Why the new SDS? The answer lies in three factors: the type of people who are *naturally attracted* to the New Left, the type of people who make up the *new influx* into the New Left, and the type of people who *lead* the New Left.

The type first attracted to SDS is the rebel, the person standing away from the crowd. He could never accept being part of the majority no matter what the majority is. For good or for evil, he can't and/or won't "adjust" to the standard customs. In an atmosphere of lingering Joe McCarthyism he'll join in a free speech movement; in an atmosphere where black students are trying to stop a course they don't like, he'll tell you that academic freedom has become the latest barrier to social change. The rebel's way of feeling superior is dependent on his vanguard, minority status, for his uniqueness, he feels, is his specially heightened sensitivity. As people move toward him, he must do something to distance himself. The law that therefore reigns among the small band of students who had always been naturally attracted to SDS is the *law of one-upmanship*.

The new influx of people into SDS during 1968, during and after the McCarthy campaign, was of a rather different type from those originally attracted. They are the former standard liberals, the Young Dem types. Only a few of them actually ever became active in SDS, but large numbers gathered around the fringes for the big events. Among these people the key word was "frustration." I have always been amazed by the fact that the emotional level of a discussion on U.S. foreign policy with a long-time activist in SDS, particularly someone in a leadership position, is *much lower* than the emotional level of a similar discussion with a former liberal now turned New Leftist. Mike Kazin spits out the word "genocide" almost matter-of-factly. The old liberals look you right in the eye and pour out venom. The leaders of the New Left do not feel frustrated because they conceive of their work as a very long and arduous process of changing American society as a whole. The old liberals, many of them only recently having come to oppose the war, became frustrated out of their minds when the war didn't end within three or four months of their politicization!

Frustration is not a healthy political emotion in the way that, say, anger often is. For anger is, as it were, a rational emotion, or at least one which leads to rational counteraction. But frustration leads to an irrational banging one's head against the brick wall, hitting out wildly at everyone in your way. The Populists and the New Deal were movements resulting from anger; George Wallace and Adolf Hitler were products of frustration.

The frustration of these students was the frustration of elitists who expected that their views would and should hold considerably more weight than those of a mere majority. Frustration with not getting results from the system is by far the most frequent reason given by kids for joining SDS. The standard line goes something like, "We wrote letters. We marched. We worked for McCarthy. But still the war went on." I have heard this argument repeated tens of times, and *never* heard anyone respond, "Yes, but did we ever convince a majority of the people that our views were right?"

Since the new influx of people came into SDS in the first place precisely because they were tired of the old route of democracy, the New Left could hardly satisfy them if it remained true to its old slogan of "Let the people decide."

Finally, there was the leadership of SDS. Most of them had been radicals for many years. They knew the arguments against the war by heart, could provide on request a rundown on American foreign policy sins from Guatemala through the Bay of Pigs. But, like a couple married for many years, the old sources of excitement were becoming routine and dull. So the SDS leadership began tasting the forbidden fruits — Lenin, Mao, Fidel. (The earlier wave of sympathy for Fidel, in the early sixties, had been based on the "Castro isn't a communist" view. Another story altogether was to seek guidance from post–Cuban missile crisis Castro.) They began to develop an ideology. They got their critique of civil liberties from Herbert Marcuse, their version of imperialism from Lenin. They were becoming more knowledgeable and more sophisticated.

And, if for no other reason than that their followers demanded it — both the naturally attracted and the new influx — the SDS leadership built the New SDS.

But just as "not not" means "yes," so the "new new" Left means "Old Left." The term *New Left* had originally been developed in the early sixties for the student movement growing out of the ban-the-bomb and civil rights demonstrations to distinguish it from the Old Left, which was viewed as insufficiently loose and free in spirit, and above all hopelessly caught up in outmoded dogmatism and clichés. The new New Left was built out of what the leaders read from the worst of the Old Left, and it was to be as dogmatic and cliché-ridden as the Old Left ever was.

They were going to "disrupt the war machine" at the Pentagon. *The idea was to provoke a confrontation,* to radicalize people through contact with hot police flesh and cold police clubs. Everyone knew in advance that there was going to be violence, even if it wasn't directly scheduled on the program. One can hardly attempt to enter the Pentagon building in massive numbers with the purpose of stopping its operations and not expect violence. As always, of course, many soft-hearted (and perhaps overly soft-headed) kids went to the "peace march" expecting some sort of love-in. (The poor parade of pacifists who consent to being used time after time by the anti-pacifist New Left never seem to escape from the innocence of pre-apple Eden. After the bust at University Hall in April 1969, a girl who had occupied the building wrote in the *Crimson*, "I had never really considered the possibility of violence.")

It was a cool Friday night late in October when I was walking down Mt. Auburn Street back from Joe's Pizza and saw the buses ready to leave for the overnight trip to Washington. I came across a girl I knew from high school.

She greeted me happily. "Hey, Steve, you want to sit with me on the bus?"

"You mean the bus to Washington here?"

"Yeah, to the peace demonstration."

"Sukie, I was just passing by. I'm not going to Washington."

She looked very surprised. *"How come?"*

"I think this so-called peace demonstration is a disaster for the antiwar movement. Sukie, let's say you're going door to door trying to persuade someone to be against the war. How would you justify to some normal person who asked you — I'm not talking about some student or something, who you could use fancy language with — why there was a *violent* peace demonstration?"

"How do you know it will be violent?"

"You'll see!"

"But, Steve, don't you have to do something against the war? This is the only demonstration going on now."

"I know that. But I think this thing will do more harm than good."

"Steve, I just think that if you're for peace you should go. You're the most right-wing leftist I ever met!" There was no anger in her voice, or in mine.

In the middle of the next week SDS scheduled a rally in Harvard Yard to hear participants in the demonstration recount the cops' violence. (The term "pig" had not been invented yet.) In a sickening display of manipulation, Jared Israel of PL, who had opposed the Pentagon march as a "revisionist" show, kept control of the microphone and exhorted the crowd to "fight back" against "these murderers." "They're right here on campus. Cop violence isn't any disruption of the 'normal' process in America. It's just the other face the rulers are forced to show when the people become too militant. As you listen to these girls tell you how cops beat them over the head, remember that those cops are much less guilty than 'educated' Pusey or 'nice guy' Dean Glimp. Don't be fooled because they make refined dinner conversation, or 'cause they know something about art. They are the rulers — they are the *real* enemy. And we've got to attack them, right here."

It was the first time I had ever heard an SDSer put forward the notion that the university *as an institution*, as a whole, should be attacked. The previous line had been something like, "Yes, we'll attack bad aspects of the university if we absolutely must, because *even* the university can't be immune. But we're not attacking the university itself."

In after-the-fact discussions of the Dow sit-in, SDS people painted a picture of rising campus anger as the bloodied re-

turned from the Washington confrontation to surge forward
into "militant" action against the Dow recruiter. I don't think
there was much heightened anger on the campus that week, at
least not before the Dow sit-in, and indeed the sit-in took place
despite the fact that the SDS executive committee voted the
night before *not* to sit in. But the rumbling, gnawing pain and
anger of fear and hate that was there in September was still
strong the week of the Dow sit-in, and when a group of SDSers
ignored the executive committee vote and blockaded the door
in Mallinckrodt Hall (the chemistry building, which I, a good
nonscientist, had never heard of before), the other SDSers
couldn't resist joining in. They immediately presented the recruiter, a Mr. Levitt who, the word soon got around, had
brought along a peanut butter and jelly sandwich to prepare
himself for any such contingency, with notice that they would
not let him go until he signed a statement promising that
neither he nor Dow would ever return to campus.

The ubiquitous SDS loud-speaker, manned by Jared Israel
(a loud-speaker, I believe, costs some $500, and I've always
wondered where SDS got the money), was soon blaring away
in the Yard, urging people to come join the sit-in. "Smash
genocide! Smash Dow!" Jared yelled. Then, for us nonscien-
tists, he told us where Mallinckrodt Hall was located (right next
to Lowell Lec, outside the Yard).

I got over there just after eleven. There was also a peaceful
picket line going on outside (with a few SDS people urging
the pickets to go in "where the real militant action is, not just
this liberal guilty conscience stuff"). I joined it.

"Isn't that thing inside there unbelievable?" I offered to the
kid picketing next to me. "You know, this thing with trying
to force the guy to sign a statement before they'll let him go.
It's taken right from the Chinese Cultural Revolution."

"Oh, I dunno," my fellow picketer answered, pausing. "I was sort of thinking of going inside myself."

In the middle of the afternoon Dean Watson, who exemplifies the generation gap between student and business outlooks on the world, came to survey the scene. He was, needless to say, very upset. But not because he had listened to what any of the SDS people were arguing for in fights with professors, opposing students, and senior tutors on the scene. (The inside of Mallinckrodt Hall was filled with hundreds of people sitting in and fifty or so more standing up, arguing with those sitting down.) He had just come and hadn't listened. (Odds are that had he listened, he wouldn't have understood.)

Watson could only think of the trapped Mr. Levitt. And not because he has a specially kind feeling for middle-aged research chemists, recruiters, or peanut butter munchers. As he walked in and surveyed the scene he muttered, desperately, to a nearby professor, "My God, that man could *sue* us!"

All this while a slow fire was being set under Harvard.

At about the same time, post-crisis rumor has it, President Pusey was arriving back in Boston from a fund-raising trip. He had heard nothing of the sit-in. Some deans met him at the airport and promptly whisked him away to a nearby restaurant. There was no need to throw oil on the embers.

Toward the end of the afternoon bursar's cards were collected, meaning punishment.

After a long debate, and without getting the signed confession, the sit-in voted to dissolve at around seven in the evening. They issued a demand for lenient and equal punishment for themselves and urged other students to hand in their own bursar's cards in solidarity. (In retrospect, SDS has undertaken self-criticism of its Dow demand for "equal punishment." According to the current theory, if one accepts punishment for any sort of action in support of a certain goal, that is to admit that the goal was wrong. Conversely, any action — from occupying a university building up to and including murder — in support of a "just goal" is justified and must not be punished. Thus *The Old Mole*, the New Left's Cambridge "underground" paper, wrote in an article on the background to the Harvard strike that students "accepted punishment (at the time of Dow), thus agreeing with the university that their action was wrong. A demand for amnesty would have made it clear that students knew their action was right.")

The Dow sit-in threw me and many of my friends into a week-long state of depression. Not because *a* sit-in had taken place, for I think that sit-ins are a justified tactic of civil disobedience on occasion. But the goals and justification of the sit-in that one heard from New Leftists and their sympathizers under the next week of intensive political activity completed the picture of the New SDS. Added to the purposeful attempt at violent confrontation pioneered at the Pentagon march and the attack on the university as an institution pioneered by Jared Israel was now the attack on the concept of so-called bourgeois civil liberties (a term which was probably used for the first time on the Harvard campus, without jesting, since the early 1930s Young Communists used it) and the contempt for the notion of majority rule.

I got into a lot of arguments during the next days: "Civil liberties, OK. But what about the civil liberties of the Vietnamese not to be killed?"

"Not to be killed? The NLF is killing people in Vietnam, too. If it's just killing you're concerned about, I can sympathize with you. But then we should ban people supporting the Vietcong, too."

Silence.

"I suppose you think it's a civil liberty to use napalm. You know, napalm kills babies." An SDSer was arguing with me.

"Look, I hate napalm too. But let me ask you something. What's your opinion of the NLF?"

"I think they're good."

"OK. What if the NLF could get a hold of some planes and some napalm, and they felt it was needed to win the war, and they used it. What would you say?"

"Well, I'd say that if they decided it was absolutely necessary, they know best."

I was speaking at an open-air SDS rally in the Yard. "Because we believe the war in Vietnam is horrible and wrong, we have the duty to do everything we can to build a movement to end that war. But we have no right, as a minority, to impose our views upon the majority, only to try to become the majority. What would you have thought if the German-American Bund sat in to prevent collection of money to help England in 1940?" After about an hour, I had finally wrestled up front to the microphone. "In their view Hitler was fighting British imperialism — if you read the papers of that time, you'll see that's what the Nazis said!"

"What about Vietnam!" Someone cried from the audience. To bring up any other subject, even for a moment, was criminal.

"Look, the number of people against the war has been increasing steadily over the last six months, although I wouldn't be surprised to see the trend reversed in the next public opinion poll after last weekend's catastrophe at the Pentagon. Let's keep working, not give up. Let's get a majority against the war and then see what happens."

The voice shouted loud and clear from the back. "NOTHING!!"

A group of friends were sitting on the sofas in Elliott Abrams's room downstairs in Adams House, drinking beer and whining to each other about how the Dow thing showed that the New Left had now become the same old totalitarian Left, daring openly to attack civil liberties.

"What is so unbelievably, fuckingly Stalinist about their view is that they refuse to allow a plurality of voluntary activities, with different political views, each being allowed to undertake different sorts of activities in support of different goals. They would allow only those activities they 'know' are 'just.' "

"Kelman, shut up and just get drunk. It's no time to philosophize. Just say that these fucking commie bastards are out to destroy this whole university and everybody's freedom with it. It's the fucking thirties all over again. Assholes!"

The speaker was Jon Ratner. He had just joined the YPSL a week earlier, and it was during Dow he became active. The Dow sit-in galvanized into activity a number of democratic students. Ratner was one. Ben Ross, a freshman who joined the YPSL then, was another. During the April 1969 crisis, Jon was to be YPSL chairman and Ben YPSL executive secretary. But the number wasn't enough. Most students opposed the Dow sit-in, but in the majority of cases it was because they opposed under all circumstances the tactic of sitting in. Sitting in was too ungentlemanly. And, as opposed as they were to the war, they saw no reason to attack the university. Rarer were civil libertarian arguments.

There were other ominous signs. That barometer, the Young Democrats executive committee, was slowly shifting. Out of fifteen, around four on the committee had handed in their bursar's cards. They voted down 10–5 a motion to "condemn" the sit-in, and finally passed a watered-down motion with "disapprove." The *Crimson*, which during the previous spring had moderately opposed the war, voted this time by a narrow majority to approve the Dow sit-in. This was not due to a change in staff, for staffers are elected from January to January.

As I was leaving the Young Dems executive committee meeting, Hutch Jenness, a tall, violent, mustachioed SDSer, came up to me and grabbed me by the collar. He had been invited to the meeting to explain the SDS viewpoint. His head towered over mine as he breathed hard down my hair, and his hand sweat dampened my shirt. "Kelman, you were the most fucking conservative person at that meeting!"

The YPSL statement read:

In 1964 at Berkeley, students fought for the right of free speech and free recruitment on campus. We believed these principles were just then, and we believe they are just now. We believe that the best University policy is the present one, that of allowing free access to all, and we hope this policy is continued.

The argument that some specific speech or recruitment is so immoral that it cannot be tolerated is used not only by the extreme Left. The American Right has continuously argued that demonstrations against the War are directly responsible for killing American troops and Vietnamese by persuading the NLF and Hanoi to fight on. Are right-wing students therefore justified in showing through the use of similar tactics their moral indignation by preventing recruitment for antiwar activities? We think not.

While we disapprove of any attempt to restrict the rights of free speech and recruitment, we feel that nothing will be gained by discriminatory and harsh treatment of certain participants in the sit-in.

One thing that was demonstrated Wednesday was the very intense disgust with the War felt by many students, and their feeling that the University is complicit with it. We too are deeply opposed to the War, and we too believe that a special responsibility to speak out in opposition to the increasing American commitment to an escalation of the War lies with the intellectual and academic community. For this reason we strongly urge the Faculty to reconsider its refusal to take a position on the War.

The YPSL circulated a petition to the faculty supporting the statement. It got over 1200 signatures and impressed a lot of faculty people. The faculty voted not to expel or suspend anyone but to put a group on probation. (A technical punishment meaningless in fact.) There were no more confrontations during the year, and at the end of the term, it might have seemed logical to describe Dow as merely a huge letting off of pent-up emotion before the long haul of the McCarthy campaign, or as the first confrontation with the political grown-up world for many newly politicized students. Indeed, SDS declined in strength during the rest of 1968. What is more surprising, they continued to decline in strength afterward right up to the big days of April 1969. Four hundred people handed in their bursar's cards for having participated in Dow; 200 were arrested at University Hall (of whom only 150 were Harvard-Radcliffe students). During my sophomore year average attendance at SDS meetings was around 200; up to the time of the April days SDS meetings in the year which was to produce the strike averaged about 100.

Students tired quickly, even of frustration, and the level of resentment at Harvard on April 7, 1969, the day we returned from spring vacation and two days before the occupation of University Hall, was much lower than it was in the days before Dow. Many fewer students were drafted than had been originally predicted. The University Hall occupation may, in a sense, be viewed as an act of desperation rather than confidence.

Yet simply to view the Dow sit-in as the high point of a frustration whose fever pitch cooled afterward is a mistake. For within the New Left, Dow was a new beginning, not an end. The SDS ideological repertoire — including the specific arguments used against ROTC on campus a year later — is just a series of variations on the theme first written (or rather, redis-covered, from the ancient Stalinist text) at Dow.

And the ideological "development" which accompanied Dow was very important in another respect. SDS's growth has al-ways been dependent on its ability to shock, its ability to be-come steadily more extreme. But an *ideology* can become only so extreme before it falls off the political spectrum entirely. As the ideology developed into pure slave-labor camp vintage Joe Stalin, and the literary level down to the depths of the slogans in the *Peking Review*, there was nowhere left for SDS to "develop" *ideologically*.

The only way one could become more extreme was by be-coming more extreme *in practice*. And here it was a question of groping out into the darkness, of *daring* to act in ever more outrageous ways. Indeed, one of the leading SDS slogans now, taken from the *Little Red Book*, became, "Dare to struggle, dare to win." The concept of the dare is psychologically fasci-nating, for it expresses exactly the playing with fire, the fear and trembling, that New Leftists feel as they experiment with ever more extreme methods. And with the dare, as children practice the art, it is always that one tries it first. If he is successful, the others, losing their fears, follow along.

So, able to go no further with ideology, Harvard SDS learned from the Columbia building occupation and strike the notion of trying to shut down a whole university. Imagine, what an idea! A tingling, dazzling, almost sexually exciting idea! Take over a building and shut down the *whole* university. "Dare to struggle, dare to win." Harvard SDS prepared for confrontation as we all returned in September 1968 from summer vacation and the Democratic convention fiasco, because they had gone as far as they could go with ideology: now only action would shock. They prepared for confrontation before they had dreamed up the issues on which to stage the event. As soon as we came back, we saw sprayed with red spray paint (the spray gun is the psychedelic age's functional equivalent of the mimeograph machine for the radical) all over the walls and sidewalks of Cambridge, TWO, THREE, MANY COLUMBIAS!

And now, as I write, the latest dare that's been successfully tried is guns on campus. I was having pizza with my brother one night in May, during reading period, after everything had quieted down, and he informed me, matter-of-factly, "You know, in SDS now, all they're talking about with each other is guns." Before Cornell they would have never dared.

At Columbia in 1969, when SDS failed to shut the place down, their unsuccessful and brief sit-in featured rubber hoses, knives, and beaten-up students and professors. New Left brutality.

The dares go on. All this is becoming "accepted" on the campus. The moderates are quiet.

It started off so nobly, like the Garden of Eden. When they say, "These are our best youth in those buildings," they are right in a certain way. It is impossible to avoid sympathizing with the New Left, for all the evil they do, so much more than with the large part of the great American middle class out of which they spring, self-satisfied, self-centered, and self-important. One frequently comes across kids at Harvard who will openly, with a little snicker of pride, affirm to you that they are at Harvard for a degree "that's gonna help me make a bundle of money." I remember handing out a leaflet supporting some striking Harvard printers when I was a freshman. Outside the

Freshman Union it was more than one person who said to me, "What are you supporting those guys for? If they raise their wages, they'll have to raise our tuition." I remember when I was a freshman one kid who saw a "Socialism and Democracy" button I was wearing came next to me and exclaimed, "Look, man, socialism's OK for poor people. But what do *you* want it for. They'll just take away our money."

How can you help but be disgusted and repulsed? Idealism is certainly not enough, but it is a necessary start. (How can we look up to adults who begin their lectures with, "Son, I was idealistic too once, but . . .")

There is a kernel of something beautiful in almost every member of the New Left. For they have decided at some point that *that* life is not for them, that they want and choose to say no to Babbitt and business and build something where more people can be more happy. They reject the adage that we should look out only for ourselves. As Bob Telson described his roommate Kazin to the man from the *Wall Street Journal*, "He sees American society as a joyless one, and he's trying to work for a society where there's more joy." That's very far from the way Kazin would phrase it. Telson himself is a sort of a shock-the-bourgeois radical, who wore his SDS "Abolish ROTC" button on the fly of his pants and always managed to be photographed by the press during SDS demonstrations. Fundamentally, though, Telson is more interested in rock and blues than politics. But in his own way Telson hit at the kernel deep in back.

But we can't let ourselves get so distracted by the kernel that we fail to see the whole plant. And the question arises: Is there *something* rotten in the kernel, something that might lead one to expect that it would grow as it did?

The answer is yes, and to locate the rottenness we must first see that in any class society there are fundamentally two sorts of revolts against that society. The first is the revolt of those physically, socially, and economically at the lower end of the society, the revolt that demands more recognition and a better place for the lower classes. This revolt responds to the question "What's wrong with society?" with answers like "People are starving here," "Workers have no job security here," or "The rich get almost everything here." It is this revolt which has and continues (even in American so-called affluent society) to lie behind the mass movements of protest within a society, such as the civil rights or trade union movements.

The second revolt is a revolt of a section of the elite against the society. This revolt has different responses to the question "What's wrong with society?" more philosophical answers like "We have no purpose in life here," "People don't love one another here," "I am bored here," and "Everyone here is just a stupid beer-guzzling slob, who only wants me to conform to his narrow-minded standards." The elite revolt mourns the lack of culture, the overflow of cars, the ethic of keeping up with the Joneses, the intolerance against free drugs and sex, the uniformity of little boxes on the hillside, the straight clothes and short hair. And, among youth, "My parents are a drag/have sold out/don't give a shit for me/are trying to keep me down." Or, "*I* don't want to fight in Vietnam."

Both revolts are justified, because in America both criticisms can be made. And, if successful social change is to take place, these two somewhat disparate revolts must succeed in reaching at least some sort of working alliance. For neither Negroes and workers nor students and middle-class rebels form a majority by themselves. But the problems are so immense, for each revolt contains an element of contempt for the other.

The revolt of the lower classes is directed primarily at the upper classes, and it is clear that workers make little distinction between the upper class they are accustomed to and the upper class in its rebellious variety. They see the fancy clothes, the refusal to work hard, the domineering self-assurance, and who is to blame them for being just as turned off to the SDS commissars as they are to their bosses?

The early stages of the elite revolt are in fact directed precisely against those "toiling masses," of whom the New Leftists, trained in the SDS line, are later to sing the praises. Because there can be no doubt that it is above all the lower classes who are intolerant of long hair, puritan in their cultural standards, and as straight as the flagpole from which stands the American flag they love. It is longshoremen who beat up students at antiwar demonstrations, who don't love Negroes. And very few educated young people are able to cope with the complexities of what seems inconsistent to intellectuals. Among intellectuals and students, who learn their politics from books, certain ideas go together: to be opposed to U.S. foreign policy implies a certain set of attitudes on dealing with poverty, on Negroes, on Bohemianism. That most ordinary people get their politics not from the books intellectuals write but from their everyday experiences — experiences which lead them to be "progressive" on some issues and "reactionary" on others — is beyond the grasp of the intellectual. And it doesn't matter that Joe the auto worker is for a government public works program that would do more to end poverty in America than any other single step — the student rebel only sees Joe living in the little box and drinking beer *and*, worst of all, having one whole vote, no more and no less than the intellectual, with his superior vision and understanding, enjoys.

So the rotten part of the kernel of the SDS revolt is that part of the content of the rebellion which is directed, not against society's elite so much as against *ordinary people.* The revolt can then come to seek not so much a new society free from elitism as a new elite, a rebel elite, holding sway. In many of the elite colleges, such as Harvard, a tiny number of ideologues has succeeded in plastering a thin veneer of Marxist-Leninist ideology, complete with class struggle rhetoric, over the initial revolt which leads young people into the New Left. That this cadre ("cadre" is the word they use to describe themselves) has succeeded in introducing such a new ideology into SDS in the years since I was a freshman is a tribute to the frustration over the war in Vietnam which has made the first law of SDS the law of one-upmanship.

I have read no more apt description of the rotten kernel of the New Left revolt than in a polemic written during the April days of 1969 by Harvard PL against the New Left caucus faction of Harvard SDS. It is an excellent antidote to the these-our-most-sensitive-youth homilies one hears on occasion from obliging adults.

Many of us became radicals in the first place for mixed reasons. On the one hand we were angry about the war, about racism, about the countless vicious acts we saw around us. But on the other hand, we viewed America as one great wasteland, a big, monstrous, mechanized, air-conditioned desert, a place without roots or feeling. We saw the main problem, really, as: THE PEOPLE — the ways they thought and acted towards each other. We imagined a great American desert, populated by millions of similar, crass, beer-drinking grains of sand, living in a waste of identical suburban no-places. What did this imagined "great pig-sty of TV-watchers" correspond to in real life? As "middle-class" students, we learned that this was the working class — the "racist, insensitive people." Viewing things from this highly self-righteous stand, we saw the people as conformist, unaesthetic, puritanical, completely incapable of understanding our sensitivities. (By comparison, the rich at least appeared sensitive.) Even some of our apparent support for Black people stemmed from considering them to be wild romantics, living totally outside society — heroically standing apart, as we ourselves wished to stand apart.

The alienation which brought us into the movement, then, was strictly a mixed bag. While involving real anger over oppression, which obviously is good, it also involved a lot of anti-worker attitudes. When white, "middle-income" students join SDS these two attitudes often are inter-mixed.

Actually, part of our "radicalization" involved aspiring to something like the POSITION inhabited by the rulers. *The wish was to escape (as they can) to beautiful dreams, to stick one's tongue out with impunity at the great, unthinking mass.* The right-wing of SDS plays to this bad aspect of student radicalism. They say that "alienation is a stage students go through and we must get them where they're at!"

In fact, these bad attitudes are no "stage" but an obstacle, which must be defeated in people or it will turn ours into a reactionary movement . . .

In effect, in organizing, the right wing of SDS says to students: *"You can coddle your hate-the-people escape wish, you can serve yourself. You can join "*THE MOVEMENT*" and* STRIKE A REVOLUTIONARY POSE, *and it's all alright!"*

Who's in Harvard SDS? Followers of Freud would sketch out a psychological portrait of sublimated parental revolt and sexual frustration. (Bluntly put, the way one friend always does, "Kids in SDS are dissatisfied because they don't screw enough girls.") Followers of Kenneth Keniston, pace the Yale psychologist's sycophantic account in *The Young Radicals,* would sketch a different psychological portrait of youthful enthusiasm, revulsion against hypocrisy, sexual honesty, and loving adjustment to the parents who taught them the glorious ideals for which they are now so nobly struggling.

As more of a follower of Marx, I think it would be useful to apply a class analysis to the sole phenomenon to which SDS refuses to apply this method: themselves, of course. Family income: average for U.S., $8000 a year; average for Harvard, $17,000 a year; average for SDS, $23,000 a year. (Source: poll of family incomes taken in Soc Sci 125, an SDS-run course taken almost entirely by New Leftists.) Secondary school education: of the 150-odd Harvard students arrested after the occupation of University Hall, approximately 50 percent attended prep school, with the largest representation from the most exclusive ones like St. Paul's. Just over 40 percent of the Harvard student body as a whole comes from prep schools. (Source: my roommate Elliott Abrams, who performed a herculean labor of hate in looking up the high school backgrounds of each of the arrested. All sociologists should be grateful.)

In any fluid society social classes are constantly rising and falling. In the United States in the last thirty years the most conspicuously rising class has been intellectual-professionals. At the same time, one could hardly point to any major diminution of the wealth of the upper upper class. To answer the question, Who is in SDS? it is necessary to look at SDS members from both of these groups. For both bear marks of their respective class origins, and these influence their roles in SDS politics.

SDS at Harvard, and at most schools I think, could never have gotten started without the initial services of the hereditary radicals. (In many universities, although not Harvard, the New Left could still not keep going without this group.) They are radicals in the same way the Boston Irishman's son is a Democrat — by instinct. It should be noted that one of the most important reasons for the growth of the New Left in the sixties is the fact that the children of young adults of the thirties, a

radical era, have now reached student age. The "silent generation" students of the fifties were children of young adults of
the twenties, a conservative decade. Irving Howe estimates that
during the thirties and forties a million Americans may have
passed through membership in the Communist party. Many
are still radicals, if only under the table — or, to put it more
accurately, at the dinner table — today.

Around these talkative dinner tables the hereditary radical
absorbed from early childhood certain notions about who the
bad guys and who the good guys are. The father of Pete Orriss,
co-founder of Harvard SDS in 1964, was active in the Doctors
Committee to Aid the Spanish Republic in the 1930s. His
younger sister, while a student in *ninth* grade, was the New
York City high school coordinator for the 1966 spring antiwar
Mobilization. According to Nat Stillman, an early Harvard
SDS leader who joined and later left the group, well over half
of the Harvard SDS executive committee in its early days was
made up of people who identified with or were members of the
old-line Communist party, U.S.A.

The hereditary radicals come to Harvard with their political
commitments already well established. They major in social
studies or government, and (today) join the New Left caucus of
SDS. That by 1969 the New Left caucus as an organized group
had a grand total of *twelve* members (compared to over fifty
in the pro–Progressive Labor group) is a good indication that
the hereditary radicals have been displaced as the dominant
force within SDS. In fact this constitutes an important part of
the tragedy of SDS. For they fell victims to the irrationalism
and antiintellectualism which they themselves unleashed but
which later got out of (their) control.

The hereditary radicals combined the confidence and optimism of members of a rising social group with the political beliefs they had inherited from their parents. Temperamentally they are on the same wavelength as the moderates. They just happen to have different political beliefs. They get good grades at Harvard and are very skilled at writing and speaking. (The atrocious leaflets produced by Harvard SDS are mostly written by PL, although the style of the hereditary radicals has begun to deteriorate under the influence of "competition" from the ranters.)

Above all, you can *talk* with the hereditary radicals. They are human beings, not mechanized robots like PL people. Mike Kazin plays pinball and has a lot of nonpolitical friends. (Of all the members of PL, the only one known to play pinball is government tutor Alan Gilbert.) He goes out with nonradical girls on occasion. He even spoke with a reporter from the *Wall Street Journal*. (For this he was denounced as a "counterrevolutionary" at an SDS purge meeting.) The politics of the hereditary radicals is horrible, but at least one feels that they have come to it through genuinely having been convinced of it.

For hereditary radicals, like hereditary Democrats and Republicans, are not in politics for extrapolitical reasons. They have strong political opinions, and they were always taught to act on the basis of their opinions. Members of a rising class, they confidently and self-assuredly believe that their views must be right. It's as easy as that — there's simply nothing "special" for them about being a radical. (As a hereditary radical of a sort myself, I remember having been surprised, although of course I shouldn't have been, by the strong reaction of wonder and amazement that greeted the "revelation" to many of my freshman friends that I was a socialist. For me being a socialist was a matter of course and nothing surprising — but for kids from Columbus, Ohio, it's a little different. Many had probably never met a socialist before, and I was the kind of oddball they had heard they might meet at college.)

Because their politics are simply goal-oriented, the hereditary radicals are also more hesitant about purgative flagellatory activities like building occupations. It is clear (as PL alleges, although with their own pinch of conspiracy theories, exaggerations, and lies) that the hereditary radicals were less anxious and more afraid to take over University Hall than was PL. Almost none of the leaders of the New Left caucus, up to and including SDS co-chairman Kazin, were arrested. The handful of Communist party members on campus were not even in the building. Mark Dyen put it bluntly to me after the strike, "One reason that PL has gained so much new support since April ninth is that they led the building take-over, and we dragged our feet." The hereditary radicals tried to conceal their fears in a hocus-pocus of SDS rhetoric about "making sure we've built a base" and "necessary revolutionary preconditions," but the real source of their hesitancy was easier to understand. Mark Dyen, Mike Kazin, and Miles Rapoport would get no feeling of personal liberation (perhaps only a sort of satisfaction at "a job well done," which finally bringing the Harvard bastion down certainly was) from taking over University Hall. But they might get jail and expulsion.

That was more than Mom and Dad had led them to bargain for and this was why they hesitated.

At the beginning the hereditary radicals were everything in Harvard SDS. When I was a freshman they still dominated the organization, and all the freshmen in SDS came from hereditary radical backgrounds. Not only did the hereditary radicals introduce the campus to New Left thought, but they were the first to venture further to taste the forbidden fruits of Lenin and Fidel, unleashing the ideological one-upmanship which they were too intellectual to keep up with. They could not quite descend to the level of primitiveness required once the mentally ill began entering SDS and gathering around its fringes. "I wish I could give simple answers like PL does and say that the reason for racism in America is to give capitalists twenty-two billion dollars extra profits, or the reason for the war in Vietnam is so that corporations can move their plants to Vietnam and hire workers at a dollar a day," I overheard Mark Dyen say one day over dinner to some kid who was asking him how the New Left caucus differed from PL. (The twenty-two billion figure on racism is not just grabbed out of a hat. PL takes the difference between the average incomes of whites and blacks in America, one thousand dollars, and multiplies it by twenty-two to get their "precise" figure.) "Unfortunately, these answers just aren't true." (Dyen's point was that the main difference between him and PL was the latter's "sloganistic and simple-minded intellectual analysis.")

Thus the hereditary radicals lost control of their own organization. The revolution consumed its own children. The pathetic culmination came when Mike Ansara, along with Pete Orriss, the founder of Harvard SDS, was "exposed" during the strike as an agent of the bourgeoisie, a "misleader" trying to get himself "a fistful of loot." Ansara had tried to adapt himself to the new barbarism. He had moved a long way from the afternoon in November 1966 when he had urged his followers to disperse after they had asked Defense Secretary McNamara a few questions. On the night of April 8, 1969, Ansara broke for the moment with the New Left caucus to endorse PL's call for a building take-over that very night. During the two years he had exchanged neatly cropped hair for a shaggy beard and a cave-man look. He had learned how to clench his fist. (Earlier one of his leading qualifications for SDS office was viewed to be his friendly ties with many administrators.) To no avail.

The hereditary radicals — the intellectual Left extremists at Harvard — suffered a sad fate at Harvard. For they at least were good people.

The same cannot be said for the other major social stratum which provides recruits for SDS and the backbone of the new cadres recruited into the organization between the time I arrived at Harvard and April 1969. These are WASP rebels. The sight of an aristocrat who has lost the will to live is esthetically degrading. These declining members of the American aristocracy are not at all similar to the standard aristocratic stereotypes. They are neither self-confident men at the top, uncaring of those below, nor the humane, social-service oriented democratic aristocrat.

The Left should normally expect good strong hostility and opposition from the upper class — the enemy is nothing if not powerful. If some aristocrats want to rebel, though, that's their right. But the pale, delicate faces of the used-up aristocrat who goes into SDS reminds one of nothing so much as Spengler's *Decline of the West.* The American upper class has been an aristocracy produced by primitive dog-eat-dog competition, and it is only now that enough generations have passed for it to begin to produce soft, declining offspring who are not "up" to its standards.

It is in the guilty aristocrat that we see clearly politics not for politics' sake, but for self-expression, the possibility of recapturing a lost vitality that one feels too weak to create for oneself. As a freshman one of these aristocrats was beaten up at a freshman dance by some townie, in front of his date, and unable to offer the slightest resistance. In September of his freshman year he told some friends that before the year was over he would have to "fuck an Oriental girl." I hadn't seen this kid since I was a freshman until he emerged in PL during the strike.

Josephine Biddle Duke, Barnard College student, made the motivations of this group rather clear when she told a reporter for the *New York Times* that it was neither intellectual analysis nor reading Marx and Lenin that brought her to the New Left. Rather it was the feeling that one's "oppression" was being shared within the group. When workers in the early 1900s sang, "What force on earth is weaker than the feeble strength of one? But the union makes us strong!" they were expressing the reality of their situation. When heiress Josie Duke needs her SDS "comrades" to share her oppression, it is only a pitiful revelation of her own smallness.

The declining aristocrats in SDS are all, *to a man*, pro-PL. Not only is there not a single one who's been attracted by the weak reformism of the Young People's Socialist League, but there is not a single one of them in the New Left caucus, which is ideologically similar to PL but emotionally a self-confident reflection of an intellectually sophisticated upper middle class. PL's rantings are about on the intellectual level that such students, whom I always considered products of favoritism at the admissions office, can comprehend. And PL's promises of blood even before the revolution — through show trials "exposing" misleaders during the confrontation and physical attacks on New Left caucus meetings after the June 1969 SDS convention — promise a new vigor to the spineless.

During the Harvard strike, according to Dave Bruce, my roommate in my sophomore year, virtually everyone around the

exclusive final clubs was wearing red armbands. One might
think that if this represented the collective dissolution of the
aristocracy's will to survive it might indicate that revolutionary
change in America is in the offing. But the aristocracy's dissolution should not be predicted too quickly. If one had to
struggle for the fruits of riches and power, the fight would be
too much for the weak souls who make up the aristocrats in
SDS. But a beneficent inheritance law and a capitalist system
which watches after its own assures these degenerate scions un-
deserved wealth and influence without their having to work
for it. Even if some of the aristocrats permanently dropped out,
the social fluidity which has always allowed new blood at the
top will assure that the aspiring Italian, Polish, and even Negro
boys going to state colleges somewhere will take their place.

But how many of these prematurely wilted flowers will really
be willing to make a life of the violence and dirt which is in-
vigorating to prattle about but for which they are so ill-equipped?
One, two, zero? Meanwhile, many of them muse, along with
a finely featured Harvard aristocrat on the fringes of SDS,
"My friends and I alternate all the time from moods of violent
radicalism to moods of resignation. One day we'll be thinking
that American society is so disgusting that we have to go all
out to change it. But the next day we think, well, that it's so
hard to change America 'cause everybody is such a fucking reactionary stupid slob, so we should just look out for ourselves
and get all we can, 'cause there ain't gonna be no social change."

"Why didn't you occupy University Hall with SDS?" I asked
him.

"Well, me and all my friends all agreed with what SDS was
doing, and really think this strike is the best thing that's ever
happened to Harvard. But we didn't want to risk getting kicked

out. Look, as long as you don't have anything permanent on your record you can change your mind later on in life about being a radical."

These are the two social strata from which SDS recruits the bulk of its cadres and very active members. Its less active members are generally former moderates "frustrated" with democracy and similar in many ways to the hereditary radicals. They generally do little organizational work because a good many of their pent-up frustrations were dissipated through the traumatic decision to change the self-image they have of their role in society (from governor to guerrilla) and join SDS. And no categorization can give a real picture of all the individuals, with their hopes and hang-ups, who end up in SDS for their own very personal reasons.

Take the only PL member at Harvard who actually comes from a working-class background. He came to Harvard a Young Republican and originally planned to become a priest. He attempted to get elected to the YR executive committee but knew he was looked down on because of his Boston accent and loud clothes. Among the PL aristocrats, he could be revered: "Shit, man, a real worker." (It is an interesting side note that PL has one or two "show workers" whom they bring along to important meetings, dressed in denim and speaking straight Cambridge, Mass., English. One frequently sees the PL workers walking around Harvard Square weekday afternoons, indicating that they are financially subsidized by PL. That the first result of becoming a PL worker is that you con some stupid kids out of a lot of dough so you don't have to work anymore is an offer so appealing that I'm sure many crafty American workers would take it if they knew about it. PL better not let the word get around, or they're going to need much bigger subsidies from Chairman Mao.)

Or take Jared Israel, founder of Harvard PL, a very brilliant full-time revolutionary said to have a master belt in karate. He is a rebel from an Old Left family. According to Jared himself, after his father learned Jared joined pro-Peking PL, he was hospitalized with a heart attack. Then there is the case of the former liberal and officer of the Young Democrats as a freshman. Tall and clumsy, he once muttered while drunk that everyone must laugh at him behind his back. (Nobody did.) As a freshman he never dated. As a sophomore he joined SDS and almost immediately got an SDS girl friend. What led him to join SDS? I once asked him. "I was working on draft counseling last summer, and I really became convinced that the ruling class couldn't end the war."

In the Vietnam environment, where politics takes command, those with personal problems seek a cure through it. So do the alienated students, who suffer from eternal human philosophical dilemmas rather than more specific everyday problems. At least the latter maintain the sense of distance never to join SDS, remaining only on its fringes.

Politics, though, as Max Weber pointed out, is not designed for people out to save souls, especially their own. Those who go into it for that reason usually end up hurting the interests of those millions of downtrodden who seek through politics not the saving of souls but of their own lives. The Thirty Years' War taught us, or should have, that the division of labor between politics and religion is a useful one.

"How do they get that committed?" is a frequent question one hears on campus from other students about SDS. People can understand the beliefs SDS people express but have trouble emotionally identifying with the clenched fists, the wild chants, and the endless hours of work SDS cadres, like men possessed, put into the cause. Harvard people are supposed to be able to be detached and skeptical. What the average student therefore can't understand about the SDSer is his complete lack of these Harvardian qualities. "They take themselves so seriously," is a frequent complaint.

What students don't realize is that the purpose of the chants and flags, the refusal to be detached, and the fanatic seriousness is precisely bravado. These are attempts to psych up the unsure, remove the doubts and above all repress the inhibitions. Behind the average Che lies a Hamlet.

Someone knocked at my door a cold night in March. My roommate and I had made a fire the previous night, and the logs and ashes still filled the fireplace.

A tall boy with a WASPish face and blond hair, wearing a facial expression of nondescript boredom, walked in. He was brandishing two long shabby and ruffled pieces of paper in his left hand, a pen in his right. While he was in the hallway he started to say, "Would anyone here like to sign the SDS Rot-cee petition?" He interrupted himself in around the middle of the sentence when he came into the living room and saw me sitting there reading.

"Oh, this is Kelman's room?" he said dejectedly. "Well, I'll be going."

"No, come on. Why don't you sit down and stay?" I responded. I had never seen him before. I tried to be friendly as I asked him who he was.

"My name is Larry Irving, and I live upstairs." He had a sort of bland Midwest accent.

"What made you decide to get mixed up with SDS?"

"Oh, just the Establishment's bullshit, their whole way of

life and exploiting people. You know, I could always see that. I hated how they were using people and screwing people. I was pretty radical when I got here."

"How come?"

"Well, you see my dad's a banker, and I went to prep school and all that. And they just want to prepare you for a life based on screwing people. I could see that."

"Are you a sophomore now?"

"Yeah."

"But you weren't with SDS last year, were you?" I thought I surely would have heard of him.

"No. It was because I didn't know about PL and the Worker-Student Alliance caucus till this year. I thought that all of SDS was the liberal Dyen crowd. You know, I went to the first SDS meeting last year when I was a freshman. But Dyen and Kazin and those people really turned me off. They're liberals, you know, not radicals." He sounded very self-assured. I asked him to sit down on the chair next to me, and he did. "Dyen didn't even say he was against negotiations in Vietnam. He talked about shit like 'negotiating U.S. withdrawal' and nothing about supporting the NLF. And he was spouting all this anti–working class bullshit about the 'new working class' and all that. These guys were all into personal liberation and serving yourself and all that." He was talking a series of broken-record PL clichés.

"So you're pro–working class?" I was attempting to gain some little hold to enter by, some common ground that could break down the wall of rhetoric separating us.

"Yeah, that's why I like PL. They're pro–working class and don't go in for this serve-yourself liberalism."

"Yeah. You know, Larry, I think it's good that you've gone

beyond a lot of this hippie stuff, because not that many students really give a shit about real working people. And I agree with you that PL is pro–working class. But the working class they're for is an imaginary working class. I mean it's completely in their minds."

He stuttered and hesitated. The mask was coming undone. "No-o," he stammered. "I don't think that could be true. You know, they live in working-class neighborhoods, and they know a lot of workers," he added, with admiration.

"Yeah, but they're in a dreamworld. Sure, working people have grievances. They're underpaid, overworked, and they get shoved around and screwed. I agree, Larry. Why do you think I'm a socialist? Shit, man, I don't go in for any of this shit liberal stuff about workers being reactionary. I think you're right to attack that. Sure workers have grievances. But they're not *revolutionary* grievances! Shit, it's fine for rich students to go around making their little revolutions. But workers have too much to lose. How can they know how the revolution's gonna turn out? "

The crack grew. "Y-yeah, I mean I have to admit that's the one part of the PL position that I don't know if I go along with. I mean I don't know if there's gonna be a revolution here."

Blood rushed gleefully to my head. The shell had broken. The human being had come out. "Look, face it: there ain't gonna be no revolution. Look at it this way — I just read a good point in a French magazine. It was a left-wing magazine. If in May nineteen sixty-eight — with ten million French workers out on strike occupying factories, with students battling police everywhere, with the working class having a revolutionary tradition going back to seventeen eighty-nine — if there was no successful revolution *then*, we might as well forget about revolutions in advanced industrial societies. They just aren't going to happen, so we better start thinking about how best to bring change through reform."

Larry nervously drew his fingers through his blond hair and scratched the polo shirt over his chest. He played with the meager stubble beneath his sideburns. "Yeah-h-h, that's a good point I guess. I mean, I suppose I could say that it was because of the treason of the French CP that it didn't succeed in France, but I wouldn't really believe that myself."

"Look, let me suggest a few subversive ideas, Larry." He was giving in so rapidly that I didn't want to press him, to appear to be taking advantage of him. "If you agree that there's not going to be a revolution, then I think you have to face some facts and draw conclusions from them. The first is that all this bullshit about 'trade union misleaders' which PL talks about is a lot of crap. Look, working people are playing for keeps, and they're facing very powerful corporations. If you attack the trade union leadership for holding the workers back from making a revolution, you're really attacking the workers themselves."

"Yeah, but what about the trade union leaders' support for Vietnam?" He fell back to the old liberal complaint.

"Well look, if you want to try to get workers to support Chairman Mao, you can try from today until doomsday and you won't get anywhere. Look, ask the average worker why he doesn't like communism, and he'll say to you — they have no democracy there, it's hard to get consumer goods there, you can't go to the church you want there, you can't strike there, you can't speak your mind there. Is he wrong? Larry, I think the average American worker is a lot smarter along that line than a lot of middle-class Harvard kids." I waited for a protest but got none. "But if you mean changing the labor move-

ment's foreign policy so it doesn't support all the reactionary
things the government does, I think there's a chance we can
change that."

"Look, I admit that unions are the best things workers have
going for them."

"OK, good. But another fact you've gotta recognize is that
most workers consider the Democratic party to be their party.
Now that may be too bad, but it's a fact. And if you're on the
side of working people you have to recognize facts, because
workers have to live in a real world, not a student LSD-dream-
world. Now look at people on the left wing of the Democratic
party, someone like Teddy Kennedy, say. Look at the issues
America is facing now: Vietnam, or closing off tax loopholes
for the rich, or rights for farm workers, or spending billions of
dollars for public sector jobs and housing for poor people, or
socialized medicine. Look, Kennedy's for all that. Now, I'm
not saying he's a socialist. But there aren't very many socialists
around now. And to say Kennedy's OK doesn't mean you stop
building your own movement."

"Yeah. Kennedy is pretty good. That's because he has a
working-class constituency." That was pure hearsay. I was
amazed to hear it.

"Larry," I finally burst out in desperation, "what the fuck
are you doing in PL? "

"They're trying to build a worker-student alliance," he answered doggedly.

"So is YPSL. A real one."

"Yeah, but I mean you guys don't even have any hope for
revolution. I mean I just don't *know* whether we have to have
a revolution to change America or not. I keep thinking about
it, and I still don't know. America is so rich, and the workers

aren't starving. But then I tell myself, What about U.S. imperialism? Now, the people in PL argue," he paused, beginning to sound like a high school teacher, "that capitalism can maintain itself in the U.S. only by the big investments in the Third World. Now, if that's true, then the revolutions in the Third World can throw the U.S. out and lead to a depression here, and then the workers might revolt and we could have a revolution. Except I just don't know whether or not PL is right about the economic importance of imperialism in the Third World. I don't know enough facts. I wish I could believe PL."

I was shocked. I started to say, "Do you mean to tell me . . ." but halted, because that would sound too menacing. I started again. "Larry, how can you go around talking about taking over buildings when you're not even sure about what turns out to be the central point in the whole chain? I don't understand it."

There was a very long pause. I waited for him to say something, but he kept silent.

"Look, PL's argument is ridiculous," I finally came in. "The total value of U.S. investment in underdeveloped countries is around sixteen billion dollars, I think, out of a total value of all U.S. corporate net worth of something like one and a half trillion. It's really not very much. If we lost the whole Third World, a few corporations would be very unhappy, but I think U.S. capitalism would continue along fine."

Larry hung his head down as he stood up. "Look, it's late and I'm very tired. I'm gonna go now, but let's keep talking together."

"Look, you have to *think* a little and not just get caught up in this SDS thing."

"Yeah, I know."

I gave him some literature to read.

On the early morning of April 9 Laurence Irving was arrested in University Hall.

On April 12 I dropped into Lowell Lec around nine-thirty in the evening to see an SDS meeting in progress. The hall was filled. I leaned against a wall and prepared to stand up for the duration. Just as I was taking off my sport jacket, a blond figure approached me defiantly. It was Larry Irving.

His voice was stern and hardly human. "Kelman, get out of here."

"What do you mean, Larry?"

"Kelman, get out of here!"

"This is a public meeting. I have a right to be here."

"Kelman, no spies at our meetings. Get out of here." His voice was pure hatred.

"I'm staying, Larry."

"Kelman, I'm warning you. Get out of here."

I stopped speaking and merely stood there, turning my face from him and pretending to listen to the "debate." Soon he went away. There's nothing like a good confrontation to revive sagging morale — or creeping uncertainty.

A few weeks later, I was walking up the stairs in Adams House when I overheard Larry Irving talking with a friend in SDS who also lives upstairs. The friend was saying, ". . . and I remember last year when your big hang-up about SDS was that they supported black riots. You were really upset with the rioting in Washington. Remember? "

"Yeah, well that's 'cause I was a liberal then and identified my interests with the property they were destroying. I thought they were rioting against me . . ."

And Larry's lifelong devotion to the working class? Serious?

A myth? Who knows? In SDS, it is so difficult to separate out the truth once the shouting starts.

I used to believe that the comparison frequently made by seasoned adults between SDS and young Nazis in the Weimar Republic was ridiculous. For after all, people in the New Left at least have a core, however corrupted, of idealism in them, while the Nazis were self-serving. However, the semester of the confrontation I took a course in modern German history. (Ironically, the lecture scheduled for the morning of the police bust was on the aborted revolution of 1919.) I must say that the more I study the Nazis the more I agree with the comparisons.

The error that most students make is in mistaking the Nazis for traditional conservatives. And conservatism has been justly discredited among students as the pathetic and sickening expression in the ideological sphere of the self-interest of the privileged, about as inspiring as tepid, flat Budweiser. Barry Goldwater, Richard Hofstadter points out in his essay on Goldwater in *The Paranoid Style in American Politics*, attempted to compare in one of his speeches the selfless approach of conservatives with the liberal's appeal to the self-interest of special interest groups. Hofstadter quotes a nationally televised Goldwater speech:

"You have probably been reading and hearing about some of the unorthodox things I have been doing. I have gone into the heart of Appalachia . . . and there I have *deliberately* attacked this administration's phony war on poverty.

"I have gone into the heart of Florida's retirement country . . . and there I have *deliberately* warned against the outright hoax of this administration's medicare scheme.

"I have gone into the heart of our farm area . . . and there I have *deliberately* called for the gradual transition from a controlled to a free agriculture.

"I have gone into an area of rapid urban growth . . . and there I have *deliberately* levelled against the Supreme Court the charge that they have no business attempting to draw the map of our state legislative districts.

"I have done all these things deliberately . . . [because] I will not attempt to buy the votes of the American people. I will not treat any of you as just so many special interests. I will not appeal to you as if you were simply pocketbooks surrounded on all sides by self-serving concerns. . . . The American people won't sell their votes. They won't *sell* their freedom."

Very idealistic. Yet, as Hofstadter points out:

There is no record, I believe, of his appearing before the National Association of Manufacturers to urge them to be less solicitous about their tax burdens or of his appearing before segregationist audiences to urge that they move over and make some place for the Negro . . . Politics, as he practiced it, would leave certain favored interests free to continue to seek their advancement through political action while encouraging large masses of the people to commit themselves entirely to the more abstract effort to fulfill high moral ideas.

American conservatism has abandoned any legitimate claim to speak for idealism. In a way it is unfortunate that there are so few idealistic conservatives around, so that left-of-center students could realize that one may respect someone's sincerity and idealism and still have very strong disagreements with his politics. On campus today, "he's sincere" and "he's idealistic" have become defenses in themselves of SDS behavior.

Students don't realize that there also exists the idealistic "revolutionary conservatism" of the youths who were the backbone of Mussolini's support before 1922 and who won the German universities for the Nazis. Like SDS, they accuse all their opponents of being people who put their self-interest above what is right. (A Nazi youth slogan was "Common good before personal advancement.") It was the Nazis who invented the phrase "the system" (*Das System*) to describe the hated Weimar democracy of compromise and soullessness. ("The system must die so that the people can live" was another Nazi slogan.)

People often forget that the Nazis were bitterly hostile to the traditional German Conservative party, which they branded as "reactionary" and "the class war party of capitalism." The "conservative revolutionary" cultural critics in Imperial Germany, whom Fritz Stern describes in his brilliant *Politics of Cultural Despair* as intellectual predecessors of the Nazis, all broke with the conservatives of their day. As early as the 1850s Paul de Lagarde, according to Stern, was "thoroughly disenchanted with the ruling classes of Prussia and wrote scathingly of the timid, reactionary monarchy and its sporadic witch hunts. He was adrift, belonging to neither political camp; he called himself a conservative radical, and opposed all existing parties and powers." Moeller van den Bruck, whose 1922 book, *The Third Reich*, popularized the expression, wrote during the Weimar Republic, "Anyone is reactionary who still thinks the life we led before 1914 was great and beautiful, and even superbly magnificent. Anyone will be a conservative who yields to no flattering self-deception and honestly confesses that it was revolting." What the ruling classes lacked in both authors' minds was any sort of heroic and liberating vision to inspire people in common purpose, in building up the community.

Today's New Leftist shares with the young Nazi the moral

arrogance and contempt of "mere procedures" which block the way to getting what he knows is right. They share large parts of the critique of modern "bourgeois" society (a term both use, with contempt), especially of the negative effects of such a society: its stifling conventionality, its puritan respectability, its inability to inspire individuals to higher purposes. Their prescriptions may seem different but in practice turn out not to differ that much. Murdered Jews and kulaks were both presented as exploiters. And, as a speaker at a Berkeley teach-in argued some years ago, the Vietcong is all right because they only murder "unpopular people."

And the Nazis and the New Left pay each other the proper respects. Asked whether he didn't find it odd that he was a supporter of the John Birch Society when he entered Harvard and a member of the pro-PL caucus of SDS as a junior, Don Mahoney told a friend of mine, "I've always seen through liberalism." The SDS line was that George Wallace's supporters among blue collar workers were the easiest workers for SDS to reach since, unlike those who had voted for Humphrey, the Wallace supporters had "seen through the Democratic party and trade union misleaders."

Adolf Hitler said shortly after coming to power:

There is more that binds us to Bolshevism than separates us from it. There is, above all, genuine revolutionary feeling . . . I have always made allowance for this circumstance and given orders that former Communists are to be admitted to the Party at once. The petit bourgeois Social Democrat and the trade union boss will never make a Nazi, but the Communist always will. [Italics added.]

Come the mass murders and the stifling regimentation, the nontotalitarians among today's revolutionaries — and they are there, to be sure — would flinch and turn away. Some would be purged. I will never get to find out which of my friends in SDS would join in with the terror and which would refuse — either because none of them will ever have a chance to show us what they would do with power, or because, if they did, I would be shot before that *n*th round of purges came.

I can see the ones who were deceived, though, painfully and pleadingly asking themselves *why*. "*This* isn't what we meant by the revolution. *This* isn't what we wanted."

One can only quote for them the last lines of Fritz Stern's book.

Moeller — and the other Germanic critics — did not want *that* Third Reich, and would not have acknowledged the reality of Hitler's Reich as the realization of their dream.

But, we must ask, could there have been any other "Third Reich"? Was there a safe stopping place in this wild leap from political reality? Can one abjure reason, glorify force, prophesy the age of the imperial dictator, can one condemn all existing institutions, without preparing the triumph of irresponsibility?

2. The Alienated Prepare for "Liberation"

Radicalism is to root out the boredom of our daily lives.
— Manifesto of "The Enragés of Harvard," March 1969

Four days after the occupation of University Hall Nick Gagarin, executive editor of the *Crimson*, bared his soul, in the proud *Crimson* tell-it-like-it-is tradition, with a piece entitled "Non-Politics on the Battlefront." Describing his feelings inside the building, Nick wrote:

What was most euphoric was us and what we were to each other. For those few hours we *were* brothers and sisters. We did reach out and hold onto each other. . . You had to realize — whatever your politics and whatever your tactics — that we were very beautiful in University Hall, we were very human, and we were very together . . .

None of the above is very political stuff. But there was a group of us in University Hall who are not very political people. It was a strange group, not well-defined at all, that included some girls, some people from the Loeb [Drama Center], a couple of guys from the Fly Club, at least one from the Lampoon, and one in a tuxedo who had just come from a party and was drunk. There were others. Some of us didn't even know what the six demands were . . .

The people who did most of the speaking at the formal meetings were, by and large, boring and had, by and large, no sense of humor . . . The people in charge didn't want us to listen to music and laugh, because that detracted from the seriousness of the meeting. That was OK, but it was also a little frightening that within this liberated area there were hints of the same kind of narrowness that existed outside.

The political people should rethink their line on "oppressed people." We all agonize over the fate of the oppressed people of South Vietnam, and the oppressed people of black America, and the oppressed people of Roxbury. But the realization that lies just around the corner is that we too are an oppressed people . . . Any radical movement at Harvard should base itself on our own needs — the needs of the oppressed student class.

The notion that students at Harvard University form part of an oppressed student class will strike most people as so outrageous as hardly to merit further consideration. Such a reaction is understandable. For the university sanctuary is a protective womb that shelters us from the natural shocks outside, in what we call on campus "the real world." (At the end of 1968 the *Crimson* introduced a column reporting wire service dispatches and entitled simply "The Real World.") The laws against liquor and drugs do not apply to us. Only visionaries could conceive of the leisuristic future society where the general population could enjoy the "work week" we have. Students sleep most mornings till ten. Sixty-five percent of those in our age group have begun — at the lowest paid, least secure bottom rung of the ladder — a dulling job in the nonprofessional sectors of the economy or are off in Vietnam. At the same time we students are, at a cost of approximately $15,000 of our parents' money, enjoying the longest period of prolonged irresponsibility the world has ever known. To those who have been both rich and poor and know that rich is better, the life of the Harvard student is indeed an enviable one.

But that some students nevertheless do feel oppressed is an objective fact that objective reality must deal with and not simply mock. To be sure, some kids can find almost anything oppressive. I remember walking home on one rather cool late autumn day with a friend from tutorial when unexpectedly he blurted out, "Don't you find it repressive to be forced to wear clothes?" Somewhat surprised, I responded simply, "No, I find it warming." The editorial editor of the *Crimson* once sought to prove that the purpose of elementary school was not education but preparing the unmolded child for a life of psychic repression by pointing out that teachers always demanded that students arrive in school on time!

However, to laugh at such attitudes doesn't mean we shouldn't try to find their deeper content. The idle rich, I have always felt, are generally rather happy precisely because they are not idle. They are extremely busy with a thousand and one activities — in business, government, or their little philanthropies — which they can perform just because they are rich and powerful. As it is, the image of the depressed millionaire, I think, is used largely to console the rest of us "poor but happy" souls. If the idle rich were indeed idle the image would probably correspond much more to reality.

Students are today's idle rich. Being idle, well fed, and generally satisfied gives us a chance to do a great deal of solitary thinking and "soul-searching" — a term which has literal significance for us. And many of us, like Hamlet, end up thinking too precisely on the event.

Stop reading for a moment and don't think about anything else but *death*. The fact that at some time you won't have any more memories of yourself or of the world to remember reality by. You won't have anything to grasp on to that can anchor you to consciousness. You will be nothing. You won't know you were *ever* there, just like you never knew you weren't there for the eternity before you were born.

Please stop and think.

Now please ask yourself, as Hamlet and thousands of students after him have done in the ample free time we've had to search our souls, what the purpose of our day-to-day strutting around can be. Except to break the boredom of meaninglessness.

It is only necessary to reflect on death to understand why some students view themselves as an oppressed class. And in order to discern the first and most urgent plea of the oppressed student class, it is only necessary to consider the results of the idleness and attendant boredom which encourage brooding. The results are purely and simply fear and trembling.

The first nonnegotiable demand of the oppressed student class is therefore for a rapidly changing stream of sensations. New ones must appear before the old ones have become, like any routine, boring. Idleness and the attendant brooding must be avoided at all costs. And the hostility of the oppressed student class is directed against its oppressors: institutions which require routinized behavior (such as going to classes every day) or which discourage experimentation with new sensations such as drugs. The three most obvious oppressors: University, Law, Family. Of course, the incomprehensible but constantly repeated rhetoric of their SDS allies also comes in for attack from the alienated, when during crisis situations the alienated can't avoid being subjected to it. "Les enragés" flooded one of the series of Progressive Labor–controlled rallies-cum-meetings during the strike with an attack against those who "bore us in meetings that pretend to represent us (motion kills emotion)," and told President Pusey that "in PL-controlled meetings as in your dull shit-filled classes, there is only one thing to do: enjoy ourselves. That's why we play our kazoos today." In a beautiful example of the coalition of the cadres, Mike Kazin, in the first good words he had to say about his arch enemies PL all year, got up at the meeting to denounce the leaflet as "red-baiting."

It is the restless search for new sensations which makes the oppressed student class the only people on campus serious about drugs. The widely reported fact that on Ivy League campuses today nearly everyone smokes marijuana at least occasionally is misleading in a way. For the vast majority of "straight" kids who occasionally smoke do so for purely hedonistic reasons. ("A few years ago," as my roommate once said to me, "you would ask, 'What psychological problems make this kid smoke pot?' Today you'd ask the question about anyone who *doesn't* smoke. 'What psychological problems make this kid never smoke pot?' ")

But the alienated are seeking mystic crystal revelations from drugs. And it is they who "graduate" to the "hard drugs" that parents warn straight Sam about when he takes his first puff of diluted cannabis. It is from their ranks that one sees the occasional pathetic sight of the nineteen-year-old "mystic" who has emerged from his last mescaline trip having "discovered" the Life Force of the Universe, or the brilliant Harvard student reduced to the handful of monosyllables which make up a "hip" vocabulary.

The oppressed student class can't talk to anyone over thirty because older people are no longer idle, have no more time to brood. As one of their number wrote in the *Crimson*:

We might as well admit it, and risk the inevitable and gleeful *Newsweek* article that usually makes us think ten times before saying anything. It *is* impossible to talk to anyone over thirty. Think of the last few times you tried. Think of the time you tried to tell your parents why you were unhappy and why Harvard made you uptight, and that maybe it wasn't just adolescent growing pains or if it was they were a lot profounder than anybody imagined . . .

And then there was one of those god-awful family get-togethers — was it what's her face's wedding or cousin George's funeral (he was twenty-nine and died of fright)? Anyway, after fifteen minutes of kisses on the cheek and handshakes with good-natured (oh yes) ribbing about long hair and campus activism you realized the only way to survive was to get hopelessly drunk . . .

Whereupon one of the many (how many?) beloved uncles sauntered over and wanted to know why you young people were soft and told you how when he was a kid nobody had time to get depressed because they were too busy figuring out where the next meal was coming from.

You were relieved to get back to school where at least some of the people over thirty weren't really over thirty (it's only incidentally related to age) and most of the others were far too occupied writing treatises on the differences between Ramist and Aristotelian logic to bait you. Except of course for an occasional mini-confrontation with an interested, bespectacled administrator who wanted to know why you thought your boredom was more profound than that of an eight-year-old who got tired of the same old toys (you never said it was, but you were close enough to eight to remember vaguely that eight-year-old *Weltschmerz* was a lot profounder than the man talking to you).

The oppressed student class has been with us at least as far back as Hamlet. In the silent generation of the fifties it vegetated on Jack Kerouac, Zen Buddhism, and bongo drums. To the great misfortune of the rest of us, it discovered politics in the sixties.

Politics for the alienated is only a side pursuit to the above-named activities. A roommate of Mike Kazin's, who is a member of the "oppressed student class," once called Kazin, in the jargon of the "class," a "political freak." "Politics takes precedence over everything" for Kazin, something which he couldn't understand. For the alienated a "political freak" is as incomprehensible as the "business freak" who plugs away day after day at making money. The important part is not the activity, but the single-minded pursuit of anything on any constant basis. The alienated must go feverishly from activity to activity, unable to concentrate on a single one.

When the member of the oppressed student class gets swept

along on the New Left's red flag, it is on the basis of a misunderstanding. For the alienated would be the most desperately
unhappy of all people in the regimented society which the New
Left would institute. The misunderstanding is based on the
shared rebellion of the New Left and the alienated, the shared
commitment to *action*. From there, the alienated merely reinterpret New Left ideology through the purple prismed glasses
they love to wear to distort other aspects of the real world.

The question, then, is why the oppressed student class has
discovered politics now. The answer provides a clue to the
relationship between events — like the war in Vietnam — and
the development of a mass base for student extremism. For
every generation contains a core of political radicals among students. And every generation contains alienated students. They
have to enter into an alliance, on the radicals' terms, for student
extremism to have a chance as an influential force.

The simple response, that "injustices" in the outside world
lead to a growth of "protests" from sensitive students, is obviously an oversimplification. First, it would be hard to argue
that America in the sixties is a more unjust society than it was
in the Eisenhower-McCarthy fifties, when students were qui-
escent. Second, we must look at what takes place on "liberated"
campuses during events like the Harvard strike. During our
strike a group of students spontaneously set up the "Harvard
New College," which received extensive *Crimson* coverage and
was in general a favorite of the oppressed student class. While
distant pundits were explaining the events at Harvard in terms
of international issues, the course content had nothing to say
about such subjects. Here is a virtually complete list of the
courses offered at the Harvard New College; it reads like a
psychoanalyst's report on a patient.

History of the Self
Repetition and Boredom in Modern Art
Psychology of Modern Alienated Man
Aesthetics of Revolution
Lévi-Strauss and Voidness of Concepts
Artificial Life
Strike as Personal Experience
The Retribalization of Harvard
Middle Class Suburbs in American Life

At the same time a strike poster was plastered all over the university, with a pastiche of free-association ramblings that was almost embarrassing:

STRIKE FOR THE EIGHT DEMANDS STRIKE BECAUSE YOU HATE COPS STRIKE BECAUSE YOUR ROOMMATE WAS CLUBBED STRIKE TO STOP EXPANSION STRIKE TO SEIZE CONTROL OF YOUR LIFE STRIKE TO BECOME MORE HUMAN STRIKE BECAUSE THERE'S NO POETRY IN YOUR LECTURES STRIKE BECAUSE CLASSES ARE A BORE STRIKE FOR POWER STRIKE TO MAKE YOURSELF FREE STRIKE TO ABOLISH ROTC STRIKE BECAUSE THEY ARE TRYING TO SQUEEZE THE LIFE OUT OF YOU STRIKE

Far from being an idealistic reaction against society's treatment of the downtrodden, the purpose of the revolution of the alienated seems to be, in the words of a leaflet of the enragés of Harvard, "to root out the boredom of our daily lives." The alienated take up politics simply because politics is in the air as a source of people's problems. Thus the striking force for student extremism comes from a coalition of the motivated radicals and those who, for the purpose of the movement, christen themselves "cultural radicals" and who use politics to act out personal problems. Thus despite the hostility of elements of the New Left, particularly PL, to the cultural radicals ("selfish psychoactors on the stage of history," one PL leaflet branded them), the simple fact is that SDS would be nowhere as a mass

force without this group tagging along. For they provide rock
bands, light shows, and the whole carnival milieu of "liberation"
surrounding confrontation. They get sympathetic press coverage
for the entire New Left from Madison Avenue adult alienated
types who envy them secretly and thus shield the New Left
ideologues from scrutiny. Finally, they provide a considerable
part of the cannon fodder.

In order to enter politics — in order to transform themselves
from "the alienated" to cultural radicals — the oppressed student class must reinterpret their basic problems, which are in
reality eternal human dilemmas, in so-called political terms.
They must blame the "social structure" for their brooding. It
is during these tortured attempts that one's sympathy for the
alienated rapidly approaches zero.

I would like to ask Nick Gagarin, for example, exactly how
"the University teaches us inhumanity, competitiveness, and
alienation." Competitiveness, maybe. I personally don't think
so. But inhumanity and — alienation?? I would like to challenge Mark Rudd to explain how Columbia is responsible for
"our identity crisis."

How can one judge in any terms other than that of psycho-
pathology the attempt to analyze, in political terms, *the family*
as one of the "two primary structures of oppression" of *capitalist* society? ("Ivy Strike Untangled," by Dick Cluster and Jon
Schwartz, in *The Old Mole*.)

You don't deal with ancient human dilemmas by sloganizing
them or by assuming, without a shred of evidence, that a "revolution" will put an end to them. We may not know how to
create a new society or a new man, but we certainly *do* know
that you don't create it by incantations.

What is the "revolution" being proposed by the cultural

radicals? It is a revolution that would mean a change from the humdrum and everyday routines of our lives — the routines that say in the morning we have to get up to work, that if we want to buy something we have to pay for it. Because routines become boring, they seem repressive — and the alternative seems liberating. During confrontation situations, the alienated see a chance to break out of these routines and "liberate" themselves.

We had a revolution in America once. Remember New England's great power failure? For that one night, suddenly everybody was friendly and talking to strangers again. It was just like the atmosphere inside "liberated" University Hall: "We were very human, and we were very together." There was love and solidarity. Nine months later more babies were born. It was like the thrill of dancing to rock music inside the stuffy rooms of University Hall, previously reserved for pompous old men, or the beauty of posing for photos in your bell-bottoms and shoulder-length hair next to oil portraits of the superannuated lining the walls of the dean's office.

The problem with the "liberation" proposed by the cultural radicals is that it forgets that the old routines developed for a purpose. Helpfulness and love were the order of the day during the "revolution" of the great power failure, but if the power had stayed out much longer you would have seen street fighting and dog-eat-dog. No electricity is "liberating" for a while but enslaving if it lasts. Dancing in the streets is fine, but soon you begin to get hungry and thirsty. Somebody has to manufacture the beautiful clothes and the stereo records that are the spark of the revolution. The revolution against the affluent society has as its presupposition continued affluence.

Liberation too becomes a boring routine, just like the old routines. If the behavior of the revolutionary constituted the norm, the alienated would be seeking the new experience of the ordered, scholarly life.

In a way, liberation is worse than the old routines, because it is a routine that does not allow society to continue to feed, house, and shelter its people. The tyranny which has followed the liberation of the great revolutions of history is a result of the need to impose order and get back to those tasks.

Paradoxically, the member of the oppressed student class seeking liberation — and being ass-licked by adult commentators anxious to portray him as "idealistic" or "some of our most creative minds" — is of necessity a parasite on the "unliberated" members of society. Working people and the poor, those who are willing to accept the routines, interrupted only by a vacation once a year, an occasional six-pack of beer, and some weekends out fishing (and often not even that much), see that they are on the victimized end of the self-serving games of the alienated.

Thus the fundamental reason the alienated have entered politics is simply because politics is in the air. Political action is a new sensation, a new substitute for the old routines. But if the attempts to construct political explanations for personal problems is only a disaster of intellectual dishonesty, the actual acting out in politics of these personal problems threatens direct disaster for the millions of people in the world outside who are threatened by the backlash to New Left antics.

In October 1968, at a time when George Wallace appeared a very real threat in the November elections, especially in his appeal to traditionally liberal blue collar voters, and race tensions in the country were on the rise, Wallace came to Boston for a big rally. About fifty members and friends of the Young People's Socialist League at Harvard came to the rally with 5000 professionally engraved leaflets entitled "George Wallace —

Enemy of the Working Man," which attempted to show the phoniness of Wallace's appeal to the labor vote. We took the Wallace threat seriously and felt we ought to try to do something serious to try to combat it.

A contingent of cultural radicals, under the aegis of their new "organization," Harvard-Radcliffe X, took the Wallace rally as an occasion merely to show contempt for other people. They arrived at the rally, looking like a cast of extras from *Wild in the Streets*, with a sloppily printed handout which read as follows:

AMERICA

FOR

WALLACE

In Times of Fear and Stress Americans
find a leader to embody them

GEORGE WALLACE IS

THAT MAN

GOD BLESS YOU

FOR IT   GEORGE

"No man should be bound by
mere humanity."
—G.W.   1968

One need not describe the effect that this disgusting show of snottiness and intellectual superiority had on the adults at the rally. But the cultural radicals didn't care. They were laughing and cheering and shouting. They got a kick out of it, especially when an occasional poor soul took the leaflet seriously and thought that the longhairs were really behind Wallace. Very "liberating."

Shortly before this incident, the Up Against the Wall Motherfuckers SDS chapter, centered in New York's East Village, published a new "post-Chicago" manifesto on the pages of *New Left Notes*. The Motherfuckers habitually break up SDS meetings at the slightest sign that serious intellectual debate may be beginning and, in general, conduct terrorism against the notion that individual rationality is possible in a sick society. The group made the key concept of their manifesto the statement, printed in bold type, THE FUTURE OF OUR STRUGGLE IS THE FUTURE OF CRIME IN THE STREETS.

Unfortunately, many of the cultural radicals have put the Motherfucker manifesto, as updated by the desperados in the Weatherman faction of SDS, into practice. In doing so they have given the lie to the idylls of "togetherness" and "noncompetitiveness" with which they innocently paint their ideal future. For violence, too, is a new sensation, a "liberation" from the old routines. Many ordinary Americans are disturbed by the decline in friendliness and mutual respect in an overcompetitive America. But they don't see "crime in the streets" as part of the solution to this crisis. They see it as *part* of the crisis. And the perpetual disorder of "liberation" is no atmosphere for creating mutual respect.

Just as the alienated present no practical recipe for a decent society, so no conceivable political change will in itself solve the hang-ups which are at the root of their unhappiness. The hang-ups which the alienated confront head on are probably unsolvable, and therefore we human beings will simply have to learn to survive with them. In unsettling, unpeaceful coexistence, perhaps. But it's preferable to the whining complaints of the alienated about the burdens of their oppression which, in the final analysis, became themselves first boring and later just sickening examples of self-pity.

Instead of a doomed and phony effort to save *themselves* through politics, let the alienated devote themselves to saving *others*, those others not yet "cursed" by affluence. This is an approach to solving alienation through political action. If no transcendent purpose for life can be discovered, at least the alienated should seek an alternative to despair in some middle-range purpose. It is merely a cop-out for the *Crimson* editorialist to write that he doesn't want to become a doctor and save people until he's seen that the world is worth their living in. Let the downtrodden decide for themselves. At the very least, it is better to be unhappy and well fed than unhappy and starving.

An altruistic politics can "cure" alienation by giving life a purpose. But politics *based* on (and feeding on) alienation is as disastrous as the politics based on frustration which creates the New Leftist out of the moderate.

But, even if under false premises, the alienated have entered politics. They do not ask to make New Left policy, but merely to follow along as the side show of the New Left circus. From beginning to end the "political" contributions of the alienated at Harvard succeeded in casting a pall of mental illness over the whole campus. The alienated came into their own during the strike, which they viewed as a compulsory group therapy involving 6000 students. But like big business advertising which persuades us that we have freely chosen what they want us to buy, the "freedom" of "liberated" Harvard was phony and manipulated. And after a short period of time it too was to become boring to the cultural radicals, who called off the new world after two weeks for lack of interest.

3. The Moderates Prepare for Active Nonresistance

Above all, we have to make it clear that we're not out to attack SDS or set up a group trying to counter them. —

Ken Glazier, student government leader and
head of the moderate Memorial Church Group,
at an early meeting during the strike,
April 11, 1969

While most of SDS was in jail the student government forces were trying to co-opt the whole thing. Those guys are the enemy. —

Jon Harris, SDS leader, at an SDS meeting,
reported in the *Crimson*, April 11, 1969

The Harvard Corporation used ready-made operators [like] Ken Glazier. —

Challenge, Progressive Labor party newspaper.
"Pro Worker Fight Rocks Harvard,"
May 1969

There are some people who if you spit on them they'll think it's raining. —

Old Jewish proverb, learned
at my mother's knee

THAT THE NEW LEFT and the cultural radicals wanted a revolution at Harvard does not mean that a revolution was inevitable or even likely, any more than a revolution in America is likely simply because SDS wants one. Indeed, it must be remembered that before April 9, 1969, Harvard was generally viewed as the impenetrable fortress, the place where it *couldn't* happen. SDS shared this view. Several weeks before the confrontation Mike

Kazin told *The Columbia Spectator* that Harvard SDS would love to "make a Columbia" at Harvard but unfortunately didn't have the student support to do so. When the Harvard confrontation was so successful ("that fantastic strike at Harvard!" in the surprised words of one SDS national leader) it took even SDS off guard.

That the Harvard confrontation came off was due to the addition of a crucial element to the confrontation coalition: the moderates. Lavished with utterly unmerited praise in the press, the moderates in fact were the key to the SDS victory. What happened to the moderates, numerically a group much larger than the New Left and the alienated combined, is thus the key to what's happened to Harvard. For the moderates were not only the key to the near destruction of Harvard University; they had earlier been the key to Harvard's stability. They were moderate students before and after. What happened?

To understand this one must first understand why Harvard had always been considered unshakable, even at a time when so many other universities had already been victims of drawn-out confrontations. The standard theory relates the success of confrontations to the immobility and stupidity of college administrations. During the 1964 Berkeley rebellion, Professor Seymour Martin Lipset, who was driven from Berkeley to Harvard exhausted and maligned when Berkeley New Leftists somehow mistook him for the power elite, continually berated the Berkeley administration for provoking the situation by their unresponsive behavior during the free speech crisis. At the time, Lipset recalls now, he pointed out to Berkeley president Clark Kerr the example of a university nearby whose administration was open and responsive to every student request and therefore would never be subject to the same troubles as Berkeley.

The school Lipset was referring to was San Francisco State College.

According to the standard view, it was the distant aloofness of the Columbia administration which provoked the first Ivy League crisis in 1968. Grayson Kirk was seen as the classic example of the uncaring college president, shot full of corporate connections and far more at home in boardrooms than classrooms. But, as Professor Daniel Bell pointed out in an article in *The Public Interest* after the Columbia uprising, this image of unresponsiveness is far from accurate. He notes that in the year period preceding April 1968, Columbia had: (1) refused to give local draft boards, as the law required, class ranking statistics of its students, (2) temporarily suspended military recruiting until General Hershey withdrew a statement which implied that draft protesters might be conscripted as punishment for their activities, (3) canceled classes for a one-day Vietnam discussion, (4) held a student referendum on whether free recruiting by firms like Dow Chemical should be allowed on campus.

Harvard did none of these things. Yet it was Columbia University which invented the new student revolution. Columbia was the first time a purposeful attempt was made to shut a college down by permanently occupying university buildings. At Columbia University an original handful of SDSers were eventually joined by hundreds of moderates *inside* the buildings. Columbia's explosion was, one year earlier, much bigger and longer-lasting than our delayed one.

The difference between schools like Harvard, Yale, and Princeton on the one hand and Columbia, Berkeley, and San Francisco State on the other is very simple. It has nothing to do with the quality of the administration, the degree of university complicity with imperialism and neo-colonialism, or with differing levels of student concern over racism and the war in Vietnam. *It is merely that the average Harvard, Yale, or Princeton student is personally contented with his life at school, while the average student at Columbia, Berkeley, and San Francisco State is not.* The average Harvard student sees no reason to attack a place he basically finds pleasant; this is the kernel of the Harvard "particularism" which saved us from confrontation for so long.

It is an open secret that most Columbia students are dissatisfied with their lives at Columbia. Columbia starts off with two strikes against it, quite frankly, because a good portion of each year's freshman class enters Columbia as a last-choice "safe school," after having been turned down at Harvard, Yale, or Princeton. Friends at Columbia report that Harvard is a major topic of discussion around campus, mainly of the sour grapes variety. The *Columbia Spectator* even stations a regular stringer in Cambridge.

The consensus around Columbia seems to be that the school attempts to make up in quantity what it lacks in quality. Freshmen must take two dull introductory courses, Contemporary Civilization and Humanities, whose endless reading lists take up huge amounts of time. Some professors do not teach any undergraduate courses. Columbia's campus is in the middle of a slum, and students are often afraid to venture out at night for fear of crime. The campus is completely buried in the New York City metropolis. I remember when I went back home for the first time over Thanksgiving of my freshman year and visited old high school friends, it was the Columbia freshmen who were the most dissatisfied with their college.

Similar observations may be made about Berkeley and San

Francisco State. Home of the "multiversity," Berkeley uneasily
accommodates some 50,000 students, using lectures given over
television and classes taught by teaching assistants. Berkeley
exudes a miasma of alienation and impersonality. A poll there
showed only about one-third of the student body basically satisfied with their lives at the school. (A comparable poll at Harvard showed over three-quarters basically satisfied.) San Francisco State has been hit by the expectation gap between the
hopes of an articulate student body recruited out of the bur-
geoning hippie movement around San Francisco and the pid-
dling funds shelled out by Ronald Reagan for higher education.

It is not surprising that Columbia, Berkeley, and San Francisco State came under successful attack. Destroying the school
was more fun than going there.

Few things are more fun than going to Harvard. (Yale or
Princeton people I know say the same thing about their schools,
so such a bold statement might be exaggerated.) Life at Harvard
is simply too mahogany-paneled, leisure-pervaded, and female-
companioned to produce anything else but a mellow and contented majority. College students from elsewhere visiting Harvard friends arrive to remark that the bathrooms in our Harvard
suites are about the size of entire student rooms at other colleges. But this is only the first shock of adaptation. The next
shock usually comes when they discover that their Harvard
friends generally have only around fifteen hours of classes a
week, often only three or four days a week, and never beginning
before the (for us) ungodly hour of nine in the morning. They
wistfully muse over the fact that attendance is never taken in
class, or that freshmen and upperclassmen can all take virtually
any course they want. The next major blow comes when they
look at Harvard reading lists, which are not only brief (Brandeis

students were incredulous when a visiting professor from Harvard several years ago handed out the Harvard-length reading list for his course) but also heavily slanted toward real books rather than textbooks.

But the deepest pleasures of Harvard life require somewhat more exposure than a brief visit can provide. It takes time, for example, to find out about the girls.

The Harvard myth is stronger nowhere else than among non-Harvard girls, and at our mixers one encounters not only Cliffies, but girls from Lesley, Emmanuel, Emerson, Lasell, Jackson, the Museum School, Pine Manor, Simmons, Wellesley, and Wheelock, as well as co-eds from Boston University. We are spoiled into laziness. Harvard students hardly ever travel to mixers at other schools. We wait for the girls to come to us.

Harvard students date frequently (over 80 percent described themselves as dating "very often" or "just about right" in a poll shortly before April 1969) and, as my own casual inspection of our dining halls indicates, they date beautiful girls. Harvard students are in general casual about sex. (A respondent to the poll question about how frequently he dated girls inquired, "What do you answer if you're living with a girl?") It is a casualness which comes of familiarity and even routinization. When drugs were new on campus, while I was a freshman, it was hard to have a conversation where they didn't come up. Now that they're widespread, people are less obsessed. The same is true with sex.

Familiarity, to be sure, doesn't breed contempt. But it does breed contentment. It is widely recognized around campus that serenity correlates most closely with success with girls. A girl friend cures disorders from gout to bad grades. In the words of one friend of mine, "When I was a freshman I hardly ever

went out steady with any girl at all, and I was on Rank List
Four in grades, drunk all the time, and goofin' off. When I
was a sophomore I started going with this girl, and I was on
Rank List Three in grades and I was really happy. When I
was a junior I was engaged to the girl, and I was on Rank List
Two and all involved in politics and all kinds of extra activities." Of the small discontented minority at Harvard, poll results showed that a third date "seldom or never."

The role that the accessibility of girls plays in making Harvard
such an enjoyable place comes out clearly in the mean bit of
folk wisdom around campus which assumes that SDSers are discontented with Harvard because they lack feminine companionship. This theory contains a grain of truth, but it fails to come
to grips with the fact that SDSers march to the beat of a different drum. The dedicated ones are hardly concerned with
the breast size of their revolutionary cohorts. (This becomes
clear, if nothing else, from observing these girls' breast size.)
At any rate, the popularity of the sexual explanation for revolutionary discontent among Harvard students themselves indicates the role we assign to girls in our own happiness.

Girls are only a precondition, as it were, for contentment.
Harvard's view of itself would decline profoundly if we thought
that we lived for the flesh alone. Rather, getting one's bed appropriately warmed prepares one for life's real business in the
somewhat colder world outside. And for those who pride themselves as intellectuals, Harvard provides the undergraduate with
an opportunity for supping, chatting, and discoursing with assorted great minds that would surprise the adult addled by
generalizations about the impersonality of today's universities.
Students occasionally do complain about lack of personal contact with professors, but it is hard to chalk up this "lack" to

anything but laziness. The simple fact is that professors, up to and including the famous names on the faculty, are eminently available to undergraduates. One need only show a tiny amount of initiative. Professors frequently come to speak at informal house or freshman luncheons. I remember one luncheon with Professor Seymour Martin Lipset in the sanctuary of the Lehman Hall small dining room. (The crowded, noisy Lehman Hall cafeteria outside is an SDS hangout for people so alienated from their fellow students that they refuse to eat in the house dining halls. The particular day of the luncheon featured a spontaneous outburst of dancing in the aisles to the music of the most recent Beatles album, played over a mysterious loudspeaker brought into the cafeteria.) Lipset succeeded in charming and amazing everyone at the lunch with off-the-cuff answers to queries from the students present in which he referred to frequently obscure evidence from Japan, Australia, Scandinavia, Italy, the United States, in support of the points he was making. With his string-bean thin tie and crumpled suit, Lipset seemed the very human, modest, and even shy genius as he mixed this sophisticated data with references to his own childhood activities as an eleven-year-old socialist in the Bronx.

A professor can be invited to have lunch or dinner with any student at the student's simple request. It's all up to the student. As a freshman I frequently went into Professor Edward Banfield's office during his office hours to argue with the quaint conservative views he presented in his course on urban problems. At the beginning of my sophomore year I found myself invited to a wonderful party at his home which he was giving for students — and treated to some delicious native Italian food by Banfield's Sicilian wife as well as a lengthy discussion of who was to blame for the high prices in ghetto stores. To be sure, there are exceptions to the rule of the friendly professor (John Kenneth Galbraith is notorious around campus on this score), but the problem of professor reticence is no greater than that of the occasional professor notorious for improper advances toward Harvard or Radcliffe students.

Professors aren't the only ones providing extracurricular intellectual stimulation. The number of speakers who come to give lectures, raps, harangues, informal talks, and/or question-and-answer sessions is staggering. One could spend one's entire college life attending such addresses and forget about schoolwork altogether. Added to speeches is the plethora of film classics and film junk which nearly literally buries us in endless celluloid footage. The two theaters at the Square change their features around once every three days, and each weekend three or four assorted "film societies" or "film culture groups" show a different movie, frequently something like a 1953-vintage Ingmar Bergman or a 1956-vintage Japanese samurai flick. Then there are the seven bookstores and three international press stands in the immediate vicinity of Harvard Square which are favorite retreats for wasting-time browsing.

Ask a student what he likes about Harvard, and most will quickly begin talking about the diversity of the student body. The old aristocratic Harvard mold, to which the occasional Jew, Negro, or Pole entering Harvard would seek to adapt, has completely broken down. So far nothing has really replaced it. The model of the sophisticated, alienated New York Jew has caught hold fairly widely (many of the aristocrats try, unsuccessfully, to imitate it). But it is by no means dominant. For the moment Harvard remains the pluralistic society which the diversity of the geographical origins of the student body would indicate. Before I came there, I had never known a southerner personally.

I was prejudiced against football players and preppies and hesitant about anyone outside New York. Harvard is no one place writ large; the Ohio farm boy and the Washington politician's son make it exhilarating and often amusing to a New Yorker. We amuse them too, no doubt. As a freshman, kids always remarked about how I pronounced the word "talk." (An unspoken resentment exists among Harvard students over the general reluctance of most Harvard blacks to associate much with whites. Students had hoped to be able to get to know black students better.)

We discover at Harvard that other people often have interests we never dreamed of, even interests that are uninvented in our own neck of the woods. Through the vagaries of chance roommate selection hundreds of students are turned on annually to the never-imagined pleasures of drugs or lacrosse, radicalism or the stock market. The myriad achievements of the fellow next door stimulate the energies of everybody else, as used as we all were in high school to being number one. If your friend is in a band that just recorded a psychedelic rock single for a record company, then the least you can do to show how good you are is to write some brilliant poetry or start a mutual fund.

Harvard students are able to be contented because they sense deep inside that they are not enjoying themselves today at the expense of success in the future. For the upwardly mobile, a little suffering today was always justified by the promise of what they hoped was to come tomorrow. Harvard students don't have the psychology of the guy trying to make it; they feel on top of the world already. Live for today, confident that tomorrow will be no problem: this is the way most Harvard students feel.

Indeed, it is the sense of confidence which Harvard engenders about the future that helps make living today more pleasant. For thinking about the glorious future is one of the most enjoyable activities one can go about in the present. Harvard professor George Wald's widely cheered "insight" that we youth are so troubled today because we are the first generation not to know whether we will survive is incredibly wide of the mark. (One almost feels that this gross inaccuracy indeed contributed to its wide acceptance from those adults always out self-consciously to "understand" and "sympathize with" our generation.) The pall of nuclear war which hangs over us all is so pale as hardly to be noticed by students, Professor Wald to the contrary notwithstanding. If Harvard students are worried, it is mainly a worry similar to what the French call "the embarrassment of choice" — we have trouble deciding which of the brilliant futures open to us we want to take.

Adults should not be misled by a plethora of self-indulgent propaganda from "youth spokesmen" about a new wave of "rejection of material success" by today's college students. For better or for worse, youth, while they may see beyond simple materialism, are surrounded by expensive stereo systems, gargantuan record collections, overvalued clothes, and exorbitantly priced marijuana. It is particularly fashionable to wear a wardrobe that is actually extremely costly but that *looks* as if hillbillies or ghetto blacks would feel at home in it. The number of Harvard seniors applying to Harvard Business School has not decreased from where it was in 1957, in the depths of the silent, materialist generation. Harvard students continue to be extremely concerned — from my own viewpoint overly concerned — about a powerful, successful career. Students could put in long and hard hours of work, sleeping on floors and eating peanut butter and jelly, for Gene McCarthy, secure in the knowl-

edge that they were signing their names to no
end up with the FBI and damage their future
name dozens of Harvard students who would
for fear of the effect it might have on their futu
vard students are concerned about their future
happy because they have every reason to be optimistic. I'll
never forget the freshman from Indiana who once said to me,
"You know, I read an article recently that really impressed me.
It said that if you go to a state college your chances of becoming a corporation president are one in fifteen thousand, at Columbia they're one in five hundred, and at Harvard they're one
in fifty." I don't know how figures like that could be computed,
but the important thing is that they were cited, and cited with
a velvety smile of contentment.

What does personal contentment have to do with political
behavior? A great deal. Harvard students closely identify the
type of political posture they take with the life-style and self-
image they imagine for themselves. Manning tables for petitions
around Harvard one frequently encounters the Harvard student
who says something like, "I'm just one of those crazy people
who happen to be happy" in refusing to sign. I saw the relationship between political posture and self-image very clearly
with a close friend of mine who went through a rather brief
left-wing stage at Harvard. During the stage, he spoke about
wanting to work for the labor movement or at least be a labor
lawyer. But at some point he made the decision about himself
that he identified with the Establishment and began to think
of himself as a banker. His political beliefs gradually began to
shift to the Right along with his image of himself.

The relationship between self-image and political behavior is specially vital in explaining both why Harvard was always rather confrontation-proof and why we finally had our strike. For as the political atmosphere at Harvard gradually became monopolized by New Left viewpoints, moderate students came to accept important bits and pieces of the SDS "analysis." However, unlike SDS, they didn't feel it inside. Intellectual commitment was not matched with an emotional commitment to action. And this was because of a difference in self-image. While they may share relatively similar ideological views, there is a fundamental difference between the SDSer, who sees himself as part of the wretched of the earth, and the Young Democrat, who sees himself as the future secretary of housing and urban development. The *Old Mole* recognized this difference when they wrote, after the strike, that "the strike petered out [as] militant strikers were confronted with huge numbers of students who supported the eight demands but were not prepared for the changes in their lives that closing down the school would have required."

The moderates came to go along with a good deal of what SDS said, but they didn't see why they should attack the university because of it. And they couldn't buy SDS's attempts to picture students as an oppressed class. Never, in fact, do SDS leaflets receive a more hostile response than when they drone on about how Harvard University oppresses its students. During a 1967 strike of Harvard printers, which SDS supported along with a number of other organizations, a leaflet was distributed in which SDS explained, in quite reasonable terms, the demands the workers were making. Appended onto this was an entire paragraph beginning, "But Harvard does not only oppress its workers. Harvard oppresses students in many ways too." I remember the reaction of a liberal friend: "Why don't they just stick to talking about the strikers? Nobody's gonna fucking tell me that *I'm* oppressed."

Harvard was special because the moderates were happy enough with Harvard so that their unhappiness about American political developments was not directed against the university. Political beliefs were adopted in an intellectual way independent of the personal happiness which most students felt. This rift between political outrage and personal contentment has a number of positive aspects which potentially make the moderates a positive force for changing America. The moderates do not display the false sense of breast-beating and the frenetic character of the possessed which characterize upper-class radicals who base their politics on personal dissatisfactions. Having no direct personal stake in the continuation of other people's social problems in the way many New Leftists do, the moderates have a pragmatic, goal-solving approach to problems. This permits them to do something about building the things they want rather than merely attacking what they don't like. Thus, the largest scale ongoing moderate activity at Harvard is the Phillips Brooks House, which undertakes projects like tutoring ghetto kids, working at mental hospitals, or organizing welfare mothers to demand more clothing. For all the inadequacies of the PBH approach, it is an improvement on the mere destructiveness of the New Left. Even better was the widespread moderate participation in both the McCarthy campaign in 1968 and various dove congressional and senatorial races since. Unfortunately, the issue evoking this large moderate commitment was Vietnam — the one issue on which students, even Harvard students, felt personal as well as political outrage. This in turn did contribute to the moralistic and self-righteous crusading tone which the

McCarthy movement took on, limited its effectiveness outside middle-class constituencies, and helped elect Nixon when students refused to back Humphrey.

It is revealing that it took an issue like the war in Vietnam to bring large numbers of moderates out into active politics. For normally the great problem of the moderates is apathy. Apathy is the flip side of contentment. The moderates have good instincts on most of the issues, but it's very hard to get them out into the field working for their ideas. Harvard apathy is legendary around campus. It's very difficult to get many more than a thousand students (out of six thousand Harvard and Radcliffe undergraduates) even to sign a petition, much less to do the unglamorous day-to-day responsible work that any sort of political change requires.

Given their intellectual conviction that something is indeed wrong with America, the apathy of the moderates causes guilt feelings. Because SDS is "doing something," the moderates to a large extent grant SDS's own claims to moral superiority. *The moderates were psychologically conditioned for the confrontation because, having no alternative ideology to SDS's and misreading SDS's own ideas for their own, they felt guilty for not being the activists SDS people are.* During the strike, probably the most frequent reasoning one heard from moderates about why it was necessary to back SDS cited the SDSers' "commitment" and "courage" or all they had "risked" in taking over the building. (Perhaps an all-time record for clichés concentrated into one paragraph was set in a *Crimson* editorial during the strike which stated, "The moderates, for their part, must continue to demand amnesty for the University Hall demonstrators. It is inconceivable to abandon the group which at great personal risk forced the necessary consideration of the issues.") As one of Kazin's roommates said of Mike to a *Wall Street Journal* reporter, "He's so concerned over these issues, he is risking his Harvard education."

The contented moderate majority thus envied SDS for the activism which they intellectually felt they should participate in also. It was a passive envy, even a grudging envy with which the moderates conceded SDS's claim to a monopoly on idealism. The guilt feelings remained un-acted-upon for the same reasons that the contented majority did not act upon its intellectual convictions about how America needs changing. But the guilt feelings vitiated any possibility for the moderates to organize *against* SDS. And when the police bust came . . .

To be sure, the moderates' SDS envy was based partly on a misunderstanding. The misunderstanding lies in the fact that campus moderates do not understand SDS's ideology. It was with a mixture of sorrow and shock that I listened one night at dinner to Ken Glazier, leader of the moderate Memorial Church Group during the strike, answer a question I posed to him about whether he thought that SDS's goals were the same as his. "Yes, I think we have the same goals. We're just working toward them in different ways."

"What do you think some of SDS's goals are?"

"Well, for example, I think they'd like to see American military aid to underdeveloped countries replaced to a greater extent by economic aid. I think they'd like to see the federal government spend a lot more money fighting poverty."

Ken Glazier was a Harvard senior and one of the most politically active people at Harvard.

SDS people would probably begin to rage at such a description of their goals. I don't know whether to laugh or cry.

To cry is probably the best response, because it was this type of tragic ignorance and misunderstanding which aided the formation of the confrontation coalition.

SDS literature is unreadable, and therein lies the problem. The language of New Left leaflets, a mixture of crude illiteracy and 1930s vulgar Marxist jargon, is simply incomprehensible to those not specially trained in the arts of sectarianism. The leaflets therefore go unread. "SDS leaflets? I just can't figure out all the ridiculous jargon," Ken Glazier told me in response to a query. " 'Imperialism' and all that stuff. It's just a lot of fancy words."

The moderate does not read SDS leaflets. Very few follow the debates within SDS or understand the evolution the organization has undergone in recent years. Because he cannot — and refuses to try to — understand what SDS really wants, the moderate *invents* his own pleasant re-creation of SDS tenets, which by coincidence comes remarkably to resemble the moderate's own liberal ideology mixed with extreme tactics. Thus the moderate's conclusion: "I agree with what SDS is trying to do, but I don't know if I can go along with all their methods." Hardly a basis for a militant alternative movement to SDS! Indeed, the foundation is set for the grudging admiration of SDS, whose tactics, however ticklishly unpleasant the moderate may find them, "succeed in raising the issues." The question of "what issues?" and "to what end?" rarely gets posed, because the moderate assumes the New Left's goals are the same as its own. (I have always felt that to praise SDS for "raising the issues" is somewhat analogous to praising the war in Vietnam for "raising the issue" of the conduct of American foreign policy.)

The moderate flaw, the defect which leads the moderates

intellectually to cave in to the New Left, goes, unfortunately, deeper than this misunderstanding. The sad fact is that campus liberalism and the New Left have a symbiotic relationship with each other. *Campus moderates develop no critique of SDS because most of them share the elitism which is the fundamental flaw in SDS.* The liberal elitism of campus moderates fundamentally views most Americans as ignorant and reactionary and sees intellectuals as knowing best how to rule the country. The totalitarian elitism of the New Left presents "The People" as flawlessly correct and postulates that if the people do not realize the interests of "The People," SDS members should be viewed as their representatives. Liberal elitism is more wrong-headed than dangerous, its main effect being to severely hurt any possibility for mobilizing a majority of the people on the side of programs the liberal wants. The main danger is that it symbioses with the New Left's totalitarian elitism, which twentieth-century history has identified as a virus causing mass murder and oppression.

In this process of the making of a New Leftist from a liberal the most important step is to transform the liberal elitism of contempt for ordinary people into SDS's intolerant totalitarianism wherein SDS appoints itself as spokesman for the people. It is fascinating to speak to non-cadre SDSers, frequently recent converts from liberalism, speaking in terms of how "Americans are so stupid" and "we need these militant tactics to push these changes we need down people's throats." David Bruck, a *Crimson* editor, told me in the fall of 1968 that he couldn't understand why I was opposed to elitism: "After all, did a majority of the people invent the wheel?" In the fall of 1969 David Bruck wrote a *Crimson* editorial urging students to support the Vietcong. They just haven't learned the new jargon yet.

Indeed, it is this very notion that social progress is such a horrible thing that it has to be snuck in behind people's backs, or even forced down like medicine, which is the bridge over which moderates cross in order to support SDS tactics. When SDSers talk about "the system" they are referring to a thoroughly undemocratic and demonic monster. When liberals use the term it emerges bastardized. For the campus moderate "the system" is democracy, and the moderate is tempted to give up on "working within the system" out of despair over convincing a majority that his views are right. Writing before the March 1968 New Hampshire primary, a reporter for the *Crimson* recounted the story of a McCarthy volunteer who had "lost his faith in the system" as a result of his work in the campaign. What this New Leftist terminology signified in reality, it turned out, was that the student felt that the voters he had contacted were stupid. Odds are the individual in question is now in SDS, a self-appointed spokesman for the people against "American imperialism."

The narrow types of issues — consisting almost solely of foreign policy and domestic racism — which the campus moderate is concerned about assure in advance that his position will receive only minority support. For the liberal is completely unaware of, and unsympathetic to, grievances blue collar workers might have with present-day American society. Unaccustomed even to thinking about the ordinary American at all — except as an uncultured boob — the moderate is surprised when references to workers are made. When a roommate running for president of the Young Democrats suggested to an opponent that the working class might be a fruitful ally in bringing about social change, the response was, "Why take workers out of the clear blue sky? Why not housewives?" The liberal elitism talks of trade union leaders as "blue collar barons" (pace the *Crimson*). The totalitarian elitism demands only the small change that one refer to them as "trade union misleaders."

The liberal elitists have to be taught a number of very basic lessons before they cease handing over legions of the confused to SDS.

If one goes back to the debates over the extension of suffrage during the nineteenth century, one hears over and over from the opponents of universal suffrage the argument that only the educated are able to rise "above" self-interest and take the "group interest" into account. The rich and the educated had gone "beyond" the point where they based their views on personal considerations — unlike the poor, who were bound by their own selfish interests. Indeed, it was argued that parliamentary representatives elected by restricted suffrage represented those excluded also, for they had everyone's interests in mind, not just those of their constituents. There has never been any shortage of self-proclaimed saviors claiming that they understand what the people want better than the people do themselves. In 1968 Eugene McCarthy told an Oregon audience that the educated, better people were voting for him, not Bobby Kennedy, who was presumably getting the votes of slob Negroes and workers. In 1969, a new member of Harvard SDS, still displaying a mix of liberal and totalitarian elitism, commented to me, "I think that the only real revolutionaries can be people who are affluent, because everyone else is trying to make it, and only if you've been affluent can you see beyond it."

What the liberal elitist doesn't realize is just how much common, ordinary people have to teach *him*. It was unlettered Mississippi sharecroppers who taught Americans a lesson about democracy and human dignity in the 1960s. It was the German

middle class, not the workers, who went over to Hitler in the
1930s. ("The workers of Thalburg," writes William S. Allen
in his book *The Nazi Seizure of Power: The Experience of a
Single German Town*, "were known for their violent anti-
Nazi opinions.") And, while intellectuals idolized Adlai Stevenson as an intellectual's candidate too sensitive to be appre-
ciated by common people, the facts show that a majority of
trade union members voted for Stevenson while a strong majority of the college educated voted for Eisenhower. The liberal
elitist myth that the educated are the great force for social
progress, who must fight every step of the way against an unwill-
ing demos, simply is untrue.

"But isn't the majority often wrong?" How does one respond to the arrogance of such a frequently heard statement?
"Wrong" of course means "having an opinion different from
mine." To be sure, the majority is often "wrong." But how
many more times have assorted and sordid minorities, countless
numbers of them each claiming to embody Virtue and Justice,
been wrong, often criminally and deadly wrong?

A democracy may produce a Vietnam, but it also produces
questioning, opposition, and an eventual end to a Vietnam.
Students who did not question American policy in Vietnam
from the very outset, which is the case with most of us, hardly
have the right to expect that the war should end the precise
moment *we* happen to come to oppose it. In a democracy,
there is no fairer way to decide when a policy should be
changed than waiting until a majority wants a change. Should a
policy like Vietnam be changed as soon as one or a handful of
people decides it's wrong? As soon as enlightened college students as a body decide it's wrong? I would suggest that the
liberal elitists provide no alternative to democracy as a *procedure* for deciding when a policy should be changed.

"I am taking a moral stand." This phrase, frequently elicited from elitists when they are about to try to impose their views on the majority, is supposed to end discussion. "Moral stand." Who can question that? If the person is pressed, he usually follows this phrase with a comparison of his action to moral stands taken against Hitler's genocide against the Jews, which, it is stated, was a policy supported by a majority. (Arguing against a referendum on the issue of ROTC, the *Crimson* stated that genocide was a policy which could "frequently" *win* a referendum. The editorial provided no specific evidence for this cynical and unhuman assumption.) The people making such statements are rarely pacifists, and so they do not accept the equation of killing in Vietnam with mass executions for no reason in concentration camps. Indeed, few if any of them would accept the proposition that advocates of mass murder in the USSR or China should be silenced or prevented from working for their beliefs.

The basic problem, and here is the great common link between liberal and totalitarian elitism, is the simple inability to entertain the possibility that one's beliefs might be *wrong*.

Behind the concept of "participatory democracy," which was so valuable and so important during the early and genuine days of the New Left, lay a very sound core: the notion that democratic, communal decision-making and participation are not merely a means to the end of a good society but also a part of the good society itself. Men feel better and fuller as human beings through participating with their fellows in deciding things for the group. We feel respected more because our opinion is asked for and valued. This is part of what Aristotle meant when he wrote that man is a political animal. He wasn't saying that man by nature loves politics in the sense we usually mean it, but rather that man by nature likes and needs to live together

with other men in a common community. Man alone and unlistened to is synonymous with man dejected and miserable.
Paternalism fails even when it makes the "right" decisions, because it leaves unanswered the human need for participation.
(Totalitarian states seek to fill this need through the phony
participation of Nuremburg rallies and Twenty-sixth of July
Day celebrations.)

This philosophical and psychological case for democracy was
an important part of SDS in its early days. I was convinced of
it while I was in high school when it was first presented, and
I remain convinced of it. But one important aspect of the case
for democracy, I notice in retrospect, was always missing even
from the early, now abandoned talk of participatory democracy.
This is any reference to a case for democracy in terms of human
fallibility, of the possibility of any individual's erring.

Thus, when SDS rejected the vision of community in a good
society as the result of voluntary group participation and replaced it with an evangelistic community of political holy
rollers, when it replaced the peaceful day-to-day community
with the revolutionary crisis community — then the New Left
had no other argument for democracy to fall back on.

The democracy that produced Vietnam produced questioning
and pressuring against Vietnam. The rule of revolutionary elites
has produced the mass murders of Auschwitz and the extermi-
nation of the kulaks — not to speak of the deaths of the martyrs
who question the tyrants. The same applies to the underdeveloped countries. Nigeria suffered from acute problems of
tribalism from the time she received independence. But the
hostile tribes managed to avoid killing each other as long as
some semblance of democratic pluralism was maintained. It
was when the dominant tribe rigged elections and took over all
government power that a succession of military coups was fol-

lowed by the Ibo secession and the mass death, starvation, and needless misery of the Biafra war.

The elitists must be fought, and fought hard, because we recognize that the bloody history of the twentieth century has taught us that democracy, majority rule, and civil liberties are not luxuries but the alternatives to mass murder and suffering. They are a necessary precondition for any decent society. What the elitists don't realize is that the thin strand which protects their freedom to espouse their unpopular ideas is precisely the notion of the *procedure* of free speech independent of whether people like the ideas or not. This is not a value which is inculcated in a population easily — relatively few are the societies and historical periods where the value of free speech has been generally accepted. And the tragedy is that the actions of the New Left are aimed precisely at destroying this consensus around the principle of free speech.

The moderates first saved Harvard simply because they were too contented to destroy it. But we were falsely lulled into thinking that Harvard was safe. What would have been needed for that was a strong, activist body of moderates with a democratic and progressive ideology which could have been counterposed to SDS's. This the moderates did not have. Instead, they had a cloudy ideology that could merge into the New Left's and the guilt feelings which come from not acting on their beliefs in a campus atmosphere which prided action above all. (Jim Glassman of the *Crimson* wrote a Nazi-mentality piece during the strike glorifying Action and urging New Leftists with "superior consciousness" to undertake more action before "the dreary days of democracy [are] upon us, and men of action [are] despised.")

The strike was successful and the confrontation coalition was consummated for one reason: the police bust. *The outrage of the police bust was such that the moderates finally felt that they had to "do something." They couldn't sit on their asses any longer. The tragedy was that when they finally did do something the only thing they could conceive of doing was falling into SDS's arms.*

The moderates were active, and they asked nothing more than to be accepted as partners by SDS. The new SDS was fortunately too ideologically pure to recognize such an arrangement. The slightest encouragement for the alliance from SDS might have meant Harvard's death knell. Fortunately, SDSers are stupid revolutionaries, and they insisted on attacking the moderates constantly. Demands by the moderates that Harvard build more housing as a solution to the Cambridge housing shortage were denounced by SDS as attempts to sabotage the SDS fight against "Imperial City" and Harvard expansion. SDS not only refused to accept the pet moderate scheme for Student Power as an additional strike demand, they attacked it, with a maximum of incomprehensible and sectarian rhetoric, as "contradicting the other eight demands." "Student Power" was a slogan taken from the early days of SDS, and most moderates were stunned during the strike to see that SDS no longer accepted it.

The moderates' desire to be accepted by an SDS that wanted only converts, not allies, was pathetic. And SDS's contempt didn't even increase their will to resist SDS.

The legions of moderates involved in the strike did give the Harvard confrontation its own special flavor, however. The striking moderates did not want to destroy the university. They continued to like Harvard. (The moderate position was that the police bust had disrupted the Harvard community. SDS got little response from its argument that the "pigs" were an integral part of the university.) Indeed, as the strike went on, one increasingly heard from the moderates that their strike had to continue in order to prevent SDS from taking over another building. The reasoning was that as long as they weren't isolated, SDS wouldn't do anything rash. But if the vast majority of students stopped striking, SDS would feel the need to do something extreme. I'll never forget the vote at the first Harvard Stadium rally, deciding whether to continue the moderate strike beyond the original three days called right after the police bust. As I stood up to vote against continuing the strike, a moderate sitting close by cried in genuine and pitiful anguish, "Steve, you're destroying the university!"

4. The New Left Takes Control of Our Mass Media

If the YPH Executive Board means that they believe the University should expel the NROTC program . . . it might be well for the board to consider that a large proportion of present and prospective enrollees could not attend Harvard if it didn't include the program in its curriculum and give credit for its courses.

> — *The Harvard Crimson* (October 29, 1949) responding to a suggestion by the Young Progressives of Harvard that the university consider action against the NROTC program if it didn't remove a loyalty oath which required the student to name friends he might have seen at "subversive" activities.

It would be pointless, and harmful to military security, for the University to expel its excellent NROTC unit.

> — *The Harvard Crimson* (December 17, 1949)

In particular, the radicals should drop their demand that ROTC be immediately abolished and should join in demanding a student-faculty referendum that will be binding on the Corporation.

> — *The Harvard Crimson* (April 11, 1969), calling for a moderate–New Left coalition, to carry on the Harvard strike.

There is presently circulating a proposal to refer this question (the status of ROTC) to a binding referendum of the entire University community. The difficulty with this proposal is that ROTC is not a question to be resolved by a majority vote. It is a moral question, and for this reason a majority vote cannot be considered binding on those who hold a moral position which happens to be in the minority.

> — *The Harvard Crimson* (April 14, 1969), three days later.

SINCE IT IS hardly possible for them to pride themselves on the wretched quality of the reporting on their "news" pages, officials of *The Harvard Crimson*, "The University Daily, Founded 1873" (and lost God knows when), choose to pride themselves on their iconoclastic independence of majority conventions. Crimeds — *Crimson* shorthand for "Crimson editors" — view themselves as a sort of elite within the Harvard elite. They proudly boast that there are two ways to do Harvard, the normal way and the *Crimson* way. The latter involves exclusion from the normal responsibilities Harvard students face, such as course work, in return for a grueling eighteen-hour day lounging around the *Crimson* office acting important. The high opinion Crimeds hold of their own talents is so legendary that I for one have always believed that when the *Crimson* wrote that among the students inside University Hall on April 9 were "some of the best minds at Harvard" they were referring to their own reporters covering the take-over.

A claim to elite status, especially in an elite community like Harvard, must rest on a myth, a Platonic noble lie. Crimeds seek to legitimize their elite role through the myth that they are the community's conscience or, alternatively, its gadfly. To hear them tell it, they've been "going out on a limb," risking everything from loss of advertising to — God forbid — the setting up of a rival campus newspaper, by embarking on their new, bold, radical editorial line. But, by God, *The Harvard Crimson* drove ahead, oblivious to unpopularity and disdain, determined to tell the truth as they saw it, no matter how many they offended.

This image is a lie, but it is hardly noble. For any check on the editorial positions taken by the *Crimson* over the last twenty years indicates that the creature which best describes the long succession of Crimeds is not the gadfly but the chameleon. For, with not a gadfly's prick of protest or dissent, the *Crimson* has consistently been a faithful transmitter of the mood of the student power structure to the masses of students below. "Transmitter" is perhaps too passive a word to describe the *Crimson*'s role, since what its editors are feeling is a very important part of the general student mood the paper delineates. At any rate, over the years the *Crimson* has challenged the received ideas of its day with all the forcefulness and critical razor's edge that *Pravda* applies to Soviet society. In the years 1968 and 1969, what would have been bold for the *Crimson* to undertake would have been any sort of critique of the New Left. In the greatest surprise since the results of the most recent East German elections, we didn't get it.

It is amusing to follow the meanderings of the *Crimson*'s editorial pages over the years. During the late forties they presented a tough-minded liberalism, rather Left-leaning on domestic issues but cold warriorish on foreign policy. Coincidentally this was the mood of adult intellectuals at the time as well. The Young Progressives of Harvard, a product of the 1948 Henry Wallace campaign, was *salonfähig* in the *Crimson*'s eyes, but not the Harvard Youth for Democracy, youth organization of the Communist party. And, exercising their favorite function, that of designating what opinions are "in" and which ones "out" (rule #1: Crimeds are always "in"), the editorial pages spared few attempts to ridicule the HYD. Typical of the tone is a review of one issue of the group's magazine *The New Student*, where the *Crimson* wrote (April 24, 1948): "Also in 'The New Student' is a slap-dash attempt to prove that American universities are in the toils of Big Business, based mostly on a quasi-review of a book which appeared two years ago."

During the late fifties, the *Crimson* was there not only to endorse the silent generation, but to enforce it as well, by clubbing back into place anyone who spoke up. In discussing (October 4, 1957) the spate of leaflets from political organizations with which the entering freshman is traditionally bombarded at fall term registration, the *Crimson* used language that even Lewis Feuer probably would have blue penciled from his acerbically antistudent *Conflict of Generations*. "Freshmen, passing through, the post Registration gauntlet," the piece began, "must find the number and verbosity of the representatives of the undergraduate political clubs bewildering." The piece went on to record the unhappy fact that "political clubs are far more active here" than at other universities, and tried to seek out the reasons which impelled Harvard students to become politically active. These were a "lack of feminine companionship, a feeling of isolation, compensation for being frustrated in the academic and social ends of college life, and the intensely ambitious young men Harvard attracts." Oh the sick young people who became Young Democrats! The only handout the article seemed to have any sympathy for was the Young Republicans', which made a straight appeal to self-interest. "Aid to the GOP," it read, "can not be looked at as altruistic, since we must live in the future we make for ourselves."

On November 27, 1957, the *Crimson* urged the university, in view of the Sputnik launching by the Soviet Union, to reconsider its ban on classified research.

One might expect that factors ranging from the normal rules of political pluralism, to the high number of Jews on the editorial board (an old Jewish proverb states that if there are three Jews in a room there will be four viewpoints in an argument), or at the very minimum the laws of chance, would dictate that the *Crimson*, as a product of many minds, would not speak with one voice. In this way the cumulative effect of the one newspaper we have coming out day by day with the same message might be reduced.

This is not the case. Over twenty years Crimeds have sung many different songs, but always in a chorus. One searches in vain, for example, through *Crimson* files from the late fifties for at least *one* gadfly Crimed denouncing American imperialism — or for at least one gadfly in the sixties defending the war in Vietnam. True, on very important issues, such as the paper's endorsement of the Dow sit-in of October 1967, or the call for a continuation of the strike beyond the original three days in April 1969, minority editorials (called "On the Other Hand") have appeared. But those signing these minority views never seem to propagandize for their point of view on a day-to-day basis in the paper. (This is probably out of a sense of journalistic ethics which the majority fanatics are either ignorant of or believe must be yet another sacrifice to the "liberation struggle.")

Crimeds enforce conformity among their own number with the same tactics of proclaiming who's "in" and who's "out" as they use in the university as a whole. John Herfort, an editor who attempted to dissent vigorously from the new *Crimson* New Left line, was mocked, ostracized, and hounded by other editors. Even a year after he graduated letters sent to the *Crimson* criticizing some of their editorial stands or news bias (and usually never published) received marginal comments from Crimeds like, "Why doesn't somebody send this along to Herfort?" or "Is Herfort back again? Take cover."

Through all periods, it should be noted, the Crimed's self-importance, and view of his own future as advisor to kings, remains constant. Over twenty years the *Crimson* has maintained a patronizing, know-it-all style. Crimeds continue to treat freshman candidates for positions on the newspaper like personal chattels, providing the only remnant of fraternity rushing left on campus. (Even the aristocratic final clubs aren't as bad.) Editors habitually address each other with a pretentious codelike three-letter initial system — for example James K. Glassman becomes "jkg" inside the doors of 14 Plympton Street. They hang all letters to the editor up on the bulletin board for snide comments by the editors. And the paper is run like a huge in-joke. "Art" photographs appearing on the front page are frequently pictures of *Crimson* editors. The paper had the nerve to waste enormous amounts of column inches on the editors' own, and stillborn, "Conspiracy Against Harvard Education" launched in the winter of 1969. The "conspiracy," which consisted purely and simply of some seven Harvard students, all Crimeds, was directed against the "lack of creativity" in Harvard classes. Its sole event was a weekend rock concert. (It was nervy of *Crimson* editors to dare venture any criticisms of education at Harvard since, spending the entire day at *Crimson* offices, they've never experienced it.)

Because Crimeds over the years have inevitably seen their future roles as being in elite positions in the society, even *Crimson* radicalism is a unique "establishment radicalism." By this I do not mean the "sellout" pseudo-radicalism of which *Crimson* and SDS people accuse men like Michael Harrington, Bayard Rustin, or Irving Howe. I mean the term in its literal sense: *Crimson* people see their role as introducing New Leftism *from above*, not by popular revolution, but by infiltrating the Establishment. Look at the political activities of the two most active Crimeds: Jeff Alexander tried to take over the unrepresentative and largely meaningless student government at Harvard, and

Jim Glassman tried to raise $500,000 from rich Washington friends for a radical magazine he was to edit upon graduation. Despite their destructive verbal radicalism, very few Crimeds are willing to risk their Establishment future by engaging in political activism. At least five Crimeds participated in the occupation of University Hall and, if they happened to be arrested, got themselves released by presenting themselves as "reporters." Most *Crimson* editors even refuse to sign petitions! The university must suffer the consequences while they keep writing away.

The point is that the *Crimson* didn't adopt its new pro-SDS line because of a duty to tell the truth regardless of fear of favor. It did so because a majority of the editors of the *Crimson* were incurable intellectual conformists, shifting with amazing sensitivity with what they sense as the dominant currents.

The *Crimson* embraced SDS politics very late in the game, only after the alliance between the motivated radicals and the cultural radicals gave the Harvard New Left a mass base. As late as the spring of my freshman year, while opinion on the war was still split on campus, the *Crimson* had a cautious stop-the-bombing position. The next fall (with exactly the same editorial board as it had had the spring before) the paper sensed the new winds. In a series of on-the-spot reports by Jim Glassman on the Confront the Warmakers Pentagon march and their endorsement of the anti-civil libertarian Dow Chemical sit-in, the *Crimson* began its new line. It hasn't changed since.

Once the *Crimson* shifted, it was determined to magnify the new direction of the wind into a hurricane, with gales of biased reporting. Minute coverage of every step SDS was taking became the order of the day. The *Crimson's* pages concocted a mythological substitute for SDS's ideology, a cultural-radical tinged New Leftism, which could be substituted in students' minds for the harsher reality SDS was presenting in its own leaflets and statements.

The *Crimson* presented students, in the year-and-a-half period leading up to the April 1969 confrontation, with roughly the following succession of arguments: (1) Sure, we don't agree with everything "the radicals" say, although you have to admit that they're right about the fact that "the system" refuses to give us the changes we want; (2) We shouldn't get lost in an endless succession of words, arguments, and debates. The most important thing is action; (3) SDS is the only group doing anything; (4) SDS is really pretty good after all, except for the Progressive Labor "extremists" who are trying to prevent a coalition between moderates and the "moderate" New Left caucus; (5) SDS is the only show in town. We all have to get behind it.

As a result of numbers one to four, number five became a self-fulfilling prophecy.

Making a case for the first four points wasn't easy. The myth that the "moderate" New Left caucus was confronted with the "extremist" Progressive Labor faction was invented out of whole cloth. (In the June 1969 SDS convention the "moderates" expelled PL for being "counterrevolutionary traitors" and charged that PL "has chosen to ally itself with the class which runs this country.") To push the "action is all" outlook on normally wordy and nonaction oriented Harvard students, the *Crimson* treated us, over a two-year period, to a series of assaults on the concept of reason. Jim Glassman brazenly proclaimed on the paper's pages: "Action is its own reason for existing. Rebellion can only be understood by a rebel, who knows that the only 'reason' for rebellion is the pleasure (or whatever feeling) of rebellion itself. Revolution for the hell of it, because there is no other reason big enough for rebellion." Nick Gagarin wrote, "It is in the nature of a place like Harvard to make us distrust emotions. The exercise of reason is, after all, what leads us to *veritas:* we think, therefore we are . . . Anyone who was in University Hall during the occupation, however, like anyone who was in the Yard when the bust came, should think back on the emotions of that experience. Emotions are our guts; without them we are but thinking machines."

So the *Crimson* glorified the unthinking machine. It was in the tradition of the Harvard New Left social studies tutor (whose tutorial was entitled The Politics of Irrationality) who once told me that the New Left should stick to emotions because the facts unfortunately were never on its side. Stream of consciousness became the favored style of its feature pages. Journalistic muckraking, which the paper used to do a good job of, gave way to dadaism of the printed word. To enshrine action, they denigrated reason.

But the most persistent and most important contribution of the *Crimson* was to overrepresent systematically the activities of SDS and underrepresent those of other groups. Since most Harvard students had no direct experience with the events described and knew or did not know about them only on the basis of *Crimson* articles, the continued manipulation went on without the knowledge, but only the suspicions, of most of the Harvard community.

The process by which most political news gets into the *Crimson* is somewhat unusual. Aside from confrontations or important faculty decisions, little political news is objectively "made" at a university. A typical news story might be that X or Y group is "working on," say, organizing welfare mothers in Roxbury or "demanding" a certain change on campus through

a petition. Leaders of an organization who want to have the
Crimson report a given story appear at the paper's offices near
the Yard and try to persuade a Crimed to "run a story." Every
afternoon, when the "night editor" for the next morning's paper
is preparing the layout, a succession of supplicants are pleading
their cases.

The Young People's Socialist League was a new organization
on campus, only two years old, during the year of the confrontation. The treatment of the YPSL, which potentially might
have been an important alternative to the New Left on campus,
was a case study in the *Crimson*'s attempt to discredit any
alternative to SDS on campus. *Crimson* editors openly admitted that they despised the YPSL's attempt to present a
democratic Left critique of SDS. Crimed Jeff Alexander once
told me that, of the many bad things about the YPSL, the
worst was that they are too rational. *Crimson* President Joel
Kramer once said that in his opinion the YPSL was the worst
political organization on campus. Above all, the YPSL's style
of politics wasn't "in"; it seemed "straight out of the thirties."
It was "old"; the *Crimson* above all was sensitive to the "new"
and different.

It is a little-known fact (for obvious reasons) that the YPSL
was the first Harvard organization to begin action on the ROTC
issue in the year of the confrontation. Toward the middle of
October the YPSL began circulating a petition arguing that
ROTC enjoyed "special privileges" on campus (free use of
entire university buildings, academic credit for nonacademic
courses, etc.), and that in a democratic community special
privileges could be granted only by democratic consent. The
petition therefore called for a student referendum to vote on
ROTC's special privileges.

When the petition had over 500 signatures, Henry Fetter was

told by the *Crimson* that the YPSL ought to come back with
its petition when it had a thousand signatures, and then the
paper might run a story.

Around a week later SDS began its petition, calling for the
abolition of ROTC on the grounds that "what ROTC is doing
is bad." When the petition had under three hundred signatures
(only after several months of very intensive door-to-door canvassing did the SDS petition on ROTC finally gather a few
hundred more signatures than the YPSL's petition), the *Crimson* ran a lengthy article about SDS's new anti-ROTC drive.
Several days *afterward*, in response to a threat to sit in at the
Crimson office, the paper ran a piece on the YPSL petition,
inevitably creating the impression, coincidentally similar to
Crimeds' own view, that "all YPSL ever does is react to SDS."

When the time arrived for the next step in the ROTC issue,
getting one's position introduced for consideration by the faculty, the *Crimson's* coverage was again outrageous. One Tuesday in early December the *Crimson* announced in a headlined
article, on the basis of an interview with an SDS leader, that
Hilary Putnam, a professor of philosophy, was going to introduce the SDS position to the faculty. Putnam was out of town
at the time, the article said, and could not be reached for comment. On Thursday, with Putnam still out of town and absolutely no new information on the story, the *Crimson* repeated
the identical story in a lead headline! Meanwhile the YPSL
had arranged with Seymour Martin Lipset, professor of social
relations and Berkeley refugee, to introduce the referendum position to the faculty. Wednesday afternoon a group of three
YPSLs went to the editorial offices. After being told that a
story would run the next day, they were informed Thursday
afternoon by the editors, after no story had appeared, that

Lipset couldn't be contacted by phone to confirm what we had told the *Crimson*. (The same morning the lead story on Putnam had been run, on the basis of hearsay, while Putnam was out of town.) Friday again no story was run. "We forgot to follow it up." (At this point the YPSL petition still had over two hundred more signatures than the SDS petition.)

Saturday morning YPSLs threatened a sit-in again. (This idea, whose only purpose would be to get publicity from the Boston press about the *Crimson*'s biased coverage, was discussed among the more bitter elements in the YPSL all year.) The Crimeds promised to try to follow up the story. Monday morning there was again no story.

"We talked to Lipset at home," an editor told Henry Fetter, "and he said he wasn't sure he was going to introduce the motion."

We called Lipset. "Sunday afternoon someone from the *Crimson* called me up and started firing all sorts of questions at me. He wanted to know if I could repeat the exact text of my resolution, and he had all sorts of iffy questions about what my position was on applying referenda as a general matter of university policy, on restructuring the university, on everything. Of course I didn't know the resolution by heart, so I gave him the gist. He got so insistent that finally I told him to call me back in the office on Monday."

"But you said you'd introduce the resolution?"

"Of course."

"Sounds like the third degree."

"It was typical *Crimson* treatment," was Lipset's short but expressive reply.

A week after the original Putnam story the Lipset story appeared, amidst a lull in the ROTC discussion and to be ignored

in the future in *Crimson* stories. The *Crimson* had succeeded
in the unmaking of a story, and the YPSL campaign had difficulty in being taken seriously afterward. The *Crimson* never
talked about the referendum, and it was difficult to keep up
the momentum of the campaign without press coverage. (Indeed, the YPSL's referendum and special privilege arguments,
as well as the YPSL's presentation of the civil liberties issue
involved in the right to participate voluntarily in ROTC, received more coverage in SDS attacks on it — it was variously
designated the "YPSL-Lipset position" and later the "YPSL-
Lipset-Hoffmann position," after Stanley Hoffmann — than
it did in the news pages of the *Crimson*.) During the strike,
the YPSL ideas emerged, phoenixlike, again. The Memorial
Church meeting, the morning of the police bust, called for a
binding referendum on ROTC. The final resolution passed by
the faculty on ROTC, on the basis of which the ROTC program chose to leave the campus, used the exact language that
YPSL and only YPSL had used in objecting to ROTC, by saying that military training programs should not be granted "special privileges." (The moderates had criticized ROTC for "academic impropriety"; the New Left for doing "bad things.")
Thus the valid ideas the YPSL had been trying to bring up all
year were diffused into the community's subconsciousness. But
the organization itself was unable to challenge SDS's image as
monopolizers of activism and idealism in the Harvard community. It was unable to develop as a strong counterforce, an
alternative idealism to the New Left's. The process is a vicious
circle. Alternative activities to the New Left's are not presented.
Alternative organizations appear to be doing nothing and then
have trouble gaining new recruits. They then lack the manpower to undertake dramatic new activities.

Examples could be multiplied. When Michael Harrington, socialist leader and author of *The Other America,* spoke at Harvard for the YPSL, the *Crimson* ran no story. There were over seven hundred people in the audience. When Ernst Mandel, obscure Belgian Trotskyist, spoke for SDS before a crowd reported by the *Crimson* as "under fifty," a story was run. A story on research by YPSLs for a leader of the Democratic party on income redistribution, research which was to be used in a "soak the rich" shift to the Left by the Democrats presaging the tax reform issue, was rejected as "unimportant" by the *Crimson,* although a scoop on any hint of a shift in Democratic party in this direction would no doubt have interested the *New York Times.*

The question is, What of it? What is the practical effect of the change in the *Crimson* on the growth of the New Left politics? An answer, oddly enough, must begin with the theories of Herbert Marcuse. Marcuse became a hero of the New Left caucus in SDS through his explanation of the problem, always grating to totalitarian revolutionaries, of why the American people never seem to appreciate the obvious efforts of the revolutionaries on their behalf and, indeed, appear to despise the radicals.

Marcuse chalks it up to "repressive tolerance," the notion that the freedoms people seem to enjoy are really phony, since the masses have in reality been manipulated by capitalists into a "false consciousness" which opposes their "real interests." As one New Left caucus "theoretical paper" (arguing why elections were meaningless in America) argued, imitating not only Marcuse's ideas but his turgid prose as well, "The manipulative consciousness-producing mechanisms eliminate the chance for counterthought to the existing system." Translated into English, this means that the masses don't support the New Left because the press brainwashes them. In one of Marcuse's memorable phrases, the people have been persuaded that "their chains are fun to wear."

This argument lies literally at the center of the New Left caucus's ideology and justifies in their own eyes ignoring "bourgeois" civil liberties and "bourgeois" democracy. (Irving Howe once challenged New Leftists to give an example of a non-"bourgeois" civil liberty.) SDSers, though, have managed to produce "counterthought to the existing system" despite the alleged fact that "the manipulative consciousness-producing mechanisms" have "eliminated" the possibility for it. Their "higher consciousness" justifies anything.

(It should be noted parenthetically that the Progressive Labor party people hate Marcuse. He has even been denounced, in an article in the national PL magazine entitled "Marcuse — Cop-out or Cop?" as a CIA agent for his work with the OSS during World War II. In PL's view, the people haven't been taken in by the press's "bourgeois propaganda." They already are on the verge of revolution, held back only by "trade union misleaders." If the people seem to hate revolutionaries, this is because they confuse them with the alienated hippies whom the New Left caucus coddles.)

To be sure, propaganda from powerful elites and its influence on the opinions of masses of people is a problem in the United States. Yet a number of uncomforting facts stand in the way of the attempt to use this to explain away everything. Big business has propagandized continuously against labor unions, social security, Medicare, Keynesian fiscal policies, public utilities, and so forth — yet the propaganda has been unsuccessful.

The majority of people favored such ideas anyway. The vast majority of Americans favor plugging up tax loopholes for the wealthy in spite of a huge and expensive campaign in favor of these loopholes. About 80 percent of Americans have supported in Gallup polls the idea that the government should employ anyone who cannot find a job in the private sector, despite constant agitation by business against such socialistic ideas. In fact, what SDS seems most worried about is that, despite SDS's own admiration for totalitarian regimes in Cuba, China, and elsewhere, the overwhelming majority of Americans oppose communist totalitarianism. To SDS, the only possible explanation for such a fact is an ideology foisted upon the people. Could it not be that people look at the suppression of civil liberties, trade union rights, freedom of religion, and democracy in communist states and — more intelligently than the SDS elite with its superior "consciousness" — decide that such a system is not for them?

What does this all have to do with the *Crimson*? The point is that "brainwashing" by the media has not been as great a problem as might have been feared because *most people do not form their political opinions primarily on the basis of what they read.* They form them on the basis of their everyday experiences in the real world. An employer can play beautiful music and broadcast comforting nostrums over the PA system of his factory, but his workers will feel their discontent anyway and react against it. People at the lower end of the social ladder are for a more equal society in spite of what they might read about the land of opportunity, simply because their everyday experience contradicts it. Despite the written myth of the universal "middle class" in America, almost all blue (and many white) collar workers, when asked to identify themselves as

"workers" or "middle class," choose the former. The exception
to this is, of course, foreign policy, where people have no personal experiences and therefore are dependent for their opinions
on what they read. Here the problem of press manipulation
is much more serious.

Marcuse's theory is in fact a classic example of the misper-
ception of intellectuals. Intellectuals themselves base their
lives on the printed and spoken word and chronically over-
estimate the importance of words on those outside their world.
Since intellectuals, by and large, have no experience with being
poor, black, Vietnamese, or oppressed, *their* political opinions
on virtually every subject are formed by what they read. They
make the mistake of assuming that the same is true for most
Americans.

Here is where they err, but in their theories they reveal
something about manipulation and the intellectual community
itself. For intellectuals are subject to the same brainwashing
in almost *every* field as most Americans are in foreign policy
matters. And what applies to intellectuals in general goes
doubly for Harvard students, who have been sheltered all their
lives from any firsthand encounters with reality and are uniquely
dependent on what they read and hear.

Thus, paradoxically, the theories of Herbert Marcuse about
"repressive tolerance" apply most accurately to communities
like Harvard. The effect of the New Left taking over the
Harvard mass media has been crucial in spreading the mood
that allowed the Harvard confrontation. Simply through constant repetition, notions once regarded as ridiculous — the idea
that Communist China is more democratic than the United
States, or that freedom of speech is meaningless — became respected subjects for intellectual debate. New Left terms of

reference — such as the view that all that had to be proved was any given individual's association with the U.S. government, at any time for any purpose, in order to discredit the individual — osmosed through repetition into the student mind.

But above all, and most dangerously, the *Crimson* spread the idea that the New Left was both "where the action is" and the monopoly outlet for youthful idealism. Playing on both good and evil emotions among young people — idealism and conformity — the *Crimson* bears a major share of the responsibility for the fact that, when the moderates finally decided to do something, what they decided to do was to come close to destroying Harvard.

5. The University Is Chosen as a Target

THE RESEARCH was painstakingly gathered by rummaging through Harvard's confidential files during the seizure of University Hall, by checking and backchecking obscure records in the stacks of Widener Library, and by looking through *Standard and Poor's* at the Business School. The result of months and even years of amateur sleuthwork, a "group of movement researchers" presented the Harvard community in the last days of April 1969 with its findings. The eighty-eight-page booklet, a ponderous mixture of psychedelia and polemic, was entitled *How Harvard Rules*. It came too late to serve the hoped-for inflammatory purpose, for students were tired, and Harvard's brief confrontation, for the year at least, was over. Very quickly SDS salesmen, desperate, were discounting the booklet from its one-dollar cover price down to a quarter or even a dime. (Literature discounts are almost unheard-of in the New Left — the accounts gotta be kept balanced.)

Yet *How Harvard Rules* is important, for it gives an insight into the level of argument and evidence which today is accepted not only as *part* of the campus political dialogue, but as the thought of "our best minds" and "most creative students." Creative indeed are the minds which can weave out of the facts "uncovered" in a document like *How Harvard Rules* the tale of malfeasance summarized in the booklet's dramatic conclusion that "anyone who believes that universities are either neutral, truth-seeking institutions, or centers of human knowledge committed to genuine social development is living in a world of fantasy."

A typical example of the booklet's argument is contained in the list of research contracts that various professors have had with the State Department.

HOW HARVARD ADMINISTERS THE EMPIRE:
STATE DEPARTMENT AID CONTRACTS

Country "Served"/ Title/ Recipient/ Dates/ Value

Current Technical Service Contracts as of June 30, 1968, from the Agency for International Development

Worldwide/ Grant to conduct a research study program relating to the impact of health on economic growth oriented toward developing countries/ Harvard, President and Fellows/ 6/28/63–3/31/69 / $206,822.

Worldwide/ Research study of liver disease and possible dietary causes thereof in Uganda/ Harvard, President and Fellows/ 9/7/66–9/7/68 / $26,330.

Worldwide/ Research study directed toward comparative studies of resource allocation and development policy/ Harvard, President and Fellows/ 5/31/67–11/30/69 / $722,882.

Worldwide/ Research study program to determine the influencing factors on fertility and family planning acceptance/ Harvard, President and Fellows/ 6/25/68–12/24/69 / $60,909.

Worldwide/ Research program directed toward improving the nutritional value of rice/ F. J. Stone, Harvard School of Public Health/ 6/30/68–6/30/70 / $228,076.

Panama and Central America/ Assistance in the study of and planning for business management and development/ W. Skinner, Harvard Business School/ 6/15/63–6/30/69 / $1,080,463.

Panama and Central America/ Assistance to Central American Institute of Business in developing a permanent institute for graduate education in business administration/ W. Skinner, Harvard Business School/ 1/1/67–6/30/69 / $423,220.

Western Nigeria/ Development of comprehensive secondary schools/ Harvard, President and Fellows/ 3/1/62–6/30/69 / $2,396,263.

Africa/ Nutrition improvement/ Harvard School of Public Health, F. J. Sture/ 5/20/68–6/30/68 / $2,000.

Chile/ Master tax reform program in Chile/ O. Oldman, Harvard Law School/ 7/1/66–9/30/69 / $393,500.

China*/ Motivational development of managers for industrial enterprises in China/ Center for Research and Personality/ 1967/ $17,850.

Central America/ Business management in Central America/ Harvard Business School/ 1967/ $947,380.

Worldwide/ Research study program relating to the importance of health in economic growth, oriented toward developing countries/ Harvard, President and Fellows/ 1967/$85,756.

Mexico/ Project to transform traditional subsistence agricultural community into a modern organized production unit to produce for the market/ Harvard, President and Fellows/ 1967/$264,342.

After reading the eery title "How Harvard Administers the Empire," I was, frankly, surprised that the list showed up *nothing* nefarious at all. (Unless SDS considers accepting government money to suffice for a verdict of guilty in itself, in which case SDS's own Harvard course for academic credit, Social Relations 148/9, financed under a grant from the U.S. Department of Labor, would qualify for the executioner's block.) I had, to be honest, expected that somewhere among the hundreds of

---

* NB that in State Department slang "China" means Taiwan.

professors there must have been at least *one* who did research
for the government on why fascist dictatorship was the best
alternative to communism in Asia, or on techniques for putting
down labor unrest. Needless to say, this would have proved
nothing but the fact that there are some reactionary professors
at Harvard. But even by SDS's own careful investigations, the
way "Harvard administers the Empire" is through research on
"improving the nutritional value of rice" or developing a "master
tax reform program in Chile."

The melange of criticisms which the New Left makes on
different college campuses, custom-tailored to each school but
inevitably reaching the same conclusion that the university
must be "struggled against," indicates well that the decision
was first reached to attack the colleges, and the justifications
were sought afterward.

An obvious or legitimate target on campus — such as secret
research, censoring of political views, or special favors for the
ROTC program — need not be present. For the New Left
critique of the university is as wide-ranging as it is contradictory.
If the college requires students to live on campus, it is subject-
ing them to "oppressive" dorm life and acting *in loco parentis*.
If it allows them to live off campus, it is shamelessly disregard-
ing the surrounding community and driving rents up. If the
college is doing large amounts of government research on current problems, it is an "action university" far removed from
the tasks of independent scholarship. If, as in the case of
European universities, little such research is done, the teachers
are engaged in a "fetichism of knowledge" unconnected with
the real world.

Although many liberal students justify SDS confrontation
politics as a "last resort" to get action on a campus issue, it is

clear that SDS doesn't regard university disruptions in that
way. Mark Rudd, leader of the Columbia revolt in 1968, told
a Harvard SDS audience that the Columbia SDS demands
themselves had been insignificant — that he "didn't even know
where the Morningside gym site was," and that the Institute
for Defense Analysis was "nothing at Columbia." There is only
one "issue" in these confrontations: whether or not American
universities should be destroyed.

It wasn't always this way. Commentators on student movements like Seymour Martin Lipset have remarked that the only
unusual aspect of the otherwise true-to-form student rebellion
of this generation is that, for the first time, the revolutionaries
are making their university itself a target of protest. "In the
thirties," Lipset, himself an activist at the time, remarks, "we
viewed the university as a staging-off point for activities in the
real world."

The reason is that student revolutionaries have usually realized what a good thing they have going on the campus. For,
just as the student has been *the* revolutionary class in modern
society, universities have far more frequently been thorns in
the side of ruling classes than their faithful minions. Survey
after survey shows that students emerge from colleges further
left politically than when they came in. Revolutionary movements from Young Italy in the 1840s to the Narodniks in
Russia — up to and including the American New Left in the
1960s — were launched into inhospitable environments from
sanctuaries provided in relatively free universities.

For this reason, universities have always drawn ire from
conservatives, from the time Metternich directed the Carlsbad
Decrees of 1819 at nationalist German universities to Joe Mc-
Carthy's attacks on "Kremlin on the Charles" and pinko professors. William Buckley complained in his best-selling *God*

and Man at Yale that the reason students turned left during their college days was simply that they were being indoctrinated with left-wing views. Since Buckley's tract a series of less sophisticated broadsides, such as the works of one Professor E. Merrill Root, have become John Birch Society staples.

Indeed, the distance between the values of the campus and those even of "enlightened" America outside came home painfully to many moderates at Harvard after the police bust in April. Many, after having read the *Times* condemnation of police violence at the Chicago Democratic Convention, were sincerely hurt and dismayed to see the paper support the calling of police at Harvard. Similarly, while most liberal adults regard college faculties as dangerously vacillating in standing up to student disrupters, student moderates hope that they *might* be able to get the faculty to move far enough left to their positions. Indeed, it is the view that the universities are so far "ahead" of the rest of America which serves to remind moderates in normal times, just as it traditionally had reminded radicals, that an attack on the university would be mad. Before the Harvard strike, one moderate expressed a widespread consensus outside the New Left when he stated that "Harvard is good because it opens up people's minds to things like the war and poverty. If America's in a bad way today, it's because more people haven't had a Harvard education."

Although always a haven for "subversives," the universities have generally escaped rather easily from the repression that such activities often encounter in the society as a whole. Oddly enough, this is precisely because of the elite status enjoyed by universities and deplored by the New Left. Strikes by Spanish workers in the sixties were met with guns, while student rioters got off with clubs and suspended prison terms. One Spanish leader explained why: the ministers knew that their sons and daughters might well be among the student demonstrators. The events of May 1968 in France were followed by a quick reform in the governing structure of French universities, while no such changes took place in the factories. As Harvard student Arthur Waldron wrote in *The New Leader*, the only building in the world which several hundred people could expect to occupy and be immune from punishment is a university building.

Looking back on the history of Harvard radicalism, the Young Communist League in the thirties devoted few attacks on the university as an institution. The first issue of the *Harvard Communist*, published in January 1935, did present a line on the nature of the university which would sound familiar today.

The University is an important part of the educational system whereby the present ruling class seeks to maintain ideological domination over all the other classes . . . [By looking at the governing bodies of Harvard] we can immediately see that the class which directly and indirectly rules the country also rules Harvard.

Yet the words were merely *pro forma*, and this was the last attack on Harvard as an institution to appear in the pages of the *Harvard Communist*. Subsequent issues praised some of the administrators ("The appointment of James M. Landis as dean of the Harvard Law School is a step forward in the liberalization of the university," they wrote in November 1937) and requested university cooperation in the 1936 "student peace mobilization" ("We regret the university could not show its sympathy with the cause of peace to the extent of calling off classes," they wrote afterward). SDS leaflets in 1969 said that all administrators were "cops" who, despite any appearances, "necessarily have to take the side of the ruling class." And any proposal which the university accepts SDS regards as unaccept-

able or a "co-optation." The purpose of the faculty's acceptance
of the black students' demands, SDS said, was to "undercut
the other demands."

The Young Communists at Harvard in the thirties justified
themselves in terms of past Harvard men, like Sam Adams or
Henry David Thoreau, who "have been heretics and rebels
for truth's sake." Furthermore, they were not contemptuous
about the value of a university education. Indeed, their intellectual elitism seems strangely in character with the dominant
Harvard elitism. (Just as the antiintellectual elitism of today's
New Left, which enthrones to absolute moral authority a series
of vulgar slogans, is a mutant part, but still a part, of that same
tradition.) "The best Harvard," wrote the *Harvard Communist*
in December 1936, referring needless to say to themselves,
"can give America a true national leadership." The communist
is "the modern educated man," the publication, now neatly
offset rather than crudely mimeographed, wrote a year later.
At one point the *Harvard Communist* attacked sociologist Pit-
kim Sorokin, a favorite target since he was an exile from the
Soviet motherland, for saying that he'd rather be ruled "by a
man of plain common sense on the street" than by a social
scientist. This populist expression of faith in ordinary people
by Sorokin was, strangely enough, strongly denounced by the
Young Communist League. Did not the educated in fact know
more than others, especially those educated in Marxist social
science? "To paraphrase," the *Harvard Communist* retorted
sarcastically to Sorokin's view, "all the people know more than
any of the people."

What "new insights" might the New Left today have gained
which suddenly led them to choose, from all the far-from-

perfect institutions in society, the university as a fundamental
object for attack at all?

The New Left critique of the university finally comes down
to something more fundamental — and, depending on your
reading of it, more sinister or even more trivial — than secret
research or ROTC. *The universities graduate the people whose
skills keep capitalist society functioning.* Corporation executives
serve on boards of trustees of universities in order to make sure
that the supply of docile, trained manpower continues. Universities graduate lawyers specializing in tax loopholes, doctors
who set up rich practices and avoid the health needs of the
poor, government leaders who get us into Vietnam, and
businessmen who overcharge consumers. The *How Harvard
Rules* pamphlet spends endless pages documenting the hardly
new revelation that many powerful people have graduated from
Harvard. A leaflet issued by Queens College SDS points out
that Queens, a public college whose students are mostly working and lower middle class, serves a "crucial role" in graduating
"technicians and middle level administrators" for government
and business.

Such revelations are almost tautological, for obviously almost everyone with professional skills graduated from *some
college*. The evil curse which is associated with such information is maintained only by mystical incantations. "The university is a means by which the bourgeoisie perpetuates its own
dominance in society by setting the criteria by which learning
is judged," a Harvard friend once told me. Even any idealism
which the university may seek to instill is perverted. "Func-
tionaries and bureaucrats *must* be socialized into the conviction that the tasks they perform are somehow connected to a
Western Heritage and are, therefore, legitimate in terms other
than self-interest," *How Harvard Rules* tells us.

What we are never told is exactly which aspect of the training itself makes the doctor serve the rich rather than the poor, the architect use his skills constructing luxury dwellings rather than low-cost apartments. Unless one is trying very hard, it is difficult to blame the university for the society's priorities. The very same university could produce the very same doctors, and if the government socialized medicine those doctors would be serving the poor tomorrow. The same architects produced by the same universities could be building new towns next week if Congress gave them the go-ahead.

If anything, there are a few more professionals who use their skills to serve people because of the modicum of idealism which some universities succeed in instilling in them. If anything, there are a few more middle-class people who succeed in breaking out of the class structure imbued from childhood because of insights they gain at universities.

One problem with this generalized SDS critique is that it becomes at this point so enmeshed in obscure jargon like "repressive tolerance" and slogans like "Harvardization of the mind," that most students, following along while familiar topics like CIA funding, bacteriological warfare research, and ROTC were being discussed, trail off and stop listening. It is this unique ability of the New Left to numb people into inattention through mystic rhetoric which aids their chances, because many students end up participating in a venture to destroy their university when they thought they were trying simply to right a certain wrong.

All these criticisms have the unmistakable air of makeshift *ex post facto* jobs. The real reason why the university has been chosen for attack now and it wasn't in the past is that *this generation of radicals, isolating itself in an unprecedented way*

*from the population at large, has for the first time had to at-
tempt to obtain a mass base for radicalism on the campus itself.*

Although student revolutionaries appear in almost every generation, they have never even tried to get a majority of students
committed to revolution. First, almost all students were from
upper-class backgrounds, and the aristocrat-rebel is an always-
present, but statistically rather small, phenomenon among the
aristocracy's children. Second, there were all sorts of oppressed
people outside who looked like excellent objects for radical recruitment.

This last point is the most important. It is in fact not so
much that people in the past were more revolutionary than
people are now, as the student revolutionary of today often
assumes in an unbecoming fit of nostalgia. It was just that the
downtrodden were *unorganized.* The workers whom students
organized in the thirties were seeking the same elementary
goals as workers seek today, but their powerlessness concealed
what the students would have perceived as their sellout. But
inevitably the workers, once organized, joined what revolutionaries saw as the Establishment. (In other words, having
struggled for some power, they tried to use it for their benefit.)
The students were now left alone.

Students thus nominated *themselves* as the agents of social
change. In the early days of SDS, this was by *identifying* with
the university rather than attacking it. As the Port Huron
Statement of 1962 said, "The civil rights, peace, and student
movements are too poor and socially slighted, and the labor
movement too acquiescent, to be counted with enthusiasm.
From where else can power and vision be summoned? We believe that the universities are an overlooked seat of influence."
Later, as the movement became "radicalized" but still inward-

directed, the focus was still on the universities, but now as an object of attack.

But the revolutionaries could not and cannot build a mass base on campus on the basis of strenuous revolutionary idealism. Idealism has a native attraction to it, but in practice it requires quantities of hard and often dull work that make it impractical as the basis for a mass movement. The revolution can build up its chosen campus base only by making other appeals more directly related to self-interest.

To do that you have to attack the university in order to get the support of the alienated and the cultural radicals. When the New Left shouts that classes are a manipulative and reactionary tool for instilling bourgeois ideology and should be smashed, these students use this as an excuse for cutting. When SDS screams that they must employ "militant action" to win important demands, the cultural radicals join in the building take-overs in order to have a good time. SDS could make no revolution on the campus were it not for the mass base provided by the personally alienated and existentially discontented. And to attract this group SDS must attack the institution which they feel is most directly oppressing them.

Specific "demands" against the university can also aid SDS in gaining support of the moderates. Several years ago, when moderates last found SDS literature comprehensible, SDS invented the phrase "Student Power" as a campus correlative to Black Power. Since having lost student referenda, for example, on open campus recruiting at Columbia University, SDS has rejected Student Power because of the possibility that students as well as administrators might make the "wrong" decisions. When the faculty set up an elected student-faculty committee at Harvard to administer discipline after the Uni-

versity Hall confrontation, SDS said that even an all-student
committee would have no right to punish the occupiers in any
way. "It is because the demands for which we seized University Hall are legitimate that no committee is justified in attacking anyone who occupied the building."

But the time lag from the old Student Power demands allows moderates to enter any confrontation with a whole series
of "university restructuring" demands which they invariably
hope they can use the confrontation situation to push. Thus,
with their own demands, the moderates add fuel to the fire.
This completes the tripartite confrontation coalition of SDS,
cultural radicals, and moderates, which, with the benefit of a
few friendly local "pigs," can shut any university down, realizing SDS's dreams.

Victimized by a mixture of their own propaganda and a
characteristic student overestimation of their crucial importance
to society, today's New Left also attacks the university because
it has convinced itself that if it can succeed in wrecking the
university it can close off a vital pressure point and thus bring
the Establishment to its knees. If, goes the reasoning, the
function of the university is essential to producing trained manpower for the elite, then you can stop the elite by stopping the
flow of this trained manpower.

Failing in the strength to shut down the university permanently, this strategy also provides an answer to a plaguing
dilemma over the "demands" on which SDS ostensibly seeks
its confrontations. On the one hand, in order to whip up
hesitant and unsure supporters to "militant action," SDS must
always present its demands as hitting at the basic interests of
the enemy. Of ROTC, SDS at Harvard argued that it was not
an insignificant or "symbolic" issue as many had claimed. Instead, it was basic to the interests of the Harvard Corporation.

These are men who have a tremendous stake in the policing and defense of the American overseas empire — they are among those who own what is being defended. Thus ROTC, which provides most of the junior officers who supervise the day-to-day policing and defending, is for these men a useful tool, and not one they will cast aside lightly.

Yet, if the demands strike at the basic interests of the ruling class, how will an insignificant little confrontation cause them to quake? Herein is the dilemma.

A Harvard Progressive Labor party leader excitedly revealed the answer to a panting SDS just before the take-over of University Hall. "The Harvard Corporation," he exclaimed, "wants to keep ROTC here to serve its interests very badly. But even more than that it needs to keep the supply of trained manpower coming along smoothly. That's why they'll have to give in to our demands if we can show them that the alternative is to keep Harvard closed."

The vision, of course, of students permanently, or even for any extended length of time, causing the educational system to cease functioning is rather phantasmagoric. But the vision is wrong even on its own terms. When he heard it expressed by a European student revolutionary at one international conference, Alan Bullock, historian and head of Oxford, responded, without a trace of British detachment, "If you've had any experience administering a university, you would know that there are a lot of people who want to get rid of universities. Universities aren't indispensible for the business elite. Business training could go on very well on the job itself, medical training could take place in hospitals. There are many other ways of giving technical knowledge. But universities are also there for a general discussion of ideas, and many people find that potentially subversive and want to dispense with it. But this is the purpose of the University — to get people who are going to become doctors, lawyers, or whatever, to come together and discuss ideas in general."

Chicago sociologist Edward Shils added that "revolutions can succeed if revolutionaries succeed in gaining control of institutions which the society needs on a day-to-day basis — the post office, the arsenal, the factory. But what would happen if the colleges produced no graduates for a few years? I'm afraid that, in a quantitative sense, very little. I think that in a qualitative sense we would suffer — but that is from my quaint humanistic viewpoint, one which I'm afraid would receive only scant hearing from the military-industrial complex."

Shortly after the 1968 Columbia confrontation, *New Left Notes*, the official SDS publication, wrote, "We are not yet ready to take state power. But what Columbia and soon others will have shown us is that some practical experience can be part of the process of getting ready."

"If you want to make a revolution," Shils comments, "you make it by occupying the post office or the arsenal, not the Faculty of Letters. Those of you who are revolutionaries better get back to the serious task of making a revolution. Those who think they can practice for the revolution by taking over the universities are like people who try to practice for a football game by kicking a ball around their living room. They may succeed in breaking a few lampshades, and knocking down some plaster, but they won't learn much football."

Part Three

Confrontation 1969, and After

1. The Escalation
of Unreality

I am entering University Hall in the spirit of Martin Luther
King. —

> Steven Hornberger, student body president at the
> Harvard Divinity School, speaking outside University Hall
> during the occupation.

The assassination of Martin Luther King was a great step
forward in the liberation struggle of black people. —

> Jared Israel, founder of Harvard PL and leader
> of the University Hall occupation.

Those who occupied University Hall did so out of a sincere
moral conviction about the nature of the University and
American society. The succeeding discussion has shown that
the issues raised were significant and legitimate. —

> Excerpt from moderate petition, signed by 2500 students,
> asking the Committee of Fifteen, the student-faculty
> group set up to discipline those arrested at University Hall,
> not to suspend or expel anyone.

We didn't take the building to "raise issues," but to win
the demands . . . The petition doesn't help the fight for
no punishment. In fact, by politely asking the Committee
to be easy on us it is cooperating with the Committee and
weakening the only *real* fight against punishment, the fight
against that Committee. —

> "Fight for No Punishment," SDS leaflet
> denouncing the moderate petition.

Strike education is also education about how a mass movement can be democratic. The strike is far more democratic
than the faculty or the student government . . . Decisions
of the mass meeting are made after hours and hours of debate. Anyone who supports the eight demands can speak at
the mass meeting. —

> *The Old Mole*, April 1969

WHEN A WORKER GOES OUT ON STRIKE, HE LAYS DOWN HIS
TOOLS. WHEN A STUDENT GOES OUT ON STRIKE HE LAYS DOWN
HIS BRAIN. —

> Professor Richard Pipes,
> during the Harvard confrontation

IT WAS THE END of August, and the long summer vacation was
almost over. One night, while we were both in our beds falling
asleep, my brother Mark broke the silence in the dark room.
"You know, when you're away from school, it's hard to conceive of the fact that anyone can even take the arguments you
heard during the strike seriously."

"Yeah, I know what you mean," I whispered to him.

"I mean, how can anyone believe that the reason the administration sent in the police to clear University Hall was
that they feared that SDS's demands were a threat to their
overseas investments which ROTC was protecting?"

"It is amazing, isn't it?"

The Harvard confrontation would never have been possible
without the promotion of a campus atmosphere hermetically
sealed from reality. "I am tired," my roommate said as he was
preparing to graduate in the June following the confrontation,
"of having to spend a good proportion of my time arguing
about whether Communist China is more democratic than the
U.S., or whether civil liberties should exist for ideas SDS
doesn't like."

Where else but in this dreamworld could socialists be denounced as reactionaries? Where else but in this dreamworld
could it be argued that a "course" which presented primarily
a diet of SDS pamphlets as its reading list and taught by section men whose only qualification was adherence to the SDS

ideology was no more biased than the typical course given at Harvard? Where else but in this dreamworld could the statement oft-repeated during the strike that "we've learned more during this week than in all our courses at Harvard" be viewed as anything but a pathetic admission of how little serious work or study one previously had done? Where else but in this dreamworld could "liberated" files refer to stolen documents, a "liberated" university refer to one where none of the academic functions for which a university is set up in the first place are going on, and a "liberated" student refer to one who, on the verge of exhaustion from prolonged sleeplessness and endless mind-dulling meetings, participates catatonically in a series of robot chants and parades?

Where else but in this dreamworld could students argue that SDS occupied University Hall only after going through all legitimate channels when three of the six "demands" were presented for the first time the night before the confrontation? Indeed, where else but in this dreamworld could one believe that the confrontation was about the six (later seven, later eight) demands at all? To be sure, SDS always argued self-consciously and defensively that this was the case. But they do protest too much. Certainly the American people were not taken in. One can criticize many aspects of the often crude and antiintellectual backlash which has taken place in the United States as a result of student confrontations. But Americans have been wise in seeing the "issues" and "demands" as mere pretexts. After SDS occupied University Hall allegedly as representatives of the Cambridge working class and massively leafleted the Cambridge community to this effect, representatives of the East Cambridge Block Associations (East Cambridge is the exclusively working-class part of Cambridge) voted

49–2 to condemn the confrontation and to disassociate themselves from any notion that SDS represented the community.
This unpleasant fact was hardly noted at all at Harvard. For
unpleasant facts from the real world hardly matter when unreality has escalated to the point it did at Harvard by April
1969.

The precondition which allows for the escalation of unreality at Harvard is the fact that Harvard students are, in a literal
sense, irresponsible. That is, they are sheltered from facing the
consequences of their actions. Normally, people can see if
they've made a mistake in a pragmatic way by seeing the results.
This allows people to correct mistaken decisions. In the case
of students, however, we act and others suffer for our actions.
As an Oakland black activist, reporting in *The Activist* magazine during the 1966 Brown-Reagan contest in California, commented to a Berkeley student who was claiming there was "no
difference" between Brown and Reagan, "Look, when this is
all over you can shave off your beard and go back to Scarsdale.
But I gotta live here." I can say that I have not suffered personally in any way from the election of Richard Nixon.

To be sure, a small group of committed revolutionaries did
suffer from the Harvard confrontation, that is, they were
suspended from the university. But most of those who occupied
University Hall, not to speak of virtually all of those thousands
out on strike, positively *enjoyed* the experience. Where students get pleasure from their mistakes (even if far-off others
are paying the price), mistakes can accumulate without ac-
countability. Idiocy may be nurtured in the isolation of our
warm, humid incubator, until finally, to the disbelief and in-
comprehension of the rest of the world, it hatches.

Unreality doesn't, however, incubate automatically because

of a favorable environment. Concrete steps must be taken to disorient students from any sort of bearings or points of reference to reality. Black must be made to appear white, two plus two to equal five. This task is easier because most students come to Harvard without very definite or strong political beliefs. Moderate leader Ken Glazier, who as a freshman was in the same dorm with a hereditary radical in SDS, once told me how surprised he and everyone else in the dorm were to see someone already so committed to and certain of his beliefs. Most Harvard students will confess to changing their minds back and forth on issues depending on which side's polemic they read last.

There is nothing wrong with uncertainty and skepticism. But when political beliefs are molded merely on the basis of reading and talking and not on the basis of experience, it becomes relatively easy to change students' minds by exposing them to a constant diet of one side only, especially since each active SDS member regards himself as a political missionary and harps constantly on ideology over pinball machines, dinner tables, and coffee. This pressure, all from one side, is constant and takes its toll.

The months leading up to the confrontation, though, provided special lessons in illusion and confusion to disorient students. The first such disorienting factor was the phantasmagoric "split" between the two factions of SDS, the Worker-Student Alliance/Progressive Labor party and the New Left caucus. What made this faction fight a contributing factor to the escalation of unreality at Harvard is the fact that the student body was exposed to the unreal spectacle of two groups of students at each other's throats, denouncing one another as "racists" and "counterrevolutionaries," when for all practical

purposes there was no difference in ideology between them!
What is the student to make of the momentous dividing line
which separated those in SDS who believe that blacks in America are merely a "superexploited section of the working class"
(WSA/PLP), and those who believe that, in addition, they
are "an internal colony within the white mother country" (New
Left caucus)? What of the colossal question of whether one
supports the Vietcong and North Vietnam but denounces
them for agreeing to negotiate with the United States (WSA/
PLP), or supports the Vietcong and North Vietnam and accepts their decision to negotiate with the United States as long
as the Vietcong makes no concessions (New Left caucus)?

Yet here were these two factions (which have now split into
two separate organizations) refusing to speak personally with
each other, "exposing" each other as agents of the ruling class,
and conducting purge-style "struggle meetings" against each
other — when what separated them was nothing more than
tactical differences on how best to establish a totalitarian dictatorship in America. The New Left caucus was to participate
in the expulsion of WSA/PLP at the 1969 SDS summer convention for "choosing to ally themselves with the class that
rules this country." In April 1969 the SDS National Council,
supported by the New Left caucus, stated that WSA/PLP was
"spreading lies" about the Vietcong and North Vietnam "for
the purpose of creating splits within the anti-imperialist movement" and were therefore "enemies of that movement and
working objectively in the interests of the U.S. ruling class."
Meanwhile WSA/PLP denounced New Left caucus leader and
SDS founder Mike Ansara as a misleader trying to get "a fistful
of loot" from the movement. *Challenge*, the national PL magazine, attacked the Harvard New Left caucus for arguing that

"the strike is 'groovier' education than going to classes." *Challenge* responded, "We say the [Harvard] Corporation doesn't fear personal exhilaration. It fears the building of a militant, pro–working class, anti-imperialist movement to crush ROTC and smash expansion."

To be sure, there were important differences in style between the two factions. PL's basic approach is toward organizing workers; the New Left caucus's toward organizing hippies and cultural radicals. For this reason, PL insists on strict puritan discipline from its members, who are not allowed to wear long hair, take drugs, sleep with girls, or wear unorthodox clothes. The idea is that such behavior "turns off" the workers. The mechanistic robotlike behavior of well-dressed PLers contributes to the escalation of unreality on the campus because their super-straightness is so completely out of step with the dominant Bohemianism of the campus as a whole and radical students in particular. Harvard students are disoriented by seeing those they have been told are the furthest left-wing students on campus looking like Young Republicans.

Furthermore, the very specially heightened gullible fanaticism and conspiracy theories of WSA/PL disorient students because we tend to believe that if at least one Harvard student says that something is true, there must be at least *some* case to be made for it. Shortly after the strike the Palestine terrorist group Al Fatah announced that they had assassinated Moshe Dayan, the Israeli defense minister. Soon the word got around Adams House that Stuart Soloway, a leader of the WSA/PLP caucus, believed for a full two weeks that Dayan had been killed. The reaction to this from some students around the house, though, was not that it exposed PL's gullibility, but that maybe Dayan *had* been killed. Similarly the most incredible

WSA/PLP conspiracy theories are accepted as subjects for debate simply because somebody has had the courage to print them. They claimed that the idea of restructuring the university democratically was an administration plot, being promoted by administration *agents* among the student body. *Challenge* wrote that "the administration held the demonstrators in jail until after [the Memorial Church meeting the morning of the bust] was over" in order "to guarantee Glazier/Raines' ability to control the meeting."

Members of the New Left caucus generally look and act in ways expected of radicals. However, the press created a myth/reality gap over the New Left caucus by spreading the idea that the New Left caucus was the moderate faction of SDS, opposed by the PL extremists. This convenient fiction was created because the press cannot imagine that large numbers of sincere radical students could *all* be totalitarian revolutionaries, and they therefore insist on seeing PL as a small disciplined band of outside agitators trying to subvert and take over the innocent little New Left. This disorients students, who accept this dichotomy as a matter of faith, when they see the New Left caucus again and again trying to out-revolutionary PL. During the strike the New Left caucus referred to the eight demands as "reformist" and denounced the PL strategy of radicalizing students through their fighting for the demands as "economist" (an old term Lenin used to describe the approach of simply supporting the trade union demands of workers without raising "higher" revolutionary issues). The *Strike Daily* put out by the New Left caucus argued that "the eight particular demands are not of themselves radical . . . They fail to expose, and expose in a clear way understandable to all, the manifold ways in which the university molds the form of our everyday lives into a pattern alien to our needs as individuals and social beings."

Thus while the press was presenting the New Left caucus all year as moderates, their criticisms of WSA/PLP were frequently criticisms from the Left. Many students were disoriented from a sense of objective reality by reading about New Left caucus moderation in the press and seeing their extremism in practice. Leaders of the New Left caucus are now prominent in the Weathermen, and the press is at it again. Now PL has become the moderates, faced by Weatherman extremists!

The second new factor which disoriented large numbers of students from points of reference with reality was the presence of an SDS course for credit, Soc Rel 148/9, during the academic year 1968–69. After the strike, Barry Margolin, a New Left caucus leader, boasted that Soc Rel 148/9 had played a significant role in preparing the atmosphere for the confrontation. "Even a lot of kids in the crazy sections, like the one on existential psychology taught by [*Crimson* editor] Jim Glassman and which we thought was unpolitical and ridiculous, ended up in the building."

Several aspects of Soc Rel 148/9 were unreal and disorienting. The first was the elaborate sham that had to be put up to convince people of the unconvincible — that Soc Rel 148/9 was being conducted under more or less normal academic standards, and that therefore any opposition to the course had to be based on the desire to suppress the "just ideas" (this was the terminology used) the course was imparting to students. Most of the section men in Soc Rel 148/9 were undergraduates who were required only to state their loyalty to New Left ideology. John Stephens, a member of the YPSL executive committee who took Soc Rel 148 in the fall semester and asked if he could be a section man in Soc Rel 149 in the spring, was bluntly told that his political views disqualified him. It was the "dirty little secret" of Soc Rel 148/9 that its large enrollment was in significant measure due to the fact that the course was a roaring gut — virtually everyone got A's. As a letter to the *Crimson* recounted:

Last September I attended the first meeting of a Soc Rel 148 section. I went there primarily because I wanted an A. The question of grades was raised almost immediately. Described at best as reflections of Harvard's repressive system, we declared them unnecessary. We were here to learn by free communication and self-expression. In particular, we filled that first cozy hour with a series of emotional assertions to the effect that none of us gave a damn about grades anyway. Suddenly the instructor remembered something. To make the grade curve appear somewhat realistic we need a couple C's. How about a few volunteers? Unanimous silence at last.

Yet to defend the course these obvious facts had to be covered up, even if everyone knew they were true. There's nothing like a little hypocrisy and deception to escalate unreality.

But if the sham over the course's form was bad, the content of the course was even worse in promoting the dreamworld. WSA/PLP people were assigned to about five sections each, and they roamed around from section to section of the course to browbeat hesitant students, dominate discussion, and cow opposition simply with lung power. The official list of paper topics handed out in each section by the course's leaders featured "research" assignments on "What Would the Establishment Do If Eldridge Cleaver Was Elected President?" and "How Many Wildcat Strikes Were There in the United States Last Year?" This topic would have provided the occasion for the first Harvard paper that could be handed in on a file card. A section of Soc Rel 148 I attended was devoted to a discussion of whether Walter Reuther was an agent of the bourgeoisie, and the fact that there was even a debate on the topic was mainly due to my presence and that of one other YPSL member. Normally the idea would have hardly been questioned. (The week's assignment, "Sell-Out at Ford" was an SDS pamphlet containing an abstruse and often inaccurate denunciation of the 1966 Ford-UAW settlement, without any mention of the fact that Ford workers, by a democratic vote, accepted the agreement.) Only a small number of people participated in the discussion, rather smaller than in most sections I've attended at Harvard, and some students seemed almost mesmerized by the proceedings.

One of the great myths of college is the idyllic attempt to compare the alleged soulless impersonality of Harvard lectures with the "real learning experience" provided by small, intimate sections. Since few students even in normal courses have prepared the readings, sections are generally rather lifeless and redundant affairs. Generally, students hope that the section man will more or less give a lecture. Lectures are where the bulk of learning takes place, since the professor is obviously informed on the subject. Soc Rel 148/9 had all the disadvantages of sections with the additional one that practically nobody did any reading and that most section men had no expert knowledge of the subject at all. A sophomore who gave a section on imperialism in the spring of 1969 happily confessed to me that the only non-Leninist view of the subject he had read was Joseph Schumpeter's brief and generalized essay "Imperialism," that he was ignorant of the fact that of American corporations' total assets of $1.3 trillion only $16 billion represents

investment in the entire Third World, and that in his view
the definition of the term *imperialism* was any American investment abroad. Whitewashed as promoting a "common
learning experience," the ignorance of the section men merely
contributed to the devaluation of any sort of logical reasoning
in Soc Rel 148/9 and made the sections all the more subject
to harassment by the roving PL cadres who attended multiple
meetings.

Soc Rel 148/9 played a crucial role in preparing for the
confrontation by indoctrinating a large number of wavering
liberal-radical types and especially presenting them with a sense
of the strength and invincibility of the New Left steamroller.
Once inside Soc Rel 148/9 — even if one had signed up just
out of curiosity — it was oh so much easier just to go along
with the line, be swept up into it in all its delicious phrases,
than to do the homework, have the courage, and be willing
to face the abuse that would be required to enter into active
opposition to what the course was indoctrinating. The simple
fact is that, contrary to the legend promoted by SDS, most
Harvard courses hardly present any political line at all in the
sense that they give insights or attitudes in approaching current
political problems. The simple fact is that *one* SDS course
succeeded in reversing for many students the effects of *all*
the other Harvard courses they had taken. This was because
other courses do not deal with the questions in the headlines,
preferring to assume that students can figure such things out
for themselves. The notion, jealously cultivated by course
leaders, that "Soc Rel 148/9 is no more biased than other
Harvard courses" was ridiculous.

The indoctrination was not countered, and it was difficult
for any but those with the firmest political beliefs to avoid

being sucked in by a whole year of propaganda for credit. Almost all one needed was a vague idealism to emerge from one's experience in Soc Rel 148/9 as anything from a sympathizer to a hard-liner. I personally know several people who were turned into New Leftists from the course.

Most fads are rather harmless. Students emerge largely unscathed from goldfish eating or pot smoking. But the faddish curiosity about this strange and fashionable thing called "radicalism" scarred almost a thousand Harvard students in one year.

The third factor contributing to the escalation of unreality during the months preceding the confrontation was the nature of the big debate on what should be done with ROTC. The debate was falsified because few students remembered that Vietnam was a controversial issue in American society, or that, not only were the views of most Harvard students on Vietnam not universally accepted, but they had only minority support. Because of campus unanimity in opposition to the war, SDS could present a series of arguments on ROTC that were accepted as perfectly serious, when their application to any other issue would be dismissed immediately by all but the most rabid authoritarians. The SDS argument was disarmingly simple: no individual has a right to participate in ROTC because what ROTC does ("suppress workers in Vietnam and at home") is evil. Unless one sides with the ruling class against the workers ("that's the only value judgment involved here") there can be no doubt that what ROTC does is objectively evil and therefore need not be submitted to any vote ("we are not engaged in any Gallup-Poll popularity contest, but rather a fight against an enemy"). SDS refused to make its argument on ROTC dependent on any generalized principle, such as the

inappropriateness of military training on a campus. Rather, "we
support the [compulsory] military training in North Vietnamese universities." ROTC must go purely and simply because
American foreign policy is bad.

There were some who perfectly well understood what the
SDS argument meant and even accepted the implications.
When I asked one PLer whether, since I considered SDS to be
immoral, I should seek to have *its* activities banned on campus,
he replied, "Yes. There's no 'right' to do immoral things."

During the confrontation, my brother pointed out, "SDS can
get away with these arguments only because everyone is opposed to the war here. Did you read about what one Afro group
at Tilden High in New York did recently? They demanded that
the school ban any collecting of relief money for Biafra in the
school on the grounds that Biafra was a tool of neocolonialism.
That's exactly analogous to the SDS demand on ROTC."

"Yeah, I know."

"But most Harvard kids would consider that demand to be
ridiculous, because they see that Biafra is a controversial issue."

The debate over ROTC revealed that many students completely misunderstand the very basic principles of democracy.
Like those Americans who believe that "he's our President and
now that he's elected we all gotta back him," many students,
it came out during the ROTC debate, didn't understand that
an outvoted minority need not give up its views just because
it is a minority. It should seek to persuade people and become
a majority.

I heard endless times, "So if we're a minority, what are we
supposed to *do* about the war? You seem to be saying we
shouldn't do anything."

"What you should do is very simple: you should keep trying
to become a majority. Demonstrate, protest."

Because the issue was Vietnam, this somehow seemed like a cop-out, a "do-nothing" position. "Do anything you fucking want except attack civil liberties. When a majority tries to trample on the civil liberties of a minority, it's bad enough. But when a *minority* tries to stop the civil liberties of a majority, then it's really unbelievable." It made some dent, but not enough.

In February the faculty voted by a large majority to overrule the administration's Committee on Educational Policy recommendations on how to "improve" ROTC courses and decided instead to strip ROTC courses of their academic credit and Pentagon-appointed ROTC "professors" of their tenured status. The unanimous view at the time was that the ROTC issue was over and that SDS would somehow have to find another issue over which to stage their spring confrontation. (The New Left caucus hoped that an issue could be made over attempts to introduce some academic rigor into Soc Rel 148/9, and the Worker-Student Alliance caucus began talking about Harvard's alleged attempt purposefully to drive workers out of Cambridge and transform the city into "Imperial City," a center for imperialism.)

Unfortunately, at this point the Harvard Corporation and President Pusey intervened in the ROTC situation in such a way as to allow SDS, with a generous sprinkling of the Big Lie to be sure, to "reopen" the ROTC issue.

The Harvard Corporation accepted the faculty's decision on academic credit and professorships. This was largely a formality, since in practice the corporation's "power" in such fields had been completely delegated to the faculty. (The corporation busies itself mainly with budgetary and financial matters.) However, in his letter to the faculty announcing the corporation's decision, President Pusey completely ignored the

spirit of the faculty's decision, which was to *downgrade* the
privileged status of ROTC, and spent most of the letter praising
the faculty for not adopting the SDS position of total abolition!

SDS quickly succeeded in burying the truth about the corporation's decision beneath enormous piles of leaflets maintaining that the corporation had "overturned" the faculty's decision
and alleging that this "proved" that the corporation was the
enemy — seven men who were "running" Harvard for their
personal profit. By April it took a brave soul to remind people
that the faculty's decision was being implemented. (In May,
on the basis of the no-credit, no-professor guidelines set up by
the February ROTC resolution, the three ROTC programs,
obeying a federal law which requires campus ROTC to enjoy
the special privileges of academic credit and professorial status
for the ROTC officers, decided to leave Harvard.)

Unreality had been escalated a further notch. It was reaching
the breaking point.

Joseph Goebbels used to say that if you repeat a lie often
enough, it becomes the truth. This is especially true for those,
like students, who can't test lies and truth against the daily
confrontation with the hard and real world. Thus for many
black *was*, at least in their minds, made to appear white.
Destroying the university was seen as the way to save it. Irrationality was praised as a higher form of rationalism. A Harvard
scientist's development of an improved strain of rice was viewed
as complicity with American imperialism. The innocuous, when
repeated with the requisite sense of horror, was made to appear
criminal.

But tasks remained so that the escalation of unreality could
be translated into the final conflict. Any traces of doubt and

despair from the ranks of the militants themselves had to be removed. Those who had already been persuaded of the SDS "analysis" intellectually and identified with it emotionally had to be whipped up into the hysterical frame of mind which would lead them to "put their Harvard careers on the line."

First they had to be persuaded that ROTC was important enough an issue. The SDS leadership tried to do this by arguing that, since a large proportion of the junior officers currently fighting in Vietnam come from ROTC programs, one could severely cripple the ability of the United States to fight wars like Vietnam if one succeeded in abolishing ROTC programs around the nation. (In elitist fashion, it was argued that what happened at Harvard would significantly affect what happened to ROTC programs on hundreds of other campuses.) That there is an enormous waiting list of colleges trying to get ROTC programs, or that any large decline in ROTC programs would merely result in the setting up of additional military academies render this SDS "argument" incredible. Yet never did SDS leaders become so defensive, angry, and belligerent as when anyone questioned the sacred notion that their anti-ROTC campaign was dealing a "sharp blow against imperialism." People weren't being asked to "put their Harvard careers on the line" for nothing!

Second, SDS members had to come to see themselves as part of a "world revolutionary storm" in order to undertake their confrontation. Since there is no revolutionary situation in America, such a confrontation would appear to be what traditional Marxists would call "adventurist." But, if seen in the world context, it could be argued that *no* action undertaken in the U.S. is too outrageous.

Third, SDS members had to feel emotionally the attractive

and romantic side of their suffering. What is romantic about
being clubbed by police? Frankly, I had always been skeptical
of the theory that New Leftists actually enjoyed being beaten
in places like Chicago and elsewhere, in order to prove their
revolutionary virtue. Never having been clubbed, it struck me as
rather much pain to go through in order to prove a point.
However, during the summer of 1969 I was beaten successively
by several Czech policemen during protests of the first anniver-
sary of the crushing of Czech freedom in Prague. I would not
recommend the experience: to put it mildly, it hurt a lot. But
in some ways I was grateful, I must admit, to have suffered in
some very direct way for the ideals I believe in. Better Prague
than University Hall, as I see it. But that is immaterial. The
point is that I can understand how SDSers too can come to seek
a little suffering for their beliefs and be proud of having the opportunity to be beaten. It not only gives them a feeling of moral
purification but, more importantly in this context, provides a
bludgeon with which to force the recalcitrant supporter into
the building. For anyone who didn't want to go could be denounced as (to use some of the expressions WSA/PL employed)
"yellow-bellied," "a coward," and "chicken." The compulsoriza-
tion of suffering became a leading method SDS used to goad
intellectual sympathizers into the building.

Harvard's hour was approaching, and there was nothing anyone could do about it. There was simply going to be a confrontation in the spring. This became apparent in the few days
before we went off for spring vacation. Our game was up; the
question was then only how many would participate in their
game.

On Tuesday, April 8, the day after we came back from spring
vacation, SDS called a meeting in Burr B (later changed to the

larger Lowell Lecture Hall) to "discuss the possibility of militant action" on ROTC.

Lowell Lec filled up only gradually that night. By seven-thirty, when the meeting was scheduled to begin, only about fifty people were there. It looked too good to be true. Would Harvard's particularism save it? Would the realization that only a few people would actually take the step of entering the building perhaps dissuade the SDS leadership at the last moment? I sat nervously toward the front of the large room, hoping and wondering.

A few minutes before seven-thirty my brother Mark arrived with two friends. "Ready for the circus?" I asked.

"Yeah. Do you know if anyone's going to get up to propose that they don't take over a building?"

"I don't know. Do you think it should be done?"

"Yeah. I told all my friends to come and vote against a take-over." Mark waved to a friend of his just entering.

"Yeah. A lot of YPSLs are coming also."

"OK. Well, we'll see how the meeting turns out, Steve. I think somebody should propose no take-over."

"Look, there aren't many people here yet. It might win."

"Well, I doubt it. But if it did they wouldn't dare overturn the decision of their own meeting."

But more people soon arrived. No, it wasn't a circus; it was a nightmare. The nightmare had only one purpose: to seal off the faithful from any hesitations. What they were being asked to do was part of a popular revolutionary struggle, that had to be made clear to all. Soon Mike Kazin, wearing a blue turtleneck and his new jet-black mustache, chalked the evening's slogan on the huge blackboard. It came, appropriately, from Chairman Mao:

DARE TO STRUGGLE, DARE TO WIN!

The WSA/PL leadership arrived in a group. They had brought with them sleeping bags, knapsacks, food, and knives. They were to propose seizing a building that night.

"Abolish ROTC" buttons were everywhere. Even before most of the seats were filled, people started gathering and sitting up on the stage, poised near the microphones. "Smash ROTC" chants were practiced in order to test the strength of the group.

Above all people had to feel invincible.

It was a fantastic group in its contrasts. Beautiful people with neat faces, long flowing hair, old army jackets (a sort of radical symbol these days), and bell-bottom blue jeans. Cliffies in sexy-looking dungarees. Jessie Gill, a young nurse's aid who represents SDS's recruit in the Cambridge community. PLers in neatly pressed work shirts and conservative cuffed slacks. But most striking of all were the faces I recognized here and there: the kid whom I knew as a freshman Goldwaterite now chatting with his friends in WSA, or the kid I knew as a machine Democrat sporting a beard and an "Abolish ROTC" button.

"Dave, we gotta stop this juggernaut, stall it if we can," I whispered to Dave Guberman of the YPSL, sitting next to me.

"What can we do?"

"You oughta ask at the beginning of the meeting — it's an SDS meeting after all — for a report on the recent SDS National Council meeting." At this meeting, WSA/PL walked out after they were out-Maoed by the alleged "Right" faction of SDS. Tensions were very high, and there was already talk of a split. The report would demoralize people.

"Why don't *you?*"

"They'll never call on me. Why don't you?"

The idea was dropped.

By the time Mike Kazin called the meeting to order, reminding the assembled of the slogan on the board and letting out with one burst of "Smash ROTC," Lowell Lec was crowded. It was hot, and people were already sweating in anticipation.

John Berg, representing WSA/PL, was recognized to present the first motion of the evening. Berg, although an nth-year grad student, still has a rosy face behind gold-rimmed glasses. He was wearing a baby-pink sweater and a green jacket. My first year at Harvard he had been my gov tutor, and I was by far the most radical person in our tutorial.

Berg stunned the audience with his faction's proposal. The New Left caucus was expecting a call for an immediate building seizure that night ("as soon as this meeting is over"). But WSA/PL's three "expansion" demands had been kept under closely guarded wraps. PL had been leafleting Harvard for a few weeks, with visible lack of interest from students, about how Harvard's "imperialistic expansion" was tearing down workers' homes in Cambridge and driving up rents. It would have never done to tell the truth — that in fact the main cause of the Cambridge housing crisis is not university expansion but the increasing number of students who want to live in Cambridge and who can afford to pay higher rents than workers. Most members of the Harvard-Radcliffe SDS executive committee live off campus. In addition, the traditional SDS line had always been that the house system was "repressive," and that off-campus living should be encouraged. Furthermore, WSA/PL's position was especially unreal because they stoutly rejected any notion that the only real way to solve the Cambridge housing crisis was to build more housing. The only thing to do was to stop the university from building any new buildings.

WSA/PL presented some demands about stopping the destruction of workers' apartments owned by Harvard on Uni-

versity Road in Cambridge and in Roxbury. The demands later
turned out to be largely fictionalized, and the only basis on
which PL could be believed at the meeting was blind faith, since
nobody had heard a thing about them before. Nobody bothered
to ask the question of exactly why the residents in the threatened buildings were not present or represented at the meeting.
Did they support, acquiesce in, or even know about the confrontation that was being called for on their behalf? In fact, it later
turned out that WSA/PL had not bothered to consult or inform
the people in question of their action.

Miles Rapoport of the New Left caucus, who went to the
same high school as I had, rose to present their faction's resolution. He immediately accepted the three new PL demands.
But he suggested that SDS did not know yet whether they had
enough support to take over a building. "I don't mind going
into a building if we think we can win, but we've got to build
our base first." (The expression "build our base" is taken from
the writings of Chairman Mao on guerrilla warfare and traditionally had been the province of PL rhetoric. Things were
changing.) A take-over should take place the following Monday, after a week of "intensive" dorm canvassing and "rapping,"
a series of militant demonstrations, and, all in all, a further
week of efforts to bombard students with the bandwagon psychology.

"Any more motions?" Kazin asked after Miles was finished.

Nobody raised his hand. So I did. Kazin recognized me and
I jumped up onto the stage. My heart was beating very rapidly.
I wish I didn't have to be the one. I began calmly.

"Next year tens of thousands of black and working-class kids
will not be able to go to the state colleges in California because
the higher education budget was just cut there. The same
thing's happening in Wisconsin and New York.

"You rich Harvard kids are gonna continue getting money from papa no matter what you do to University Hall. You're not the ones who suffer when everyone gets turned off by your riots and building take-overs.

"With your fancy theories you're gonna try to prove that it's the ruling class who reacts against the confrontations. That of course is untrue. Recent polls show about eighty percent of Americans want to see the universities get tougher on campus riots, and people with higher incomes are more likely to favor leniency.

"We hear a lot of talk around here about a worker-student alliance. Well, baby, if you take over this building tonight or next Monday you might as well forget about it. Because your — your — your *immature* stupidity and your fun and games will bring out the worst in workers."

There had been heckling during every line, but at this point I could barely make myself heard even through the microphone. "Let him speak!" one lone friendly voice shouted out above the din.

"SDS has become so lost in the unreality of its own rhetoric that you're unable to see that there's a fundamental difference between any society where you can organize for and propagandize for your views and one where you can't." One person yelled "Liar!"

"Oh, so there's no difference? Well, you'll find out if you succeed in bringing repression to America. You'll find out there's something worse than social-fascism, and that's fascism. As a Czech socialist who had to leave his country when the communists came to power told me, 'There's something more repressive than tolerance, and that's repression.'"

"What should we do about ROTC?" a WSAer from Adams House shouted out from the audience.

"I propose that various groups continue their activities against ROTC, but that no disruptive action be taken."

Hisses, and some applause.

Kazin wrote on the board alternative three. NO ACTION. What a death-knell term! Who likes to vote for "no action"? I insisted he change it, to "no disruptive action." He didn't.

"You made a mistake, Steve," one old friend from freshman year sympathetically told me as I walked toward the back of the hall. "You should never tell babies that they're babies."

The "debate" proceeded, and WSA/PL in particular took great pains to argue that I had slandered the working class. James Truesome Kilbreth III, square-jowled and fearsome, got up to the microphone to spit out his words, "Kelman the racist pig doesn't realize that our action is *modeled* on the great working-class struggles of the past, like the sit-ins where the workers fought hard against the bosses. You don't have to believe me. The next speaker is a Cambridge worker who'll tell you."

PL now carted out their prize exhibit, a middle-aged Cambridge-accented "worker" wearing a blue denim jacket with a peace insignia sewn on the back. The gist of his speech was summarized in the wildly cheered sentence, "Go into the building tonight! Don't wait! The working people of Cambridge will join you inside!"

What more unreality could one ask for? The "worker" received a thirty-second ovation for this gem. (During the occupation the next day, not a single worker, including Jessie Gill and PL's exhibit, showed up at the building.) Black was white. The new math was alive and well in Lowell Lec: two plus two equaled five.

The workers would join SDS in the building!!

The real debate continued. "We've built all the base we need," Jared Israel, founder of Harvard PL and former lonely totalitarian voice "unlistened" to in SDS, responded with brilliant, crisp style to the New Left caucus. His short jet-black hair and his well-developed karate-trained arms stood out as he carefully gesticulated and moved his face. "We've been sharply raising the level of antiimperialist consciousness all year. If we wait till Monday it will give the corporation all sorts of time to create smoke screens and confuse us.

"Let's be honest! If we don't go into the building tonight we never will. The corporation will crush us. Miles Rapoport and the other misleaders in his caucus know this. They don't want to go into the building at all! I say, 'Fight to win!' We go *tonight!*"

Someone rushed in through the door and asked for the floor. "I've just been over at University Hall. I don't know whether this'll influence people's votes, but there are a lot of university cops guarding University Hall right now. We'd have to fight them to get in."

"Smash ROTC. No expansion! Fight to win!!" came the chant from the WSAers.

The vote came. It was 180 for a seizure on Monday, 140 for a seizure right after the meeting, 60 for "no action," and 40 for a nondisruptive student strike.

Some people began to put their coats on and leave. But it was far from over. For at this point PL decided to re-create the hysterical and poisoned atmosphere of Stalinist-controlled meetings in the thirties. I was sitting right near the stage when the coordinated offense began. WSAers began chanting rhythmically as their leaders literally assaulted the stage and grabbed the microphone from Kazin. A group of WSAers surrounded the microphone so it could not be retaken. One drew a knife on a stunned Miles Rapoport and called him a "yellow-bellied fascist." Jared Israel took the microphone to say that the debate was not over. There would be some people who would take over the building tonight no matter what the group decided, because they knew that "these sellouts don't want to take over a building at all."

The meeting went on for another two hours and took two more votes. Additional policemen arrived at University Hall. No building was taken that night. The New Left caucus motion was passed. In the official SDS version of the meeting, it is stated that the final vote agreed to take over a building at some "randomly selected time" during the next week. In this way WSA later claimed that they had never ignored a majority vote on the seizure. My definite impression, although I may be wrong, is that the final motion voted on during that waking dream of a meeting was the original New Left caucus motion, which talked about a seizure on Monday.

The presence of police prevented any seizure that night. Most people, including the *Crimson*, left Lowell Lec with the impression that a seizure would probably take place the next Monday — unless some campus opposition to it could be mobilized. Wednesday morning I spoke with some friends about the possibility of a nonviolent defense squad, with groups of three linking arms in front of the doors of University Hall and requiring the occupiers to beat us up in order to gain entrance. This would put the moral onus, as these calculations go in the student community, on them.

While I was talking Wednesday morning the Harvard SDS executive committee was meeting in a small room in the philosophy department offices in Emerson Hall. WSA had a majority on the executive committee.

A few minutes after twelve noon, at the time of a scheduled "rally," a group of WSAers, not joined by most of the New Left caucus, entered University Hall and evicted the deans.

Most of the rest is, as they say, history. Giddy with a mixture of anger and absurd resignation at the inevitable, many of us were optimistic during the first hours. The number of people going into the building was rather small. The crowd outside was incredibly hostile, not because they loved SDS less but because they loved Harvard more. SDS speakers urging people to join them in the building were met with cries of "Vote! Vote!!" from the thousands of students filling the entire green and beautiful Yard. Wasn't it fantastic that it was such a beautiful day, really the first springlike day we had had at Harvard all year!

"Vote! Vote!!" Students were demanding a binding vote of those present on whether the building should be taken over. SDS controlled the microphone, and they controlled the speakers, but the cries were too persistent. Finally, one SDSer called for a vote. "All those in favor of taking the building!"

Fists and yelled ayes. But pretty pathetic.

"All those who favor kicking ROTC off but not taking any militant . . ."

A kid up front shouted out, "That's not what we're voting on!" The chant of "Vote! Vote!!" went up again.

The SDSer was flustered. "OK. All opposed to taking over the building!"

It was an overwhelmingly obvious nay.

Jared Israel came out of the door to University Hall and grabbed the microphone. He looked flustered too and stutteringly made the worst harangue I've ever seen him give. "OK. Now you've had your cute little vote. But don't think you're going to stop us from fighting imperialism! Your little vote was ridiculous because it included imperialists deciding on whether *we* should fight imperialism."

Rumors flew throughout the afternoon about what was going on inside the building. Some people said morale was very low and the group was considering leaving. The Yard was sealed off around five, and from that time you had to show a freshman bursar's card to get in. (The freshmen live in the Yard.) Late at night, a group of moderates were meeting in Weld common room, in the Yard, to plan a meeting for the next morning in order to condemn SDS but demand that police not be used to clear the building, except perhaps under certain very definite guidelines to prevent brutality. I got into the meeting with a freshman bursar's card borrowed from Rob Pattullo, who remained back in my room for the YPSL executive committee meeting that was taking place at the same time.

Around 2:00 A.M. a group within the moderate group tried to organize a letter of student leaders to Dean Glimp very vaguely threatening a student strike if police were used. The letter never got off the ground.

I went to sleep around 3:00 A.M. A friend slept in our room, because he refused to go talk with his roommates, some of whom supported the confrontation.

Elliott came rushing into our room, in his pajamas, a little after four-thirty to tell us to turn on the radio. "WHRB says the police seem to be gathering outside the Yard."

Half asleep, we turned on the radio. It seemed calm. They were reading, surrealistically, the statement the YPSL executive committee had passed earlier that night condemning the confrontation. "You have just heard the statement passed by the executive committee of the Young People's Socialist League at eleven fifty-seven tonight."

Just then the incredibly loud, piercing, atomic-war-like buzz of the house fire alarm exploded into the room. It was stinging, deadening, and awakening at the same time. Small groups of SDSers were running through the streets outside, yelling "Bust! Bust!!" WHRB could barely be heard in the background, ". . . We're taking you directly to our reporters outside of University Hall as our report 'Confrontation Sixty-nine' continues."

We all got dressed and ran over to the Yard.

It was 5:00 A.M. and already light. The streets were deserted. Many thoughts ran through my mind. I thought of my optimistic conversation with Professor Lipset during the afternoon in the Yard. "If the administration just plays it cool maybe Harvard can turn the tide and be the first school to defeat the New Left." He answered, "The question is whether they will be stupid enough to call the cops."

I thought how the people of Prague must have felt when they got up early one morning and saw Soviet tanks all over their city.

It was all so helpless and so absurd. The police wore baby-blue helmets. They marched in military formation. It was so stupid.

Looking back he'll probably deny it, but even my cool-headed roommate Elliott was very upset. He had been forced to flee several police charges into the crowd while watching the bust. He hadn't been hit.

At 7:00 A.M. people began gathering in the house dining hall. People were standing on the tables to speak. Very few people had gotten much sleep that night.

I hoarsely spoke, while cold sweat and dirt covered my body. I must have looked very pale, but I guess we all were. "Two

horrible wrongs have been committed in the last twenty-four
hours. First SDS occupied University Hall, and then the administration, instead of ignoring them, used the police to clear
the place. There's no reason to add a third wrong to the two."

"Strike. STRIKE! STRIKE!!"

Back in the room Elliott had his face down in his arms.
"Steve, those police were brutal! A lot of kids got hurt. You
can't just ignore that."

Once it started, it had to go its course. The media were
looking; they expected it. And it had to be done with Harvard
finesse. As someone in the *Crimson* wrote, "I have always said
that when the revolution came to Harvard, those Harvard boys
would do it with class. Did you see that meeting they had out
there among all the columns in Harvard Stadium? Harvard
Stadium — now that's class. And you seen the posters yet?
Aren't they great! Much better than anything at Columbia."

Thursday night, after the Mem Church meeting which called
a three-day strike, I had dinner in Kirkland House with Frank
Raines, chairman of the Student-Faculty Advisory Council
and one of the best of the moderate leaders. He told me
that my hunch that the three-day strike would just confuse and
disrupt the situation further was wrong. "Don't worry. The
strike'll never go on beyond three days. The three-day strike
will calm things down."

By Monday, the day when thousands and thousands of kids
were to gather in Harvard Stadium to decide whether to continue the strike, Raines and John Hanify, president of the Harvard Undergraduate Council, couldn't even get the majority of
HUC representatives to support a YPSL proposal calling for an
end to the strike. The best they could get through to be presented at the stadium was a call for a three-day moratorium.

Even that never came to a vote at the stadium. With six thousand voting, the stadium meeting came within thirteen votes of calling for an indefinite strike in support of demands which inevitably would have taken months, if not years, to accept. Finally, an extension of the strike for another three days was approved.

Things didn't calm down. Too much fantasy had been unleashed. Too many people were watching. Too many other campuses, inspired by Harvard, were exploding. (The *New York Times* began to run a daily box score on the front page.)

How can the mood of the strike be evoked?

The mood of the strike was of sleeplessness and hunger, of skipped meals as well as skipped classes, of physical and mental drainage. At one point during the strike much of the SDS leadership had to take some time off to get a little sleep. Ken Glazier, leader of the Mem Church moderates, left for Cape Cod after a week to recuperate.

The mood of the strike was of red armbands which some said identified supporters of the SDS strike for the eight demands and some said identified supporters of the "moderate" strike going on at the same time. The armbands could be bought at the local hippie boutique for a quarter. The red fists, prepared by SDSers in the School of Design, could be silkscreened onto shirts, pants, poster paper, or anything else for free.

The mood of the strike was of endless house meetings where jocks who had never before done a single political thing in their lives demanded immediate Student Power and denounced anyone who wanted to stop the strike as a sellout. It was of SDSers ringing their spoons on their glasses and standing up on tables in the house dining halls to make announcements of the latest struggle meeting, purge, mill-in, sellout, or concession.

For two weeks I experienced an almost constant ringing in my ears. Whenever I heard an airplane overhead, I would discern in back of the engine noise the chant of "Smash ROTC, no expansion!" I had several nightmares where crowds of red armbands were marching through the streets, "Smash ROTC, no expansion!" My heart jumped whenever I heard an automobile backfire. Several friends reported identical experiences. This too was the mood of the strike.

The mood of the strike was reams of printed matter, from the neatly printed administration statements placed in boxes at the house dining hall entrances to ten-page closely packed SDS exposés and curt ads in the *Crimson*. As the strike wore on and students began to latch on to the faculty as the group they could trust, SDS attacks (such as "The Faculty — Our Ally or Theirs?") began to center on the professors. The metaphor used was always one of trial, conviction, and symbolic execution. An example of an "exposure" of one popular professor by an SDS leaflet telling "Who Are the Agents?" sounded like the sentence of a "people's" tribunal:

Stanley Hoffman. Exponent of realpolitik. Has written that the Vietnam War would have been justified if the U.S. could have won it. Argued that the police bust would have been correct if only the students and faculty had first been "consulted" to make things look legitimate. Supporter of ROTC (when pressed, often likes to pretend he isn't). At Paine Hall, baited SDS by accusing us of "playing at revolution." Chairman of the liberal caucus. Committee of 15.

Later on, the leaflet stated, "House Masters are obvious agents: appointed by Pusey, they serve as an intelligence network."

Or take an ad in the *Crimson,* shortly after a student was given a harsh jail sentence for his role in physically expelling Dean Watson from University Hall:

PERSONALITY	OFFENSE	VERDICT	SENTENCE
Carl Offner	Assault and Battery	What Do You Believe?	1 Yr.
Prof. Samuel P. Huntington	Genocide	Decide for Yourself?	Scot-free

The mood of the strike was of savage in-fighting within SDS, taking place at the same time as the cultural radicals were dancing to rock bands in the Yard and in general having a wonderful time. Mike Kazin made a mistake he would never live down when he happened to leave the three expansion demands out of his speech at the Mem Church meeting the morning of the bust. He called "only" for an indefinite strike for the SDS demand on ROTC plus total amnesty. Immediately, a particularly mentally crazed WSAer began to yell out, "He doesn't speak for SDS! He doesn't speak for SDS!!" and to run literally over the people sitting in the crowded aisles of the church and onto the pulpit. Ignoring the people waiting patiently in line to speak, he proceeded to denounce Kazin for selling out SDS. WSA leaflets were issued during the strike specifically to denounce Kazin and other "misleaders." At one meeting leader after leader of the New Left caucus was subjected to attack and forced to make self-criticisms. When a New Left caucus member got up to say that, despite disagreements, everybody should act "like brothers and sisters in this together," he was hissed. (Kazin himself has now dropped out of Harvard, demoralized over the possibility of building his kind of SDS at Harvard.)

The mood of the strike was of Harvard Afro's brief but fiery

entrance onto the scene. In accounts of black militance on
campus it is often forgotten that black students generally use
the most extreme of tactics for the smallest of goals. These
goals relate generally to the narrow self-interest of black students. Manning petition tables I have noticed that black
students generally pass them by without even looking at them.
Similarly, black students generally ignore leaflets being handed
out in the Yard. There were hardly any Afro activists involved
in the anti-ROTC or other general political campaigns. There
is absolutely nothing wrong with black students' acting primarily in their self-interest, although it should lead those who
condemn workers for doing the same thing to pause. The point
is that their mood and motives are very different from those of
white students, particularly radicals.

Afro showed not the slightest hesitation in joining the strike
(after it got started) to press for a series of demands for participation on the committee to set up an Afro-American Studies
department, and then precipitously and ungraciously leaving
the strike, en masse, as soon as their one demand was met. In
the midst of large numbers of students out to save their souls,
beat their breasts, and make their revolution, Afro's behavior
resembled more that of the Mafioso turned semi-respectable
businessman. Their participation in the strike was matter-of-
fact and methodical. It was largely white students whom one
saw display the black fist superimposed on the red one which
was the symbol of the addition of the black studies demand to
the seven strike demands. Yet before their demand was met
Afro allowed the rumors to spread that it was going to bomb
Widener Library. An Afro speaker at the faculty meeting which
passed their demand told the professors that this was their last
chance to save Harvard from being destroyed.

The mood of the strike is perhaps best conveyed by individual incidents.

The Mem Church meeting the morning of the bust ended after the house dining halls closed for lunch. Most students just skipped lunch, but my brother and I went to Joe's Pizza for a bite. On the way back, walking down Mt. Auburn Street, a car tried to run us over. It was as simple as that. We were crossing the street, and instead of stopping at the stop sign, the 1950s-vintage blue Chevrolet approaching us speeded up. We narrowly avoided being hit. Nothing like that had ever happened to us before.

"Don't think the guy tried to run us over because we are right-wing social fascists," I said at a house meeting that afternoon. "You can be sure that the guy's hardly gonna be a ripe recruit for the worker-student alliance."

My brother walked around during the entire two weeks of the strike, Diogenes-like, trying to find out from SDS people what *procedure* they felt should be used to make decisions like the one on ROTC. He always hit up against a stone wall.

"I want it abolished," was inevitably the first answer.

"No, that's not my question. I'm not asking you what *decision* you want to be made. I'm asking what *procedure* you want to make the decision on ROTC."

"I don't understand. I want it abolished."

He once asked an SDS leader in a section of Soc Sci 125, a New Left–oriented course on the American economy, how he wanted the decision on ROTC made. The other people in the section looked at him with bewilderment, not understanding why he asked the question. Finally one girl got up the courage to answer. "Why do you ask, Mark? Can't you see the button he's wearing." The button said, "Abolish ROTC."

He once got an SDSer to understand the question, although getting an answer out of him was more difficult. "How do I want the decision made?" the kid finally mumbled. "Vote with your feet. Confrontation."

After the strike was over I heard a WSAer give a post mortem on the mistakes the New Left caucus made which allegedly led to the failure of the strike. "Militancy is dead on this campus, because of all the liberal attitudes kids have which the New Left caucus encourages. It's just the whole nonstruggle attitude. Take the mill-in at University Hall during the strike. I mean the New Left caucus encouraged the attitude that kids should talk to the deans, as if we have anything to say to them, as if they don't represent the interests of the enemy. It wasn't supposed to be the idea of the mill-in that we should talk to the deans. But that's how it ended up. And it was very unmilitant. One kid I know was even convinced!"

The kid he was talking with attempted a feeble and uninteresting defense of the New Left caucus.

"Now take the New Left caucus analysis of housing in Cambridge. It doesn't oppose expansion. It doesn't talk about Imperial City. It leads straight to the demand for building more housing!"

During the strike my brother and I began referring to Imperial City as Emerald City from the Wizard of Oz. That seemed somehow more appropriate.

Perhaps the most frightening aspect of the strike was the artificial form of mass "participation" which took place for the two weeks of springtime at Harvard. Students mistook mindless repetition of catch phrases and slogans for democratic discussion. The type of "participation" which flourished during the strike was quite literally of the same type as Germans experienced at Nuremburg rallies. Students were rapidly politicized behind a single point of view, and dissent became dangerous. That the participation was not genuine was shown by how short-lived it was. All year students had been supremely uninterested in the question of democratizing the university. Open hearings of the Fainsod Committee on university governance, held just a few weeks before the confrontation, attracted around twenty students. Then for two weeks in April everyone was crying that complete democracy at the university would have to be introduced or else they wouldn't permit Harvard to survive. After the two weeks were over, students returned to supreme uninterest. Quincy House, which before the strike had a reputation as the least political and most self-satisfied of all the houses, adopted the most radical resolutions at their house meetings during the strike.

The enormous growth in political interest and "discussion" during the strike did not represent any commitment to the hard work of building a new society. It represented "participation" in pleasant illusions. It was merely part of the escalation of unreality.

Soon it all ended. Surprisingly soon, in fact. The Harvard confrontation ended after two weeks, while the San Francisco State strike lasted several months and the Columbia confrontation over a month. Final exams went on completely as scheduled. Underneath a poster urging students to come to a meeting to organize an exam boycott in Adams House, a student wrote simply, "I dare you." When one of a band of student mystics

who began regular Hindu chanting and singing in front of the
Harvard Coop during the strike approached a Harvard senior
in May and said to him, "Hare Krishna!" the amused response
was simply, "And Merry Christmas to you too." SDS was unable to organize any actions protesting the disciplinary Committee of Fifteen, even though the committee was "manipulat-
ing" the student body by holding off its decisions on punishment until after final exams were over and almost everyone had
left Cambridge.

Why did it end so soon? Basically, it was simply that the
degree of alienation on which it could build any staying power
was simply not very deep. The confrontation coalition simply
collapsed, leaving SDS alone holding the ball to engage in a
series of mutual recriminations on who had "sold out" the strike,
which were as irrelevant as they were obscure.

The confrontation coalition collapsed because the factors
which led the cultural radicals and the moderates into the
coalition in the first place began working against a continuation
of the strike. The cultural radicals, who joined the confrontation coalition out of boredom, became bored with the confrontation as they found out about the superpolitization SDS
wanted to impose on it. One cultural radical who had stopped
striking even before SDS officially declared the class boycott
ended, told me over lunch, "When I finally sat back for a
second and thought about it, I realized I had been manipulated
to some extent. The SDS people are so ideological, and they
weren't willing to accept that many people weren't in the building for political reasons. I don't know how those kids at Columbia struck so long. I went to the Yard every day to watch
and listen to what was going on, but it got boring pretty soon."

The moderates, who joined the confrontation coalition out
of a loss of bearings and lack of any clear or deeply held con-

victions, saw the continuation of the confrontation demanding precisely the sure bearings and deep convictions which they lacked. The moderate, who had previously been made to doubt the certainty of a belief in democracy or in tolerance, now came to doubt the beliefs SDS wanted him to die for. In "A Moderate Goes to the Stadium," Scott Jacobs of the *Crimson* outlined the vacillation which was soon to lead the moderates out of the confrontation coalition. Speaking of himself, Jacobs says, "The moderate did not know if he wanted to change the University, he no longer knew whether abolishing ROTC was good or bad or even whether it was worth the chaos that must continue if the strike continues. The moderate did know he was tired of chaos."

Shortly after the strike was over two junior social studies tutorials met together in the apartment of one tutor in order to discuss the effects of the strike. The discussion was largely unreal, partly because the SDS people persisted in simply denying the objective existence of events that had taken place. Mike Kazin said that SDS had never expected the workers to join them and denied that the statement of the Cambridge "worker" at the April 8 meeting that the workers would join SDS in the building was cheered, while my own opinion to the contrary was hissed.

But insights managed to slip in here and there. At one point Barry Margolin, one of the more thoughtful of SDS people, ventured his own view of the long-range effects of the strike. "I think that what we've done is to radicalize a lot of students. There were twelve hundred kids at SDS meetings during the strike, and just about all of them supported striking for the SDS demands."

"How long do you think that radicalization will last?" I

asked. "Historically, the record of student radicals remaining radicals isn't very good."

"I know that. I suppose the best we can hope is that most of the kids who were radicalized will end up as liberals instead of conservatives when they're adults."

"You mean, the ultimate effect of your strike is that you've gotten more people for some future Gene McCarthy movement."

"Yeah, I would guess so," Barry answered softly.

"But I thought SDS considers liberals the main enemy, worse than conservatives?"

"Yeah, you're right. We do."

What more absurd epitaph for a year of absurdity?

2. Has Sanity a Future?

ALTHOUGH he was not the first to point it out, Karl Marx was one of the most perceptive of those who have noted that, for most people, political activity is based more or less on self-interest. Although many of his followers persisted in romanticizing the proletariat (just as many today romanticize Negroes) as some sort of never-erring and even superhuman demigod, Marx's own approach was rather different. For him, the workers were a "progressive" social force in industrial society because of the position they were placed into in that society. Freedom of speech and organization, greater social equality, expansion of education — and, eventually, in Marx's view, socialism — were fought for by the working class simply because these changes were in their self-interest. This was so even though many workers individually might have been dirty and uncultured. In the same way, the upper classes might individually have been refined and cultivated people, but their social position meant that their self-interest was directed against humanizing changes in the society as a whole.

To be sure, it is true that there are always exceptions to the self-interest rule. Especially among those whose eyes have been opened by education, there has always been a significant minority among the middle and upper classes which has selflessly expounded the cause of the downtrodden. Although the majority in these classes has always and will continue to be conservative politically, simply because conservatism favors their self-interest, voting statistics show that the socially conscious middle class is a smallish but significant group.

When it comes to voting "right" on election day, or contributing money to different organizations, one need go no further than idealism in explaining such middle-class behavior. For these are actions which do not involve huge amounts of effort; they can be done rather easily. But when it comes to organized activist political movements of the middle and upper classes, which demand of their members large commitments of time and energy, idealism is not nearly enough of an explanation. A small activist political organization may be built on the basis of the small number of saints who inhabit our world. A mass one cannot. It must be based on some form of self-interest. This is where Marx's analysis is useful in understanding the growth of mass student revolutionary groups.

What is the self-interest which motivates middle- and upper-class students in a massive way into Left politics? In underdeveloped countries, as Max Nomad argues, it can be direct material self-interest. In these lands there is usually an excess of university graduates overqualified for the well-paid positions available. Thus a mass base for a revolutionary student movement in developing countries is provided by the hunger for good positions and power in the society, which these antidemocratic revolutionaries expect to wrest for themselves after the revolution.

In Western Europe and America today there is no such direct force of *material* self-interest. The self-interest which allows student revolutionary groups in America and Europe today to grow into mass student movements is a *psychological* self-interest, or, to be more precise, the therapeutic value that acting out of psychological problems has for many students. While the first movers of student revolutionary organizations traditionally have been among the small band of saints in the hu-

man race, the social class origins of the overwhelming majority
of students, that is middle or upper class, have dictated that
the revolutionary student movement can grow only by reaching
out to the crazy conglomeration of generational animus, tribal-
istic cultism, fearful neurosis, paranoiac feelings of grandeur
and conspiracy, and other psychopathological phenomena which
are bound to affect a percentage of any population.

Mass movements based on the self-interest of "the masses"
have generally been forces for social progress, from the movements for the extension of the suffrage in nineteenth-century
Europe through the CIO in the American thirties. Mass movements based on the psychological hang-ups of "the masses"
have been one disaster after another, from chauvinistic war
hysterias which restore feelings of power to anti-Negro lynch-
ings which purge the feared sexual supermen. It is therefore
no surprise that student revolutionary movements like the SDS,
as they become mass forces and therefore need to become rooted
in student psychological self-interest, lose their original positive
aspects and degenerate into groups whose effects are destructive.

An example of this degeneration from an adult middle-class
crusade is given by Joseph Gusfield in his brilliant book on the
temperance movement, *Symbolic Crusade*. When temperance
started out in the early part of the nineteenth century, it was a
small idealistic movement which had compassion for the drinker
and attempted to persuade him to abstain. The movement
grew into a mass middle- and upper-class movement on the basis
of fears by old-line Yankee groups that their cultural life-style
was being overrun by immigrant groups and that their psychological superiority was threatened. But as it grew — on the basis
of these hang-ups — it lost the original compassion and reason-
ableness that it had as a small idealistic reform organization. It

changed its approach to what Gusfield calls "coercive reform," denouncing the drinker as a moral pervert and finally ramming through coercive legislation that only exacerbated the problem. As it grew the temperance movement became a symbolic crusade, because its alleged goal was merely a symbol for deeper-seated psychological problems being acted out in the movement.

The American and European New Left movements have similarly turned into destructive symbolic crusades. The early American New Left was composed of small groups of serious people, deeply concerned with practical and theoretical problems, hopeful of rebuilding a serious Left movement in America. Their particular contribution to American radicalism was the very explicit and repeated emphasis of the importance of democratic decision-making as the very *foundation* for any sort of new society. The primary fear of the early SDSers, often obsessive, was overmanipulation of ordinary people by middle-class radicals. Indeed, at the 1965 SDS annual convention one speaker even wondered whether SDS's community organization campaign, in which students were sent in to poor urban communities to help them organize themselves, was not itself a form of manipulation not much better than when politicians manipulate the poor!

But a student activist and radical organization cannot really grow and get large commitments from many students on the basis of such modest rationality. Most people simply demand some sort of compensation, psychic or material, for the commitment asked from them. This is especially true in America, where lingering McCarthyism makes the middle and upper classes especially hesitant to commit themselves to radicalism for fear of their precious "future."

So SDS inevitably gave up on organizing a movement of

saints and settled, as it had to, for organizing a movement of psychopaths. Sacrifices had to be made — reason, self-questioning, a sense of proportion. It was necessary to lavish praise on mass murderers to attract those who thirsted after blood. It was necessary to denounce the hated procedures and conventions — civil liberties, tolerance, academic freedom. It was necessary to revel in the primitive beauty of destruction — "burn, baby, burn."

It is interesting that an exactly analogous evolution has taken place in the West German New Left. At its beginning during the early sixties the movement consisted of a small group of young, serious students who were well-read Marxist scholars, emphasizing Marx the democrat and hopeful of revitalizing the historical Left in German politics. But as the movement grew all this was lost in a sea of slogans, rocks thrown at enemies, orgies of verbal violence, and immature posturing. In the cases of both the American and German New Left a good proportion of the honest early leadership has left the movement, repelled by the new primitivism. They are now working inside the serious democratic Left movements of their countries.

The reverse side of this phenomenon should be noted also, for it too has unfortunate implications. This relates to the behavior of a group on campus much larger than that of the potential student revolutionaries — the normal, rational students. The problem with this "silent majority" is that it will *always* be silent. During the middle of the Harvard strike, an *ad hoc* group called Coalition for Peace at Harvard distributed a leaflet urging moderates opposing continuation of the strike to be sure to attend the second Harvard Stadium meeting, where a vote on whether to go on beyond the first week of strike would be taken. In referring to the previous Monday's stadium rally, when a con-

tinuation of the strike for three days had been voted and a
motion to continue the strike indefinitely "until the demands
are met" was defeated by only thirteen votes, the leaflet asked
rhetorically, "Where were nine thousand Harvard moderates
when a vote to shut the University down indefinitely was almost
passed? We can't let a minority of the University almost do
that again!" Now, it is true that of the some 15,000 members
of the undergraduate and graduate community at Harvard, only
some 6000 stayed around to vote at the first stadium rally.

*But the unfortunate fact is that the "silent majority" is not
necessarily a force on the side of sanity, but on the side of acqui-
escence to whatever is taking place.* The vast majority of these
9000 whom the Coalition for Peace hoped would come to the
stadium meeting to end the strike were themselves staying out
of the largely empty Harvard classrooms during the strike. The
"silent majority" gives its passive support to whatever the active
people are doing.

Something similar applies to the large groups of liberals on
campus who theoretically should be able to provide a counter-
weight to the extremists. Every year since I have been a freshman
the Young Democrats at Harvard have begun the year with the
illogical syllogism that since their views represent the center of
campus sentiment, their group should therefore be the most
powerful group around. Each year since I have been a freshman
I have watched the organization's strength decline further into
insignificance. This is partly because of the liberal elitism which
fits in very well with SDS totalitarian elitism, but in the main
the liberals are an insignificant political force on campus because
it's impossible to get them to do any political work. It is a sad
fact, which I have noted in the YPSL and Young Democrat leaders frequently complain about, that the degree of active work —

making phone calls, printing leaflets, putting up posters, walking on picket lines, knocking on doors — which students put into politics is directly proportional to how extremist they are. This is not at all surprising, since the political work the mass of SDSers do serves symbolic or therapeutic functions. "Liberals here at Harvard," as the president of the Young Democrats once remarked, "are too fucking *contented* to get off their asses."

The problem with organizing students as a force for expansion of democracy and social justice in both the university and the society thus lies mainly in the fact that they are students. As middle- and upper-class people going through a psychologically difficult stage of transition from childhood to adulthood, forced through idleness into consideration of the basic dilemmas of human existence, groups of them are subject to organization by radicals on the basis of psychological self-interest. But in order to attract them the movements organizing them must become hate-filled, intolerant, and destructive. In this process they must, through their weird and repulsive behavior, repel the vast majority of citizens in such a way that not the chances for social progress, but those for a wave of repression in the university and in the society are enhanced. In the atmosphere of the New Left sixties, when students threw cow's blood on passing taxis and cars to "protest the war in Vietnam," or shouted obscenities in order to protest the brutalization of America, how could the level of decency we have on the campus even be maintained, let alone extended? And the rest of the student body, those acting on rational self-interest, were too unmotivated to put the required energy into the struggle for progress.

This is the way things have always been with students. Never is the self-indulgent phrasemaking of students and their adult

admirers more odious than when we are subjected to their proc-
lamations that this is the most "idealistic" or most "sensitive"
generation of students ever, and shouldn't we be thankful to
them for exposing the hypocrisy of the adult world. Such inan-
ities are usually "proven" by a glib and misleading reference to
the silent generation of the fifties.

In fact, if one looks at the history of students the experience
of the fifties was the exception rather than the rule. There have
been student revolutionaries active in virtually every generation.
German campuses in the twenties were dominated by young
Nazi revolutionaries. Students were one of the most active
groups in the revolutions of 1848 in Europe. The Russian revolutionary movement in the nineteenth century was largely a
a student movement. Students provided the backbone of the
Slav revolutionary nationalist movements which helped provoke
World War I.

And the fact is that the dilemma of student revolutionary
movements — according to which they must, in order to grow,
undermine their own possibilities for promoting justice in the
society — is also ancient. Marx complained about the extremist
influence of adventurist students on the revolutionary committees
in 1848. Engels noted during the late nineteenth century what
a tragedy it was for the world that there were thousands of revolutionary Russian students. Student revolutionary organizations
have almost always been banes on the dispossessed classes they
are supposedly trying to help.

What is new about our generation is nothing qualitative, but
something important quantitatively. For the number of students
in America has grown so astronomically that we are now a major
political force simply in terms of numbers. (There are more students in America today than farmers.) This does not necessarily

mean, as many of us assume, that just because we are more numerous, students are more *powerful* now than before. During the nineteenth century, students were a tiny group recruited out of the elite in basically nondemocratic societies where powerful mass organizations like labor unions and socialist political parties did not yet exist. Both because they were an elite and because there were few others organized, student revolutionaries were rather powerful. (The same conditions — of a tiny student community, which is nevertheless powerful because of its elite status and lack of competing organizations, exists in underdeveloped countries today, and student revolutionaries there have overthrown governments almost singlehandedly.)

If students are to be powerful today we must abandon the approach of the previous generations when students were a tiny elite and learn to take advantage of our numbers in democratic politics. And until we accept, deep down in our hearts, the idea of one man, one vote, we are not going to be able to change either our universities or our world. For people resent students self-righteously telling them what to do about everything.

Intellectuals should have an important function in the process of social change, and that is by coming up with ideas and programs in the common interest of various disadvantaged groups, so that these groups can come together instead of fighting and polarizing against each other. So our potential role need not be just one of providing numbers; it can be one of providing ideas also.

It is clear that students potentially *could* be an important positive political force in American society. The question is, how likely is it that they will be? Any optimism here must be based on a leap of faith. The hope must be in nurturing and protecting from deformation that kernel of youthful idealism — still believ-

ing the nice moral rules we learned as children and naively wanting to see them put into practice — which is what is good and
hopeful about us.

Yet in our idealism lies a paradox and a nightmare. Shortly
after the Harvard strike was over I saw, for the fifth time since
I came to Harvard, Humphrey Bogart's *Casablanca*, one of the
Harvard student's favorite films. Bogart has always been admired
at Harvard for the streak of selfish cynicism in him, and every
time I've seen the film Bogart's lines in Casablanca like "I don't
stick out my neck for no one" have been wildly applauded by
Harvard audiences. Except this time, shortly after the strike,
when they were met with embarrassed and total silence. I had
always been disgusted to hear kids applaud previously, and the
stunning reaction this time set me aback. People couldn't applaud such selfishness so shortly after engaging in what many
themselves regarded as the most idealistic and self-sacrificing
thing they had ever done.

The paradox was that the effect of this burst of active idealism
was so different from that which most who undertook it had in
mind. They loved Harvard, yet they shook it and almost destroyed it. They respected scholarship, yet they replaced it with
slogans. They deeply hoped for a better America, yet they
moved the country to the Right.

The nightmare is that it can be the most idealistic who introduce the most terrible systems of degradation and unfreedom
we can imagine. We need not wait for the SDS tortures and the
SDS jails to learn that lesson of history.

But the paradox and the nightmare are too horrifying for the
mind to cope with. For this reason alone our hearts cry out for
a decent idealism, an idealism which does not consume itself
in vindictiveness and moral superiority, an idealism which does
not become corrupted and degenerate.

Can decent idealism be the basis of a mass activist movement? *Does* sanity have a future at Harvard? In the final analysis it may be a sort of cop-out even to pose the question, for a rational answer might leave us overly pessimistic and dejected. That must not be. For if we do not work for a decent student idealism, who will? And, if not now, when? If we do not labor with all we have within us to give sanity a future at Harvard, then the answer to the question will surely be no.